LOCOMOTIVE ENGINEERS

OF THE
GWR
DENIS GRIFFITHS

PSL

Patrick Stephens
Wellingborough, Northamptonshire

Dedication
For PATRICK, my son and friend

First published in 1987

British Library Cataloguing in Publication Data

Griffiths, Denis, *1943 –*
    Locomotive engineers of the GWR.
    1.   Great Western Railway——Employees——
Biography   2.   Railroad engineers——
England   ——Biography
    I.   Title
    625.1′0092′2   TF64.G7

    ISBN 0-85059-819-2

*Patrick Stephens Limited is part of the
Thorsons Publishing Group*

Printed and bound in Great Britain

10 9 8 7 6 5 4 3 2 1

Contents

Acknowledgements   4

Introduction   5

1. Brunel: The beginning   7

2. The nineteenth-century men   19

3. The twentieth-century men   34

4. Chain of command   50

5. Design influences and construction   61

6. Nineteenth-century locomotives   73

7. Twentieth-century locomotives   94

8. Testing and innovation   113

9. Carriages and wagons   129

10. Standardization   143

11. Influence abroad   154

12. Western heritage   163

   Appendix   175

   References   176

   Index   182

Author's acknowledgements

It is impossible to undertake any historical research without access to published and unpublished documents, the majority of which are held by libraries and museums. Many individuals at such establishments have offered considerable help and, generally, they are unknown by name. Acknowledgements are, therefore, due to the staffs of Bristol City Reference Library, Swindon Reference Library, the Science Museum Library, the Library of the Institution of Mechanical Engineers, Liverpool City Library and the National Railway Museum Library.

I am indebted to the unknown people at Britain's preserved railways for the efforts they have made in restoring the locomotives and rolling stock we can all now enjoy. Special thanks must go to the Great Western Society at Didcot and to the Severn Valley Railway.

A number of individuals have assisted greatly in my research, including Tim Bryan of the GWR Museum, Swindon; Mr Langley of Bristol Reference Library; Mr Trayherne of Swindon Reference Library; Mike Williams of the Brunel Society; and Mike Diggle of the Mechanical, Marine and Production Engineering Department at Liverpool Polytechnic. My other colleagues in the same department at the Polytechnic have also offered constructive criticism. I am also grateful to two friends, Geoff Johnson and Chris Surridge, both of whom have provided invaluable help.

All line drawings are by the author. Unless otherwise credited, photographs are by the author or form part of his collection.

It is normal for any author to offer thanks to his family for their tolerance during production of the work. In that respect I am no different as my wife, Patricia, and children, Sarah and Patrick, have had to suffer anti-social behaviour from me whilst I researched and typed. The family members showed understanding as they were 'dragged' about the country visiting preserved railways, and they even helped in providing some of the photographs.

Introduction

The Great Western Railway attracts far more affection and devotion than any of the other three post-grouping railway companies. We all have our favourites in any sphere and the railway enthusiast has his favourite company as well as his favourite class of locomotive, but why do so many choose the Great Western? Analysts have attempted to define the reason but with little success. Many present-day devotees will hardly have known the Great Western as an independent company and the majority will never have experienced the railway during its last normal operating period, prior to 1939. Nostalgia plays an important part, as does the delight of childhood memory, no matter how illusory. Without doubt a major factor in deciding a preference is visual attraction. Steam locomotives and rolling stock provide visual impact and colour the enthusiast's feelings for a railway, but beauty is still in the eye of the beholder.

This book does not attempt to analyze the reasoning behind any choice of favourite company, nor is it intended to be another book in praise of the Great Western Railway. It is, however, intended to provide an insight into the lives and work of those men who gave the GWR its visual impact, the Chief Mechanical Engineers. Their locomotive and rolling stock designs are what most people consider to be, however erroneously, the heart of the Great Western. Whilst it must be admitted that each of the railway companies produced excellent designs, no attempt will be made to compare performance or even construction. Any design should only be considered in the light of the work it was expected to undertake and judged accordingly. The GWR Chief Mechanical Engineers designed locomotives and rolling stock for that company's services and to suit track gradients and other conditions on its lines. The overall design criterion was in effect 'horses for courses'.

Several attempts at interchange trials were made over the years but the results were usually confused and if they did not suit a particular party some excuse could always be found. The skill and knowledge of driver and fireman are of paramount importance in any test, but individuals differ even from day to day. Coal quality has been a ready-made excuse, but should anybody be surprised? After all, a good designer will have his boilers constructed to suit the type of fuel available in his region. Different criteria govern the shape of firebox required to burn good Welsh steam coal efficiently compared with, say, hard Yorkshire coal. Railway company designers had no need to develop 'universal' locomotives.

Unlike the other three post-grouping companies the Great Western Railway did not come about from the amalgamation of a number of smaller concerns but in essence absorbed a number of minor companies. Though these minor concerns possessed locomotives, rolling stock and engineers, the impact on the GWR was minimal. Continuity was the hallmark of the Great Western and its engineering traditions were no exception. In the 112 years of independent existence of the GWR only six men occupied the chair of Chief Mechanical Engineer (the title was changed from Locomotive, Carriage and Wagon Superintendent in 1916). One of the other post-grouping companies had five in twenty-eight years.

There are many books available detailing the history of the Great Western Railway and there are volumes illustrating the locomotives and rolling stock. Several works have been published concerning the lives of certain engineers who form the subject of this book; the life of Isambard Kingdom Brunel has been well documented but much of the engineering character of the man is generally overlooked. Though some repetition of information already available will have to be made, this book aims to give the reader an appreciation of the engineering problems each man faced and the reasoning behind the solutions.

In engineering, as in every other walk of life, people have differing ideas as to how problems should be solved and those ideas are based upon knowledge and experience. The Chief Mechanical Engineers of the GWR came from very different backgrounds and each received his training in a different environment with only one, Hawksworth, being trained at Swindon, the GWR engineering shrine. Why then did GWR engineering design show such apparent continuity, with the absence of major upheaval which was obvious on the other railways? Apart from Gooch each appointment of CME came from within, an heir-apparent being chosen well in advance. Though each new man had his own ideas there was never any need to make immediate changes as he would have been in a position to influence, to some extent, his former 'chief', possibly getting ideas tried in advance. Careful planning ensured that, apart from wartime and the early years, locomotives and rolling stock were up to the tasks in hand. Even during the broad gauge run-down, motive power, by way of the 'convertibles', allowed operation without real disruption.

The line Brunel gave the GWR was straight and flat, at least between London and Swindon, and this eased the burden of the locomotive designer to some extent when it came to providing motive power for high speed. A comfortable loading gauge provided room for locomotives and rolling stock to 'expand', allowing the designer to produce plant for the job in hand rather than to suit the space available. Steep gradients on the South Devon banks presented problems but the region was relatively small and could be dealt with by special designs or adjustments to running schedules. Even in Wales special designs operated as necessary: again it was 'horses for courses'.

Engineering, though, is not merely the final product: it is also how it is achieved and maintained. Swindon and other outposts of the empire kept abreast of modern practice and in certain respects were leaders, in Britain at least. Good design and accurate assembly reduce the need for maintenance as wear is less of a problem. Availability is increased and the railway as a whole benefits. Standardization means that fewer parts are needed even with a large number of different classes, and this in turn reduces costs and down-time due to the non-availability of parts. From Gooch onwards the lessons of good engineering practice were not lost on the Chief Mechanical Engineers of the Great Western Railway.

Unlike the other post-grouping railways, and many of the pre-grouping railways, the GWR Locomotive Department was responsible for running as well as manufacture and maintenance.

That placed additional work on those in charge but also provided an advantage in that maintenance schedules could be arranged to suit the works. Careful planning and the skill of those responsible was needed to ensure success. Properly constructed locomotive sheds with repair facilities had to be built throughout the system and carriage/wagon maintenance had to be organized. Fuel and water supplies had to be arranged with the water properly treated if necessary.

All of this and more came within the remit of the Chief Mechanical Engineer/Locomotive, Carriage and Wagon Superintendent. Naturally, no one man could attend to all matters within his domain, but there has to be a 'Top Man' to take the credit and the blame. This book is about those 'Top Men'. It does not seek to denigrate the work and effort of those who laboured within the engineering department of the GWR, but space does not permit mention of everybody concerned with each project. Some will be mentioned, but, hopefully, the reader will accept that the Chief Mechanical Engineer is given the credit because he, ultimately, had the responsibility. All projects involving the men are not covered: the book is not intended to detail their work but is about the men themselves as engineers and their part in shaping the Great Western Railway. I trust that the book will provide some insight into the character and ability of the Chief Mechanical Engineers by considering examples of their work, practical and published, on and off the railway.

1. Brunel: The beginning

The Great Western Railway was Brunel. He shaped it, breathed life into it and gave it style. Isambard Kingdom Brunel was nothing if not original. Not for him the accepted practice merely because it was the way that others tackled the problem. Solutions to problems were not routine; each engineering task had its own difficulties which had to be dealt with accordingly. Why, he questioned, did all railways have to be constructed to the 'coal cart' gauge of 4 ft 8½ in just because George Stephenson had made his first lines to that guage? There was no logic behind that dimension, merely tradition, and Brunel was not a man of tradition; he was an engineer and a good one. He was in fact a civil engineer, not a mechanical engineer, and there is a distinct difference. Brunel's adventure into the realms of the mechanical engineer and his 'originality' were to cost some of his employers dear. That does not, however, detract from the genius of the man but illustrates admirably his powers of persuasion.

Merchants and prominent citizens of Bristol had considered the proposition of a railway connecting their fair city with the capital as early as 1824, but the plans were short-lived. Autumn 1832 saw the first positive action with the formation of a committee to investigate the practicability of the project. An initial meeting in January 1833 was favourable towards the plan, which meant that an engineer had to be appointed to survey the route and prepare an estimate of cost. At the time there was a notable lack of experienced railway engineers and the committee was faced with a difficult task. A number of names were advanced including that of W.H. Townsend, a local land surveyor who had surveyed and was then charged with constructing the Bristol & Gloucester Railway. Despite the grandiose title that line was, in fact, only a ten-mile 'coal gauge' tramway.

Brunel had a reputation in Bristol, having been successful in the competition to design a bridge across the Avon Gorge at Clifton. He had also carried out improvement works for the Dock Company. Fortuitously the Dock Company had representatives on the Railway Committee and one of these, Nicholas Roch, proposed Brunel for the position of surveyor. By a single vote the committee appointed Brunel to carry out the preliminary survey. He was, however, not to work alone as Townsend was to assist him. For a fee of £500 the men set about their work though Brunel was not enthusiastic about having a partner no matter how subordinate he was.

Isambard Kingdom Brunel: Engineer to the Great Western Railway Company (courtesy of the National Railway Museum, York).

It had at one stage been suggested that each of the names proposed to the committee be allowed to survey his own route and that the lowest estimate be accepted. Brunel made it known that he would have no part in such a scheme and wrote to the committee in the most forthright of terms. 'You are holding out a premium to the man who will make you the most flattering promises. It is most obvious that the man who has either least reputation at stake, or who has most to gain by temporary success, and least to lose by the consequences of disappointment, must be the winner in such a race.'[1] Brunel would survey only one road between Bristol and London; that road would be the best, not the cheapest. Throughout his career Brunel adhered to that philosophy, refusing to place financial matters above engineering considerations and his own high standards.

Brunel's road went by way of Chippenham, Swindon, the Vale of the White Horse and the Thames Valley to Maidenhead. The London approach could be dealt with at a later time. For a sum of £2,800,000 Brunel considered that the line might be constructed and, at the end of July 1833, the committee set about the formation of a company. The typically Brunelian title Great Western Railway was adopted and the major tasks of raising finance and obtaining a full survey could then commence.

For that work many assistant surveyors were required with Brunel superintending every stage of the progress. A major failing in the Brunel character was that he could trust nobody to carry out his instructions; he felt that without his constant presence work would not be done. That may have been the case with some but was certainly not the case with all. Daniel Gooch, having received a scolding from Brunel for unloading one of the early GWR locomotives without consulting his superior, was prompted to make the comment, 'One feature of Mr Brunel's character (and it is one that gave him a great deal of extra and unnecessary work) was, he fancied no one could do anything but himself. . . .'[2] His presence on the road would be constantly required and the only solution was a form of mobile office. To that end Brunel designed and had built his famous black britzska, known to the surveyors and construction gangs as the 'Flying Hearse'.

All projects with which Brunel was associated are, understandably, referred to as his though he will have had little to do with the day-to-day superintending. In many cases he would not have carried out the survey or design work. Ultimately, however, he was responsible as any contract would have been under his name. With a dozen or more projects in hand at any one time (he lists eleven in his diary at the end of 1835), an extensive staff of assistants had to be employed. A letter sent to all members of his staff indicates that thirty-three people came under his direction during 1850.[3] Each of the major projects required a Resident Engineer, possibly with an assistant, whilst other engineers were required to superintend contracts. As he failed to trust many of his personnel it is not surprising that Brunel felt obliged to dash about the country checking on the progress of work.

It is unnecessary to describe in detail the events leading to the eventual passage of the GWR bill through Parliament but without the efforts of Brunel, and certain other people, the railway would have been long delayed. With capital not forthcoming and with an urgent desire to get their bill before Parliament as soon as possible, the Directors decided to apply for powers only for the ends of the line, leaving the section between Reading and Bath for the next session. At the Committee stage Brunel underwent a most rigorous period of questioning but proved himself equal to the task, making many friends and admirers in the process, one of whom was George Stephenson. Stephenson was questioned by the Committee as to the merits of Brunel's proposed route and offered the comment, 'I can imagine a better line, but do not know of one so good.'[4] Despite those efforts the bill was lost and another, for the complete line, had to be submitted for the next session.

Debate during the 1835 session was just as intense but the proposers of the GWR bill were well prepared and their case was well presented. Engineers such as Joseph Locke, Charles Vignoles and George Stephenson all expressed approval of the line chosen by Brunel and of his estimates. On the last day of August 1835 the bill received the Royal Assent and the Great Western Railway came into being. Isambard Kingdom Brunel had played a major part in the victory and with some pride, on 26 December 1835, he could write in his neglected diary:

> What a blank in my journal! And during the most eventful part of my life. When I last wrote in this book I was just emerging from obscurity. I had been toiling most unprofitably at numerous things—unprofitably at least at the moment. The Railway certainly was brightening but, still uncertain—what a change. The Railway now is in progress. I am their Engineer to the finest work in England—a handsome salary—£2,000 a year—on excellent terms with my Directors and all going smoothly. . . .[5]

To many people the broad gauge is synonymous with Brunel and the Great Western but in the original Bill for the railway the narrow, or 4 ft 8½ in gauge was implied if not actually specified. (No copy of that bill has survived to allow checking.) Certainly in the 1835 Bill there was no mention of a specific gauge and it is likely that such an omission was at the instigation of Brunel, whose mind must have already been engaged in consideration of the advantages of a more substantial width between the rails. Exactly when he decided upon a 7 ft gauge is not known; even the great man himself was uncertain. 'I think the impression grew upon me gradually, so that it is difficult to fix the time when I first thought a wide gauge desirable; but I daresay that there were stages between wishing that it could be so and determining to try and do it.'[6]

His reports to the GWR directors during September 1835 were specific; he wanted a broad gauge with 7 ft between the rails. The second report of 15 September lucidly explains the case for that gauge which had been proposed in the first report dated a day earlier. That second report has been reprinted in full in volume 1 of MacDermot's *History of the Great Western Railway*, so it is unnecessary to detail it here. The main arguments in favour of that gauge were a very mixed bag, some being quickly dropped when obvious defects could be seen. Frictional resistance and the centre of gravity of rolling stock could be reduced by the use of large diameter wheels, with the coach or wagon body being placed between the wheels. The passenger safety problems of such an arrangement seem to have escaped Brunel, but that part of the argument was quickly dropped when they were pointed out. Other reasons for the wider gauge were sound: there would be more space for higher powered machinery (which would be more accessible for maintenance), smoother riding and increased steadiness, particularly at the higher speeds for which Brunel had arranged his road.

The major disadvantage, that concerning break of gauge, lay in the proposed joint London terminal with the London & Birmingham Railway. Brunel conceded that point but did not consider it a major obstacle. Breakdown in negotiations between the two companies effectively erased that objection. At a board meeting on 29 October 1835 Brunel's proposal came up for discussion and was adopted with a large majority. The Great Western Railway would be different; it would have 7 ft between its rails.

It might be supposed that Brunel considered his 7 ft gauge the only one worthy of application, but that was not the case. He dealt with each line in isolation, looking at all possibilities and deciding upon that which most suited the circumstances. A broad gauge provided for high speed but required large radius curves and hence plenty of space. If the space was not available a 7 ft gauge would not be possible. Directors of the Taff Vale Railway wanted a 7 ft gauge but the engineer told them that it would not be suitable due to the sharp curvatures. They then suggested a gauge of 5 ft. That he was against as it would present difficulties in obtaining locomotives and rolling stock. Standardization of gauge had many advantages and obtaining running equipment was one of them. At that time, April 1839, Brunel could consider himself an expert on the procurement of non-standard operating stock. The Great Western had nothing else. Being able to connect the line with another was of major importance and the expected

main line near the coast must be of narrow or broad gauge. His report was blunt, 'This main line will not be a 5 ft gauge; it will be either a 4 ft 8½ in or a 7 ft—the latter you cannot have and therefore the former offers the only chance.[7]

In designing his track Brunel would also show originality. He was not going to be tied to stone block supports as used by the Stephensons and most other railway engineers. The broad gauge demanded its own type of road. Uppermost in the mind of the Great Western's engineer was the desire for high speed and smoothness of running, so his track had to allow for such operation. Longitudinal timbers or baulks provided a continuous support for the rails, these baulks being of American pine about 15 in wide and 7 in deep. At 30 ft intervals double transverse ties or sleepers held the longitudinal timbers together and preserved the gauge. Joints in the longitudinal timbers were made at the double sleepers with pads providing support for the connection. Between each set of double ties were single transverse ties. This arrangement connected both tracks together as the transverse sleepers had a length of about 24 ft.[8]

All timbers had been kyanized in order to minimize the risk of rotting, and tar was liberally spread upon exposed surfaces, both wood and iron. Bridge rails of 44 lb per yd resting upon hardwood packing were connected to the baulks by means of screws which passed through holes in the rail flanges. Screws for the whole of the double line between London and Bristol cost in the region of £20,000.[9] It was soon discovered that the 44 lb rail would not effectively carry the heavy trains and so relaying with 62 lb rail had to be carried out soon after the first section of line was opened to traffic. Replacement of rail was not a major problem, nor had it caused any real inconvenience, but another aspect of Brunel's baulk road design did lead to serious difficulties.

Brunel advocated the use of piles driven into the ground and connected to the double and single transverse sleepers. This, he postulated, would keep the track firmly in position and level. Beech piles, 10 in in diameter, would be driven at least 7 or 8 ft into the original ground. In cuttings that presented no difficulty but on embankments very long piles might be necessary. Although inconvenient and costly that was not the problem; only when operations commenced did the evil manifest itself. Ballast had been driven under the longitudinal timbers but the relatively soft ground of the embankments gradually compacted as trains passed over. Subsidence occurred and the track sank, but only between the piles which then acted as

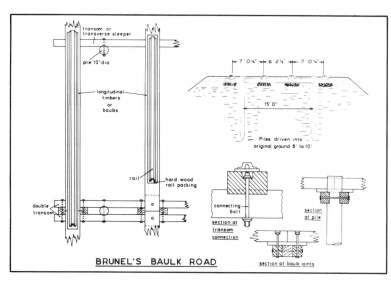

BRUNEL'S BAULK ROAD

supports. The track assumed the characteristics of a roller coaster and riding became very unpleasant.

A number of shareholders became anxious about the cost of the track and also the broad gauge in general. Shortly after the first section of line, between Paddington and Maidenhead, opened on 4 June 1838 the directors indicated that they would request a number of eminent engineers to investigate the line and its working. In fact Brunel himself had suggested to the board that two or three other engineers be called in to report on the permanent way which was causing concern.[10] The scrutiny required by some people turned out to be more far reaching than Brunel contemplated. Two of the three engineers initially approached, James Walker, President of the Institution of Civil Engineers, and Robert Stephenson, declined but Nicholas Woods agreed. Later John Hawkshaw, engineer of the Manchester and Leeds Railway, was also called upon. It is unnecessary to detail the events or the reports of the two men as they have been given space in MacDermot's history of the GWR and in the two major Brunel biographies. Needless to say, Brunel was not happy about his engineering qualities being brought into question but he continued with his tasks and awaited the reports from the two investigating engineers.

Brunel knew that there were imperfections in his road and had already decided to make modifications, particularly in the abandonment of the piling system. However, both reports were loaded against him and when visited by George Henry Gibbs, one of the directors, on 14 December 1838 he looked to be in a very dejected state. The engineer told Gibbs that '. . .the evidence which was accumulating against him appeared to be too great to be resisted

without injury to the Company, and therefore he was prepared to give way.' Though the dice seemed loaded against him Brunel was still certain that his propositions were sound. Gibbs recorded in his diary, 'He had no vanity of any kind. If it were necessary to yield, he had no objection to it being said that he had been defeated, for he felt confident in the correctness of his views and was sure he should have opportunities of proving it.' Statements of that nature indicate many aspects of the Brunel character. Though his convictions regarding the broad gauge were strong he was not arrogant and was more than willing to subordinate his own feelings to the interests of his employers. He would not, however, brook the idea of working with another engineer:

> . . .but if it was proposed to connect another engineer with him, he could not see how such a scheme could possibly work, for which he gave his reasons, nor could he understand the meaning of a consulting engineer. He gave us clearly to understand that he could not and would not submit to either of these alternatives, but that he would resign his situation as engineer whenever we pleased.[11]

That must have been the blackest period in the career of Britain's greatest engineer.

When others about him seemed to be losing their nerve, Brunel's strength of character showed through. His plan was fundamentally correct and he knew it. Daniel Gooch alone appeared to have unyielding faith in his chief and worked tirelessly to support him. Modifications brought about incredible improvements in locomotive performance which, with Brunel's convictions still firmly holding, brought victory over Woods, Hawkshaw,

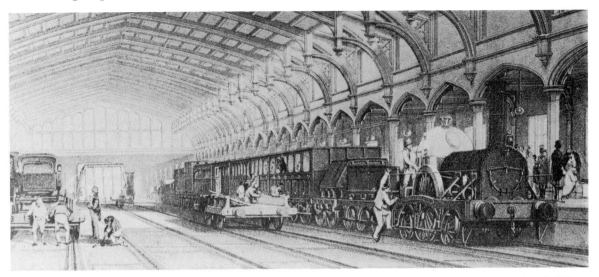

Dr Dionysius Lardner and the disenchanted shareholders from the north. A passionate meeting on 9 January 1839 heard all of the arguments and by a show hands supported Brunel. Unwilling to accept defeat the shareholders from Liverpool demanded a ballot. Next day the shareholders voted in favour of the broad gauge continuing and all dissension ceased.[12] With but few changes in the permanent way structure the road continued towards Bristol.

Though he was Engineer to what he considered 'the finest work in England', Brunel still undertook other commissions even if, as mentioned previously, these were carried out by other members of his staff. As far as Brunel was concerned they all added to his stock, although some were rather beneath him. An entry in his diary on 26 December 1835 illustrates some of the projects for which he had been contracted and his feelings for them.

> Merthyr & Cardiff Railway—This too I owe to the GWR. I care not however about it. Newbury Branch—. . .almost beneath my notice now. It will do as a branch. Cheltenham Railway—Of course this I owe to the Great Western—and I may say myself. Do not feel much interest in this. None of the parties are my friends. I hold it only because they can't do without me. . .However, it's all in the way of business and it's a proud thing to monopolise all the west as I do. Suspension Bridge across Thames—I have condescended to be engineer to this—but shan't give myself much trouble about it. If done, however, it all adds to my stock of irons.

Could the Engineer have then been developing attitudes of self-importance and superiority? An entry regarding the Bristol & Exeter Railway, the survey for which was undertaken by William Gravatt, one of his first assistants and who had worked with him on the Thames Tunnel, shows feelings of gratitude. 'This survey was done in grand style—it's a good line too—and I feel an interest as connected with Bristol to which I really owe much—they have stuck well to me. I think we shall carry this bill—I shall become quite an oracle in Committees of the House.'[13]

The need to speak in public had been forced upon Brunel but he did not relish the idea. It was necessary to perform before Committees in Parliament and also to persuade potential shareholders to part with their money. The Brunel tongue was effective and his personality striking. Many an individual as well as company director and shareholder came under his spell. He could speak well but the information he presented would always be based upon sound reasoning and fact. Unfortunately, in a few cases his enthusiasm seemed to get the better of him. Even then his projections would still be based upon correct engineering principles and not supposition. Mechanical practicalities would let him down, not the concept. His disastrous adventure with the atmospheric system on the South Devon Railway is the prime example.

In order to allow for high speeds with the locomotives then available Brunel arranged his lines, whenever possible, so that the gradients were reasonably easy. In all of the early railways with which he was associated lack of finance did not restrict his plans. A railway in South Devon between Exeter and Plymouth would extend the broad gauge westward, adding to the empire, so naturally Brunel became interested. Traffic in the region would not be as great as in the more populated areas but a railway was considered essential. Even the board of the GWR considered that to be so for it was the Great Western, together with the Bristol & Exeter and Bristol & Gloucester Railways, which subscribed a major part of the finance.[14]

The South Devon countryside had a decidedly different appearance from that of Wiltshire or Somerset and there was no way of avoiding the hills to the west of Totnes without a massive and expensive detour. Heavy earthworks and tunnels were also ruled out on the grounds of cost. Locomotives then available were not suitable for stiff gradients but the pace of locomotive development was rapid, a fact Brunel seems to have missed. A solution to the problem lay in the atmospheric system as devised by Messrs Clegg and Samuda. Conventional locomotives were not required, the propelling power coming from stationary pumping houses. The system needed a large pipe to be placed between the tracks and in that pipe ran a piston connected to the pulling car. Steam driven pumps evacuated the pipe ahead of the piston whilst air was allowed into the pipe behind, thereby forcing the piston, and hence the train, along. To allow for connection of the piston to the pulling car and also to provide an inlet for the air, the top of the pipe was slit and sealed with a continuous leather valve.

As adhesion of locomotive wheels played no part in the drive, steep gradients could be managed with ease, thus reducing the cost of earthworks. Single line working could carry the same amount of traffic as a double line of conventional railway, again reducing the costs. Rail and ballast costs would be lower as no heavy locomotives had to traverse the line. The operating costs of pumping houses, every three miles of line, would be less than that of conventional locomotives. These were some of the arguments put forward by Brunel in favour of the system. He even produced detailed costings showing a saving of £67,000 compared with a locomotive system. Needless to say, the South Devon Railway directors were convinced and adopted the plan.[15]

At that time very limited experience of the atmospheric system had been obtained and then only on short lines in good conditions. The coast of South Devon was to prove a different trial ground. Brunel based his arguments upon information gathered from the operation of a short length of track laid out by the inventors and on the branch line between Kingstown and Dalkey, near Dublin. George Stephenson wanted nothing to do with the idea, considering it to be 'a great humbug', and his son Robert was no more enthusiastic.[16] What attracted Brunel to the system is difficult to imagine as mere novelty did not intrigue the engineer. Generally he was a man for whom only sound and practicable suggestions had merit. Why did his judgement fail him in this instance? It appears to have been his understanding of the mechnical engineering aspects which let him down.

There were likely to be mechnical problems and

Atmospheric railway train system.

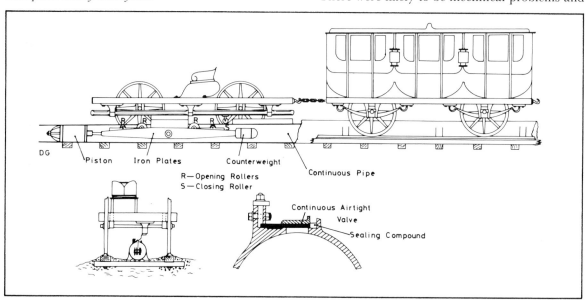

Brunel was aware of this, but he dismissed them in a rather casual manner. His report to the South Devon Railway board included the brief statement, '. . .the mere mechanical difficulties can be overcome. . .'.[17] That might have been the case if the technology available had been better and if money had been without restriction, but money was in short supply. Brunel had advocated the installation of an electric telegraph system on the line, not only for public use but also to warn a pumping house of an approaching train. A pump might then be operated only when a train was about to enter its section of line, thereby reducing fuel costs and wear on the machinery. Without the telegraph, pumps had frequently to be kept in operation for prolonged periods because a train was running behind schedule. Leakage at the leather pipe seal resulted in additional pump work. Failure of pumps and their steam engines resulted in delay and necessitated the use of locomotives. Robert Stephenson's major objection to the system was that each section depended entirely upon the functioning of a pump. If that pump failed then the whole line was out of action as nothing could move in either direction until repairs were executed. Brunel appeared blissfully unaware of the consequences of mechanical breakdown.

The first trains worked the line from Exeter to Teignmouth in May 1846 and to Newton Abbot in December but they were pulled by Gooch locomotives, the pumping equipment not being ready. Not until September the following year did atmospheric service trains operate to Teignmouth with an extension to Newton in January 1848. Initially the trains worked well with better than expected speeds being obtained and many passengers expressing satisfaction at the lack of smoke and ash. Only with prolonged operation did defects manifest themselves. Leather seals on the travelling pistons became damaged whilst passing through the valves which isolated the sections of pipe. The basic requirement of stopping at a station and starting again became a problem if the train stopped short or the pipe was not effectively evacuated. The sealing of the longitudinal valve gave increasing problems. Water built up in the pipe during wet or stormy weather and rats, who took a liking to the whale and seal oil used to coat the leather strip, would be drawn into the pipe when it was evacuated for the first train of the day. As the pumps were not fitted with filters and discharged straight into the engine house, conditions could be unpleasant with dead rats, mice and oily water being ejected.[18]

More importantly, the rat corpses damaged the pumps and failure occurred. Though efficient pumps were essential, the atmospheric system stood or fell by the effectiveness of the longitudinal valve. Sealing compounds helped to maintain performance but the cod oil and soap compound required frequent application. The leather itself was, however, the problem as nobody knew what prolonged exposure to partial vacuum and weather would do to its structure. Sun caused drying out whilst frost froze the water in the leather; in both cases the resultant stiffness caused the material to tear and sealing was impaired. A totally unexpected and fatal condition resulted from the chemical reaction between the tannin in the leather and the iron oxide in the plates which backed it. Iron oxide removed the tannin converting the leather to a useless tissue.[19] Any form of seal quickly disappeared and the trains stopped. To present-day observers the use of an untried material for such a critical purpose might seem strange, especially as Brunel was so good an engineer. That might be the most inexcusable part of the fiasco but Brunel was never as conservative as the Stephensons; he was prepared to push back the bounds of knowledge, and his works showed that. Some failed but most succeeded and in doing so improved the lot of many people.

By June 1848 it became obvious that a complete replacement valve would be needed, the cost being in the region of £25,000 for the section of line then operating on the atmospheric principle. Without other action deterioration of that leather must take

Atmospheric railway pumping house, Starcross, Devon.

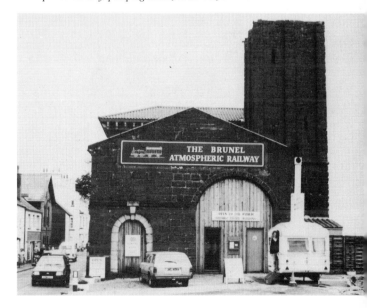

place within a relatively short period. But there was no other remedial action which might be taken, only leather was available as a valve material and it could not be protected against the environment. Brunel acknowledged that and bowed to the inevitable; the atmospheric experiment had to be abandoned. In a lengthy report dated 19 August 1848 he presented all the facts and his recommendation to the directors. The valve was the problem and Brunel considered that Samuda and the patentees of the system had a responsibility for not pointing out potential problems. Litigation would have resulted in no solution and so the matter was dropped. The directors agreed with Brunel and reported to the shareholders that they '. . .have arrived at the conclusion, with the entire concurrence and on the recommendation of Mr Brunel, that it is expedient for them to suspend the use of the Atmospheric System until the same shall be made efficient at the expense of the patentees and Mr Samuda.'[20] From 9 September that year the line was operated by locomotives and remained so.

Without doubt Brunel was wrong to advocate the use of such an experimental system. His, and other people's, lack of knowledge about the properties of leather resulted in the fiasco. But he had an optimism regarding the solution of mechanical problems which bordered on fantasy. He was a brilliant civil engineer and expected others to have the same skills and ingenuity in the mechanical world. Unfortunately that was not the case.

As Engineer to the Great Western Railway Brunel had responsibility for all items connected with any branch of engineering. That included the provision and operation of locomotives together with rolling stock. The embryo GWR had no facilities of its own thus putting manufacture in the hands of outside contractors. But which manufacturers would supply the stock and to what design? Surprisingly Brunel was willing to leave detailed design to the manufacturers he considered suitable, only laying down certain conditons. In June 1836 he sent a circular letter to a number of locomotive manufacturers requesting that they tender for the supply of motive power.

> The particular form and construction of the engines will be left to your own judgement, the object of the Company being to induce manufacturers to turn their attention to the improvement of locomotive engines and to afford them an opportunity of introducing such improvements as may suggest themselves when unchecked by a detailed and particular specification of the parts. . . .

Fine sentiments in the cause of mechnical engineering development but not those which a single railway company should have been propounding if commercial logic had prevailed. The letter then indicated the few conditions.

> A velocity of 30 miles per hour to be considered as the standard velocity and this to be attained without requiring the piston to travel at a greater rate than 280 ft per minute. The engine to be of such dimension and power as to exert and maintain without difficulty— with the pressure of the steam in the boiler not exceeding 50 lbs upon the square inch and with a velocity of 30 miles per hour—a force of traction equal to 800 lbs upon a level. . .tender with a supply of fuel and water for one hour's consumption. The weight of the engine, exclusive of the tender, but in other respects supplied with water and fuel for work not to exceed 10.5 tons, and if above 8 tons to be carried on six wheels.[21]

This very broad specification indicates Brunel's open mind on mechanical matters, particularly with regard to the locomotive, design of which was still in its infancy. It might have served him better had he studied mechanical engineering in more detail or at least employed a mechanical engineer in his office. Unfortunately the engineer of that period was still very much expected to be a 'jack of all trades'. Although in many respects Brunel was more than a match for Robert Stephenson, the 'Geordie' had greater skill in mechanical matters regarding machine design and construction. Considering the training Robert received at the side of his father that was only to be expected.

Five manufacturers responded, agreeing to supply locomotives under the conditions laid down. Mather, Dixon & Co. and Tayleur & Co. of the Vulcan Foundry each contracted for six engines; Sharp, Roberts & Co. were to supply three, whilst the Haigh Foundry and Hawthorn's of Newcastle would each produce two machines. The two locomotives supplied from the works of R.& W. Hawthorn were to a patent of T.E. Harrison of Whitburn, later to be associated with the North Eastern Railway. It is uncertain whether the contract was with Harrison or the Hawthorn company. An approach was also made to Robert Stephenson & Co. but they had a full order book and could not meet the time requirement. Fortuitously for the GWR a locomotive destined for overseas became available and Stephenson aproache;d Brunel to see if he would take it. A contract was agreed in July 1837 and, following adjustment of the wheel gauge, *North Star* arrived at Maidenhead in November.[22] As it turned out, fortune smiled upon Brunel and his employers

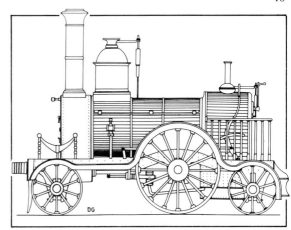

Vulcan, *the first locomotive steamed on the GWR, built by Tayleur & Co.*

Lion. *Built by Sharp, Roberts & Co.*

when financial uncertainty prevented that foreign order from being completed.

Even though he left the design work in the hands of the builders, Brunel requested that plans of the locomotives be submitted for aproval. To what extent any changes in design came about is unknown but it would appear from the resultant products that few were required. If Brunel did ask for changes to be made then proposed designs must have been rather weird as many of the machines eventually delivered were odd to say the least. Most did not even comply with stipulated conditions, mainly on account of weight. Presumably Brunel realized that the weight restriction was totally unreasonable as many narrow gauge locomotives of the period did not even meet it. Some of the Vulcan engines weighed in at nearly twice the maximum amount.

Two locomotives were turned down because they did not comply with the details given in the submitted plans. Haigh Foundry decided to depart from the usual practice of cranked axles and adopt a geared form of drive in order to meet the condition of 30 mph velocity with a maximum piston speed of 280 ft min. The drawings had indicated a minimum distance between gear wheel and rail level of 17 in, but when assembled at Paddington in July 1838 there was only a 10 in gap.[23] In view of possible impact with objects between the rails the locomotives were not accepted. (Gearing, in the ratio of 3:2, allowed the use of 6 ft 4 in diameter wheels and was adopted by another manufacturer, but most decided to employ large diameter driving wheels.) Changes had to be made but exactly what they were is unknown. In later years the machines appeared with conven-

tional cranked axles and considerable controversy built up concerning the gearing, many being of the opinion that references to it implied the valve gear. As designed, approved by Brunel and delivered, *Viper* and *Snake* had a form of gear drive. At a meeting on 30 August 1838 the directors agreed to take them subject to certain conditions and it is likely that one of these was replacement of the gearing as soon as convenient.[24]

Large diameter wheels had no obvious disadvantages as far as Brunel was concerned and he passed plans utilizing them, although the original intention had been to limit diameter to 7 or 8 ft for passenger engines. Why the Engineer desired a piston to move no faster than 5 ft per second is difficult to understand; there was no sound reason for keeping it so low, particularly when narrow gauge locomotives of the period attained twice that speed from 5 ft driving wheels and 18 in piston stroke when running at 30 mph. Whether the reasoning lay in a conservative attitude, with which Brunel was not normally afflicted, or a lack of understanding as to the workings of the steam engine cannot be known. In all of his projects requiring steam plant he had little to do with the machinery, leaving that side to the experts, the builders, and rightly so. But why stipulate such amazing conditions? The answer must lie in a lack of understanding, a mental block in an otherwise brilliant engineer. Perhaps that is as well.

Large wheels allowed compliance with the piston speed condition but imposed problems regarding another of the conditions. Big wheels were heavy and Brunel had stipulated a maximum weight. In the end none of the manufacturers kept fully within that restriction but no comment

appears to have been made. By that time Brunel probably realized that such a weight restriction was almost impossible to meet. The locomotives produced to the patent of Thomas Harrison did at least go some way towards achieving Brunel's aims. A separate power unit kept weight on the driving wheels within the restriction but the ball and socket steam pipe connection to the boiler presented many problems during operation. *Thunderer* had a power unit of 0-4-0 form with the 6 ft coupled wheels geared up in the ratio 2.7:1, whilst *Hurricane* had a conventional 2-2-2 arrangement with 10 ft drivers. For each locomotive the boiler (on its own set of wheels) had a large firebox but this was divided into two separate longitudinal compartments by an intermediate water space and it suffered from the disadvantage that lighting up was a problem. If the fire in one part of the firebox burned well it had the tendency to extinguish the other fire resulting in delay.[25]

Mather, Dixon & Co. delivered *Premier* during

November 1837 and *Ariel* the following March; however, it was *Ajax*, delivered in December 1838, which attracted attention. All Mather engines were not constructed to the same pattern and *Ajax* had 10 ft diameter plate wheels. Brunel knew of the plate wheels and the proposed diameter as early as July 1837. On the 27th of that month he wrote to the manufacturers complaining that he had received no plans of the wheels. In the same letter he seemed to approve the use of 10 ft diameter wheels, or at least made no objection to them.[26] The singular objectionable feature of large plate wheels appears to have eluded Brunel, namely the effect of side winds. A sail-like 76 sq ft upon which any wind might act did not help stability. It is difficult to comprehend why a normally fastidious engineer like Brunel can have let such a patently defective scheme be applied to engines for his line. Again it forces the point that he was not a mechanical but a civil engineer. Such an obvious wind barrier would never have been found in one of his bridges.

In all of his schemes Brunel sought to instil a sense of beauty; his designs not only had to function but also be pleasing to the eye. His tunnels and bridges which survive exhibit that aesthetic charm he felt to be important, and the locomotives also had to be attractive. Maybe that had greater priority than performance. In a letter to Harrison prior to delivery of his second engine Brunel laid out his feelings.

Lastly let me call your attention to the appearance— we have a splendid engine of Stephenson's, it would be the most beautiful ornament in the most elegant drawing room and we have another of Quaker-like simplicity carried even to shabbiness but very possibly as good an engine, but the difference in care bestowed by the engine man, the favour in which it is held by

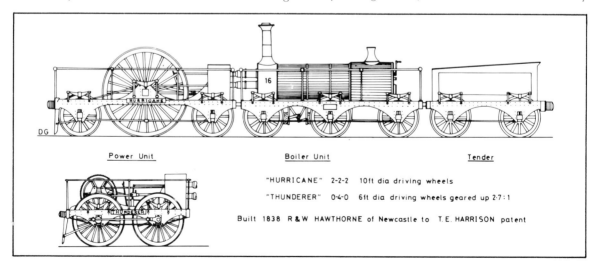

Power Unit	Boiler Unit	Tender

"HURRICANE" 2-2-2 10ft dia driving wheels

"THUNDERER" 0-4-0 6ft dia driving wheels geared up 2.7:1

Built 1838 R & W HAWTHORNE of Newcastle to T.E. HARRISON patent

Left Teign, *originally called* Viper. *Built by the Haigh Foundry.*

Below left *Harrison patent design articulated engines* Hurricane *and* Thunderer, *built by R. & W. Hawthorn.*

Right Ajax, *with 10 ft diameter disc wheels. Built by Mather, Dixon & Co.*

Below *The broad gauge* Iron Duke, *in final form. Mixed gauge track is laid in Bleadon Hill Cutting (courtesy of the National Railway Museum, York).*

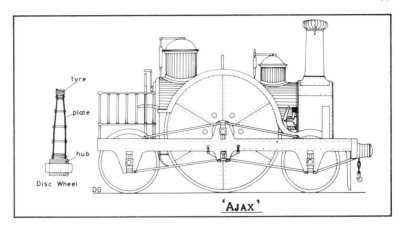

'AJAX'

others and even oneself, not to mention the public, is striking. A plain young lady however amiable is apt to be neglected. Now your engine is capable of being made very handsome, and it ought to be so.[27]

Most commentators have had little to say regarding the beauty of those early GWR engines but overall the term 'freaks' has been liberally applied.

Without doubt Brunel failed as 'locomotive procurement officer' and certainly cost the GWR money and time as well as damaging its early reputation. It would appear that he was much better at selecting men for engineering positions. Why nobody was employed to supervise the acquisition and maintenance of locomotives before any contracts had been made is difficult to understand. Brunel had overall responsibility and seemed capable of manipulating the board to agree to any proposition he made. It has already been shown how Brunel felt that nobody but himself was capable of performing all but the most mundane of

tasks. An obviously important task concerning the purchase of the line's first engines could not be left to anybody else. Engineer to the Great Western Railway meant sole responsibility for everything connected with the building and operating of the line. That included signals and locomotives. As time progressed it became obvious, even to the assiduous Brunel, that a full-time engineer would be required to supervise the locomotive department. For the GWR and British locomotive development it is fortunate that Brunel had the foresight and skill to judge the qualities latent in the young Daniel Gooch. Perhaps it is propitious that Brunel held on to control for so long. If a locomotive engineer had been appointed earlier it is certain that Gooch would not have been considered on the grounds of age, or rather lack of it. Fortunately that was not so, otherwise the history of the Great Western Railway would have been very different.

Right *The GWR system and the extent of the broad gauge lines in 1868.*

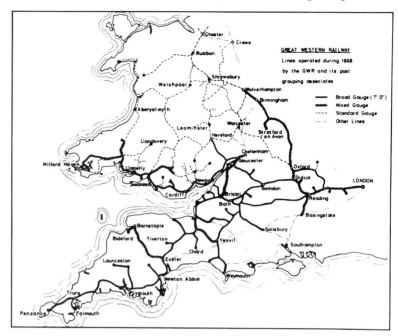

Below *Brunel system of signals for broad gauge lines.*

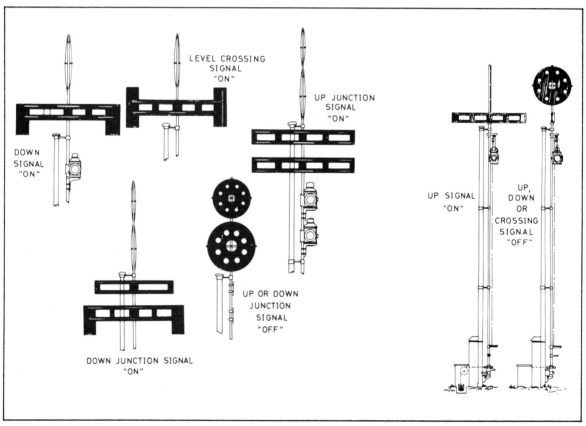

2. The nineteenth-century men

1. Daniel Gooch

Certain events in the history of any organization are often looked upon as being critical to the development and prosperity of that concern. Without doubt Brunel's decision to appoint the young Daniel Gooch as locomotive engineer of the Great Western Railway ranks amongst his most successful. For that railway it was momentous, not just in locomotive terms but also for survival. During July 1837 Brunel was given permission to advertise for a works manager who would be responsible for maintenance of the locomotives then on order. At the time Daniel Gooch held a somewhat temporary appointment under his elder brother Thomas, who was engineer of the Manchester & Leeds Railway. That line was then under construction but the work did not appeal to Daniel. He had feelings for the 'iron horse'; he was a mechanical, not civil, engineer. Work with locomotives, that was the aim and at once he wrote to Brunel (see Appendix 1).

The two men met in Manchester on 9 August 1837 and Brunel was obviously impressed with the applicant for he immediately offered him the post. How many others had applied is not known but Gooch was the ideal choice: his pedigree in locomotive engineering made him a natural complement to Brunel and his enthusiasm for the broad gauge an admirable partner. Later in life Gooch recorded, 'I was very glad of this appointment, as I felt it was a permanent thing in which, by attention and perseverance, I might hope to get on. I was also very glad to have to manage the broad gauge, which filled my mind as the great advance of the age, and in the soundness of which I was a great believer.'[1] As the memoirs were written many years after the event, it might be supposed that enthusiasm for the broad gauge was included to suit posterity; that does not do justice to the honesty of the man. The board approved of Brunel's choice and on 18 August, a few days before his twenty-first birthday, Gooch took up his appointment.

Born at Bedlington, Northumberland, on 24 August 1816, Daniel Gooch was soon to discover the world of engineering for his father, John, worked at the local iron foundry. George Stephenson and that other well-known engineer Joseph Locke were family friends, thus providing vital stimulus during their regular visits to the Gooch house. When his father took up a position at the Tredegar Iron Foundry the family went with him and Daniel obtained an apprenticeship at the works. Enthusiasm for engineering never wavered and he was a dedicated worker, but the folly of others nearly cost him his life on two occasions. Whilst working in the cylinder of a large air pump Gooch was nearly squashed by a descending piston set in motion by an inattentive worker. A short time later somebody decided to fill the air chamber of a furnace blower with powdered lime whilst he was working in the space. The lesson was not lost and, in later life, Gooch dealt severely with the neglectful or careless workman.

The death of his father in August 1833 interrupted that training and Gooch left Tredegar with his mother to live in Coventry. Within a matter of weeks Daniel had secured a place at the Vulcan Foundry where his real contact with locomotive building began. Nominally under the control of Charles Tayleur & Co., the Vulcan

Daniel Gooch, first Locomotive Superintendent to the GWR.

works formed part of the Robert Stephenson locomotive manufacturing empire. It was conveniently placed for the Liverpool & Manchester Railway as well as the new railways being constructed in the north and Midlands. Whilst at Vulcan the young Gooch again threw himself into the work, learning about machines and men. He made friends with many people and became very well liked though he did not much care for the social life.

A number of Vulcan engines were supplied to the Liverpool & Manchester Railway and as part of his duties Daniel had to ride on the engines which had just been delivered in order to assess performance. This he enjoyed and would obtain footplate rides whenever he could. Driver Jim Hurst regularly saw Gooch on the footplate and the two developed a regard for each other. Hurst was, however, rather eccentric in his driving habits and was eventually dismissed in June 1836. Later that year, following his appointment to the GWR, when Gooch was looking for drivers, the foreman of the L & M's locomotive works at Salford, a Scotsman called Sandy Fife, suggested Hurst. A meeting at Fife's house was arranged. Hurst subsequently recalled the meeting, 'He at once recognised me, gave me a warm greeting and spoke of the old days, and our interview ended in his engaging me as an engine driver for the Great Western at 6/8d per day.'[2] Gooch would later encounter Hurst at regular intervals, sometimes possibly regretting the day he engaged him, for the driver was never conventional.

After a year at Vulcan, ill-health forced Gooch to spend some time with his mother at Coventry, and a short while later he obtained permission to work at the Dundee Foundry in order to gain further draughting experience. Within twelve months he returned to Stephenson but at the Newcastle works. In the drawing office he had contact with the latest ideas in locomotive practice and became involved with construction for gauges other than the Stephenson standard. Gooch had been instructed to prepare drawings of locomotives destined for a 6 ft gauge line in Russia and he also had contact with plans for engines of 5 ft 6 in gauge required to fulfil an American order. The advantages of so much space between the wheels was not lost on the young man barely eighteen years old. Later in life he could, with all honesty, say that he believed the broad gauge to be better than the narrow. In June 1845, following a Parliamentary fight over the Oxford, Worcester & Wolverhampton Railway, an embittered George Stephenson accused Gooch of betraying the gauge in which he had been reared. Gooch remained firm, believing,

'I was not only fighting for my convictions, but also for my employers. . .'.[3]

Seeking advancement, during October 1836 he threw in his lot with a group of people desirous of establishing a locomotive works in Newcastle. Disagreement between the parties resulted in the escapade being short-lived, and by March of the following year Gooch was without a position. Before obtaining the temporary post with his brother Thomas there was a spot of courting to be done. Daniel had known Margaret Tanner from Sunderland for some time, the couple having met when she visited her aunt in Gateshead. For a week during the middle of April the two were regularly in each other's company and on the 17th of that month, '. . .she went with me to the museum alone, and we left it engaged.'[4] Neither in love nor in engineering was Gooch slow to react when he saw a true opportunity.

Without employment the young suitor had little to offer Margaret but she must have known the worth of her future husband. One day as they walked together over Sunderland bridge she pointed out the motto cast on the bridge; '*Nil Desperandum*'. Gooch took the message.

At a salary of £300 per year Daniel Gooch began his long association with the Great Western Railway, and one of his first tasks was to inspect the locomotives then under construction for the railway. They were not impressive, 'I felt very uneasy about the working of these machines, feeling sure they would have enough to do to drive themselves along the road.'[5] But they were all that the Company had and he would have to make the best of it. One by one the engines were delivered and the new Locomotive Superintendent knew he had work on his hands. Hard work would be no problem but keeping the assorted machines running when the line opened certainly would. During May and June of 1838 the recently married Gooch was forced to spend many nights away from his bride, practically living in a carriage at the engine house, Paddington, as he tried to cajole the excuses for locomotives into performing another day's work. There was only Stephenson's *North Star* and the six Vulcan engines upon which he could rely with any certainty.[6]

Unfortunately, some people laid the blame upon Gooch and not where it squarely belonged, with Brunel. George Henry Gibbs, a director of the GWR, friend of Brunel and normally a very fair man, was not at all happy with the situation at the end of the first year. 'Our engines are in a very bad order and Gooch seems to be very unfit for the superintendence of that department.'[7] Why Gibbs should have come down so strongly against the

North Star, *the Robert Stephenson engine upon which Gooch based his designs.*

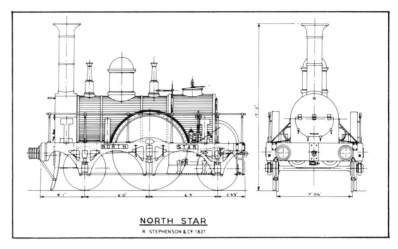

young northerner is difficult to understand as Brunel certainly was satisfied with his work and nobody could have been more enthusiastic or hard working. Possibly the reason lay in his youth and direct northern manner. With the failure of so many engines in the first few months of operations the directors called for reports from Gooch and Brunel. Up to that time the Locomotive Superintendent had reported only to Brunel and he felt himself to be in a difficult position as his report would be scathing about the design of the machines. Naturally, that would reflect upon Brunel; however, he had no option but to comply. Brunel was angry but only in an initial letter to Gooch and he continued to give him a free hand with the stock, knowing that what had been stated was right. 'His good sense told him what I had said was correct and his kind heart did me justice.'[8]

Inevitably, Gooch was given the order to prepare designs for new locomotives which would have to be delivered quickly and in quantity. That matter will be discussed later but Gooch worked tirelessly at his task, having the assistance of draughtsmen he had appointed: one of these was Thomas Crampton, later to be a renowned locomotive designer in his own right. The resultant 'Firefly' class was an immediate success and spawned many other designs. Gibbs had been proved wrong and the GWR had a locomotive fleet of which it could be proud.

With the line nearing completion the provision of repair facilities between London and Bristol exercised the minds of Brunel and Gooch. Eventually they settled on a spot close to the town of Swindon where a junction with the line to Cheltenham existed. The depot commenced repair operations early in 1843 and delivered its first locomotive, *Great Western*, during 1846. Over the

following years the locomotive works and the township of New Swindon, which grew up around it, expanded dramatically.

Throughout the early years Gooch and Brunel worked together in fighting off assaults from narrow gauge interests, the battles continuing in the boardroom and Parliament as well as the public press. Such conflicts are well known and need not be repeated, but in many respects it was only the unstinting efforts of Gooch which provided the broad gauge party with the ammunition with which to fight off the outside interests. He was not prepared to bandy words just for the sake of argument; if proof was needed he obtained it. Gooch locomotives were superior to any others; the designer knew that and would show the world. To do so meant the construction of dynamometer car and the development of an indicator device in order to measure the power produced by the locomotive. In his experiments he was meticulous even when necessity demanded that he perch on the buffer beam of a locomotive going at 60 mph in order to obtain indicator diagrams. Nobody could criticize his results or methods of testing. In 1851 the eminent engineer and author D.K. Clark commented, 'Mr. Daniel Gooch is the only experimentalist whose results are worthy of implicit confidence.'[9]

Gooch only ever took out one patent and that concerned the coating of rails and locomotive tyres with a layer of steel. Over the years the royalties amounted to something over £5,000, but overall the inventor was displeased, not with the amount of money he received but due to the difficult situation which existed with his employers. It led him to the conclusion that engineers who worked for companies should not take out patents and that the patent laws which then existed were wrong. He believed that '. . .absence of a patent law would not retard invention; the human mind will scheme and study for the pleasure of the work and the honour of being the originator of a real improvement would be sufficient stimulus.'[10] It is worthy of note that Brunel never took out a patent and held the same views about them.

Financial matters never really troubled Gooch for he always held firmly to the belief that debt had to be avoided. Apart from his salary he was able to boost his income by taking pupils, a step approved of by the directors. His brother John considered that a premium of £400 should be charged for a four-year term of training.[11] The salary paid by the GWR increased to £550 following the opening of the railway, with an increase of £150 being made in January 1841. Following the gauge battles of 1845 an award of £500 was made in gratitude for Gooch's efforts in putting the GWR case.[12] In January 1846 his annual salary stood at £1,000 and five years later it had risen to £1,500, but not before some unpleasantness intervened. At the end of 1849 a committee set up by the directors in order to investigate costs suggested that the salaries of company officers should be reduced. The Locomotive Superintendent would get only £700 instead of £1,000. Naturally Gooch objected most strongly and the shareholders backed him, but the *contretemps* taught him a lesson: his position and salary rested with directors who might be changed at short notice. The GWR did not offer a job for life. Believing, in fact, that his position was secure he had turned down a number of better paying offers, one of them from Locke on the Grand Junction. An interview with Russell, the chairman, resulted in approval being given for the taking of outside work as a consultant, such work paying handsomely.[13]

On the domestic side life progressed very satisfactorily. Daughters Anna and Emily were born in June 1839 and July 1840 respectively, both at the rooms he had rented in Paddington Green. A first son, Henry, was born in December 1841, followed by Charles in January 1845 and Alfred during March 1846. Frank, born in July 1847, completed the family which could then move into the recently built house in Warwick Road, Paddington. Gooch was devoted to his family as he was to his friends. The death of Brunel devastated him, 'I lost my oldest and best friend. . . .He was a true and sincere friend, a man of the highest honour, and his loss was deeply deplored by all who have the honour to know him. . .I shall ever feel a deep sense of gratitude to Mr Brunel for all his kindness and support from the day I first saw him in 1837.'[14] Both daughters married before the age of twenty, a situation not to Gooch's liking for

he wished them to have stayed at home a little longer. This is a natural reaction in most fathers who never feel their daughters are grown up enough to marry!

Outside activities provided a valuable income and added variety to life. Gooch was becoming a skilled entrepreneur with interests in a couple of collieries and Brunel's steamship, *Great Eastern*. During 1863 a partnership was formed with Whitworth of Manchester, the purpose being the manufacture of guns to Whitworth's designs: 'My chief object being to place Harry there as a future provision for him, and I also thought the gun work would be an amusement for me when I retire from the Great Western Railway.'[15] Already he was thinking about retirement from the railway but wished to make provision for his younger brother, William, to follow him as Superintendent. William had been appointed Works Manager at Swindon in 1857, with the tacit understanding that he would have charge of the Locomotive Department when Daniel retired. Unfortunately, amalgamations with the West Midland and South Wales railways brought new members to the board and a new chairman in the form of Richard Potter. Disagreements within the board during the early part of 1864 determined Gooch to resign, but only after receiving assurance from Potter that the agreement regarding William would be kept. Gooch resigned his position and Potter reneged on his agreement. Potter had already offered the position to Charles Reboul Sacre of the Manchester, Sheffield & Lincolnshire Railway, but Gooch made his feelings known to the directors and they turned down the appointment. The appointment of Joseph Armstrong met with his approval and Daniel Gooch officially left GWR service on 5 October 1864. Naturally, William Gooch also resigned and Daniel set up a company to purchase the Vulcan Foundry where William would be installed as Managing Director. He remained there, and the company thrived, until his retirement in 1892.

There is no doubt that Daniel Gooch, though a hard taskmaster, had the admiration of all in his charge because he was fair and stood by those who followed his instructions, even against other company officials. In the words of Jim Hurst, '. . .he was a man who was rather stern and always wanted the work done well, he appreciated a good servant, but a bad one stood no chance with him. He'd have the work done his own way, and plenty of men to do it.' One official was overheard to complain to a colleague, 'I don't know how many times I have complained of that Hurst, but it's not the slightest use, Mr. Gooch will take no notice of my letters.' The colleague replied, 'You might have saved yourself the trouble, you may be sure that Hurst has been working according to his Superintendent's orders.'[16]

Gooch had been one of the founding fathers of the Swindon Mechanics' Institute, a body established to further the education of those employed by the Great Western at Swindon, and it was to that body he bade farewell on 31 August 1864. He had been President of the Institute since its founding and rejoiced in the good it had done for the community as well as the workforce. Brother William was Vice-President and both gave up their positions solely because the rules indicated that serving officers of the GWR only could hold such posts. As a departing gift he offered the Institute a number of shares in the New Swindon Improvement Company. The £10 per year yielded by the shares was to be devoted to the granting of two prizes for students who displayed the greatest proficiency in mechanical drawing. Showing signs of great emotion, Daniel managed to finish his speech and then, following a few words from William, the Gooch brothers were given a prolonged ovation.[17] It is interesting to relate that the final occupant of the Gooch chair as Locomotive Superintendent, F.W. Hawksworth, was a recipient of that Gooch prize for drawing.[18]

Away from the railway, Daniel Gooch kept himself occupied with many projects including, in 1865, his first attempt to lay an Atlantic telegraph cable using *Great Eastern*. Though the attempt failed, Gooch returned the following year with another expedition which proved not only successful in laying a new cable but also retrieved the first and completed that. For these feats Queen Victoria made him a baronet. 1865 also saw Gooch returned as Member of Parliament for Cricklade, but it was not work in which he held much interest for he never actually spoke during a debate. Freemasonry did attract him and from 1850 onwards he played an active part in the affairs of that organization, holding many offices and forming a number of Lodges. Later in life he described his connections with Masonry as 'useful' and also 'a very pleasant part of my life'.[19] This work is not, however, a Gooch biography and space does not permit more than a brief mention of his works not connected with GWR engineering.

With the unpopular and extravagant Potter holding the reins, matters on the Great Western became serious and confidence declined. The Railway was in serious danger of bankruptcy when, to his surprise, the directors offered Gooch the chairmanship. His initial inclination was to refuse, wishing to have no further connection with Potter and those who had wronged William.

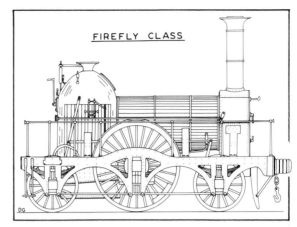

Gooch 'Firefly' class locomotive design.

However, good sense prevailed and Gooch became chairman of the GWR, bringing the railway to more prosperous times by careful control of the finances. The situation had been so bad just before he took office that James Grierson, the General Manager, expressed the opinion that 'Next Monday morning the Railway will be in the hands of a receiver.'[20] Gooch held the position until his death on 15 October 1889. His wife Margaret died during June 1868 and despite his children and grandchildren, the baronetcy and successful business ventures, her departure was a savage blow. His diary and memoirs contain many remarks of a deep and sincere nature showing his love for the lady who had been at his side through the years of trial. His second wife, Emily, whom he married towards the end of 1870, eased some of the grief and she survived him by twelve years.

2. Joseph Armstrong

Following the resignation of Daniel Gooch and his brother William, and the rejection of Sacre, Potter's nominee, the only realistic option left to the board was the appointment of Joseph Armstrong as Locomotive Superintendent. Armstrong had been assistant to Gooch with responsibility for the Northern Division, situated at Stafford Road, Wolverhampton. That section at Wolverhampton had been inherited when the Great Western Railway absorbed the Shrewsbury & Birmingham and Shrewsbury & Chester Railways in September 1854. With them came Joseph Armstrong, who had been responsible for the locomotives and rolling stock of both railways. In appointing Armstrong the board set a precedent of continuity which lasted throughout the existence of the GWR. As it turned out, the new man had greater responsibility

Joseph Armstrong.

than Gooch for he was also to be in charge of carriages and wagons. During the latter years of the Gooch era Mr J. Gibson had been Carriage and Wagon Superintendent, but he also resigned in 1864, as did Edward Wilson. That gentleman, based at Worcester, was in charge of the narrow gauge district which had been formed when the West Midlands Railway was absorbed.

Joseph Armstrong was born in Bewcastle, Cumberland, on 21 September 1816, the fourth son of Thomas Armstrong and a descendant of a Scottish border clan. Following a seven-year spell in Canada, during which two more sons were born, the Armstrong family returned to England and a home at Newburn-on-Tyne. Joseph attended Bruce's school in Newcastle, where Robert Stephenson had received his early education, and during those formative years had contact with the local colliery locomotives. Naturally, his mind turned to mechanical matters and when he left school an engineering position was found at the Walbottle Colliery under Robert Hawthorn, the father of Robert and William, founders of the

famous locomotive building firm, R. & W. Hawthorn.[21] Within a short time Joseph could consider George Stephenson, Timothy Hackworth and Edward Woods as intimate acquaintances, if not friends. At the young age of twenty he obtained a position as an engine driver on the Liverpool & Manchester Railway, Edward Woods being the Locomotive Superintendent.[22]

During 1840 he moved to the Hull & Selby Railway, working first as a driver and then as foreman of the running shed and repair shop at Hull.[23] George Gray was responsible for engine design and it is likely that Joseph Armstrong found the designs interesting. In all probability Gray was more than satisfied with the work of his foreman, for when, in 1845, Gray moved to a similar position on the London & Brighton Railway Armstrong followed him, taking up the post of foreman at Brighton. Two years later a more experienced Joseph returned northwards in order to take up the post of Assistant Locomotive Superintendent at the Saltney works of the Shrewsbury & Chester Railway. When the Shrewsbury & Birmingham Railway opened in 1849 both lines were operated together by a committee, with the S&BR locomotives being maintained under contract at the Wolverhampton base by Johnson & Kinder. The contract expired in 1853 and Armstrong became Superintendent of the combined locomotive stock, moving his base from Saltney to Wolverhampton. That was the position when the GWR obtained control over those railways and instructions then came from Paddington.

The Northern Division of the GWR, for which Armstrong had charge, consisted of all narrow gauge lines and broad gauge lines as far south as Oxford. Only Daniel Gooch was above him and he didn't interfere on the 'coal cart' lines.[24] When the West Midland Railway was absorbed its Locomotive Superintendent, Edward Wilson, had charge of the narrow gauge lines and Armstrong, under him, retained control over the lines north of Wolverhampton. He also, under Gooch, retained control over the broad gauge lines as far south to Oxford.[25] That peculiar situation lasted only one year as, in 1864, wholesale retirements allowed Armstrong to gain full control, becoming the GWR's first Locomotive, Carriage and Wagon Superintendent.

Unlike Gooch, who lived in London and operated from an office at Paddington, Joseph Armstrong took up residence in Swindon. With him went his wife, Sarah (née Burdon), together with five surviving sons and three daughters. Strictly speaking the move was to Swindon 'New Town' as the 'Old Town' still remained a distinctly separate community perched up on the hill. The 'New Town' *was* the Great Western, having been created to house the employees at the locomotive and carriage works, and its population in 1864 amounted to some 7,000 souls. The company built a residence for its new Superintendent as up until that time there had been no necessity for such a house, Gooch only commuting to Swindon when required. The secluded brick-built dwelling, alongside the main line a little to the west of Saint Mark's church, was named 'Newburn House' after the small town on the Tyne where Armstrong had grown up.

The works dominated Swindon and Joseph Armstrong was, naturally, a very prominent figure, but the respect he engendered did not result from position, it was truly earned. He took an active interest in the Mechanics' Institute and was always willing to provide practical and financial support from his own pocket, not that of the Company. During 1864 a committee was formed to consider means of providing sickness and superannuation benefits for GWR drivers and firemen. From that grew the Mutual Assurance Sickness and Superannuation Society, of which Joseph Armstrong was the first President.[26] He gave unstinting support and all encouragement to the society which not only provided pensions but also looked after widows and orphans.

Civic responsibilities were not taken lightly: for many years Joseph Armstrong held the position of Chairman of the New Swindon Local Board, which was the town council. He also became a director of the Swindon Water Company, holding the firm belief that all workers had a right to a wholesome water supply. Aware of the dangers which lurked in any manufactory, the Locomotive Superintendent became a fervent promoter of the establishment of an accident hospital. He never advertised his public works but felt a deep sense of duty in any task associated with the town and its people.[27]

Devotion to his family was matched by devotion to duty at the works and he approached his job with enthusiasm and dedication. Though he cared for the well-being of the workforce he would tolerate no dereliction of duty and severe penalties would fall upon any malefactor. At work he was hard and a strict disciplinarian but away from the railway he was tolerant and generous to a fault. At times he was so generous he would be imposed upon by undeserving cases, but he preferred that course to seeing somebody suffer hardship. On one occasion he had to dismiss a man for a serious breach of regulations and he would not change his mind even though others begged him to do so. The man had a large family and so Armstrong supported them financially until other employment had been found.[28] Actions such as that were typical and from them it can easily be seen why Joseph Armstrong was held in such high esteem.

Armstrong was a devout Wesleyan, serving as lay preacher at the local chapel. The Swindon Methodist community had, in 1869, acquired the former GWR workers' hostel in Faringdon Road and converted the place for use as a chapel; the building now houses the Great Western Museum. A deep Christian belief obviously directed the Armstrong character. Holcroft, in his book *The Armstrongs of the Great Western*, relates an incident where a local merchant tried to bribe him. It took some time for Armstrong to realize why the money had been passed over but when he did, the notes

Tartar, *an Armstrong rebuild of Gooch's 'Iron Duke' class.*

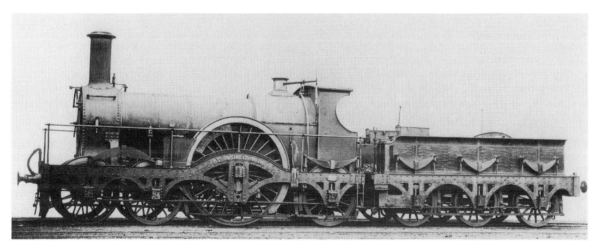

were sent flying out of the office door with the threat that if the owner did not immediately follow he would be propelled by an Armstrong boot.[29]

With his removal to Swindon Joseph Armstrong left his brother George in control at Wolverhampton, but there was no suspicion of nepotism as George was simply the best man available, having been deputy in the Northern Division for many years. In 1868 William Dean was brought to Swindon as Chief Assistant and likely successor. Dean, then only twenty-eight years old, had been assistant to George and Works Manager at Stafford Road, but he was enthusiastic and possessed considerable ability. Naturally, George considered that his seniority put him next in line to the 'crown', but Joseph felt differently. Such a move would have appeared suspiciously like nepotism and could not be countenanced. Anyway, George was only six years younger and unlikely to remain in office much after the departure of his brother; reality was to be different.

During the Armstrong era gauge conversion began in earnest and much of the work was aimed at providing locomotives and rolling stock to meet the changing circumstances. Few new broad gauge locomotives were required and needs were met by rebuilding the older Gooch designs. Whenever that was not possible 'convertibles' were constructed which could be readily arranged to run on either gauge. No other locomotive designer has been faced with a problem of that nature and though the machines were not beautiful in broad gauge form they served their purpose admirably. In 1867 the directors decided that the GWR should construct its own rolling stock rather than purchase the items from suppliers and so a carriage works had to be built. Building was completed in 1869 and James Holden moved from Saltney as the first Carriage and Wagon Works Manager. These were exciting and energetic times at Swindon but the burden was heavy on the shoulders of a zealous Joseph Armstrong.

It is a measure of the man that he produced locomotives and rolling stock to meet all requirements without services being disrupted and without the need to call in contractors. His reputation extended far beyond the boundaries of the GWR not only amongst engineers and directors but also amongst the working men. Meetings of the Institute of Mechanical Engineers, of which he was a Member of Council, brought him regularly to London, as did meetings at the 'Civils'. William Dean, as his assistant, grew to know Joseph Armstrong very well and became aware of many facts which did not become public knowledge because, although in a position of considerable

power and influence, he remained a very private person, maintaining his quite and retiring manner. Dean knew of at least one extremely tempting offer made by a rival railway which was turned down because Armstrong was happy with the people at Swindon. Great Western Railway directors were also known to consult their Locomotive Superintendent upon many matters which had nothing to do with the locomotive and carriage side of the railway.[30] The engineer had a 'feel' for people which was almost unique, but then he understood the enginemen and factory workers, having been in similar positions himself.

That 'feel' also extended to selecting good engineers upon whom he could rely. The selection of William Dean for future high office illustrates the gift he had for being able to see potential in subordinates though they were still young. Another was his own son Joseph who, upon leaving school, became a pupil to his father at Swindon and later made evident his obvious talents. Only tragic death prevented continuation of the Armstrong dynasty.

Gauge conversion and railway expansion due to the absorption of other lines increased the workload greatly, for not only was there a need to maintain the availability of satisfactory running equipment but new depots had to be constructed and manned. New express narrow gauge locomotives had to be designed and these included the famous 2-2-2 'Queen' class of which No. 55, *Queen*, was the progenitor, a locomotive regularly used for hauling the Royal train. The Armstrong 0-6-0 standard goods engine commenced production in 1866 and over the following ten years nearly 300 were turned out at Swindon in order to meet most freight requirements on the system. Facilities for the production of such large locomotive numbers and rolling stock were not won lightly. Planning and organization took time and effort. When, in 1876, the GWR took over the Bristol & Exeter, South Devon and two railways in Cornwall, the workload increased and Joseph Armstrong drove himself harder. He did not have to prove anything, everybody knew of his engineering skill and devotion to duty, but his employers had a railway to run and he had to provide the locomotives and rolling stock. Too late he realized that there was a limit to the work even his body could stand.

During the latter months of 1876 it became obvious that Joseph Armstrong's health was failing simply because he was worn out. Many friends urged him to take a rest but he would not listen. Following a collapse during a visit to Newport in May 1877, the GWR directors pressed the matter and he agreed to a three months' leave of absence,

The Armstrong Memorial at St Mark's Church, Swindon.

The details on the memorial stone to Joseph Armstrong. The inscription reads, 'The Lord knowest the days of the upright and their inheritance shall be for ever.'

allowing for a holiday in Scotland. Whilst on the journey northwards a stop was made at Matlock Bath where, on 5 June, he collapsed once more and died. The diagnosis was a seizure, nowadays known as a heart attack.[31] Only sixty years old, Joseph Armstrong had many more years to offer the GWR but that was not to be.

His death had a great effect on those at the factory and the townfolk in general. Mourning was widespread and the loss deeply felt. On the day of the funeral, Saturday 9 June, the town came to a halt with shops being closed and throngs of silent, grieving workmen with their families lining the streets from 'Newburn House' to St Mark's church. Black cloth draped solemnly from closed shops and other buildings whilst those who payed silent homage along the roadside also wore black. Sir Daniel Gooch, company directors, GWR officials and notable engineers from other railways all came to pay their respects, but it was the mass of some 6,000 ordinary people along the funeral route which illustrated the love and affection the life of

Joseph Armstrong had generated. His body was laid to rest in a corner of St Mark's churchyard alongside that of his son George who had died, aged twelve, four years earlier.[32]

A memorial collection in 1878 raised £550, but it was considered that a statue or similar monument would be inappropriate. The money, therefore, was donated to the Lifeboat Institution in order to purchase a boat which would help to save the lives of those in peril at sea. It is certain that Joseph Armstrong would have approved. Stationed at the Cornish fishing village of Cadgwith the self-righting lifeboat, *Joseph Armstrong*, was 33 ft long and 8 ft wide and was propelled by ten oars. The boat rescued many from the sea including forty people from the Cunard steamer *Brest* which went aground between Cadgwith and the Lizard. The original boat was replaced in 1887 but the new boat received the same name.[33]

As expected, the board appointed William Dean

Left *The lifeboat* Joseph Armstrong *stationed at Cadgwith.*

Right *The details on the memorial stone to 'Young Joe' Armstrong.*

to the post of Locomotive, Carriage and Wagon Superintendent, but the new 'boss' had the sense to leave George Armstrong in control at Wolverhampton and there he remained virtually his own master. In character the two brothers were entirely different with the younger George being much more outgoing and vociferous. With the appointment of Dean to the top job it is claimed that he responded in characteristic style, declaring he cared for no man and would not be taking orders only giving them.[34]

As mentioned earlier, George was the youngest son of Thomas Armstrong, having been born in Canada in 1822. Upon leaving school he followed Joseph around, joining him at the Hull & Selby Railway in 1840 then moving to Brighton with him. Their paths diverged for a while as George moved across the Channel to become an engine driver on the Nord Railway in France. He found himself much in demand as trained French drivers were in very short supply. All went well until 1848 when the second French Revolution began and the Englishman found himself in a foreign argument much against his will. Unwilling to become involved he returned to England and found employment as a driver on the recently opened Shrewsbury & Chester Railway, thus rejoining his elder brother. Promotion to locomotive foreman quickly followed and he was in that post when the GWR took over the railway. Working closely with his brother, the talents of George soon blossomed and it was no surprise when he became Superintendent of the Northern Division following Joseph's move south.

William Dean became his assistant and also manager of the Stafford Road works. The two worked well together but the partnership came to an end in 1868 when Dean moved to Swindon. Work at Wolverhampton was not as spectacular as that at Swindon but the task had its many difficulties, foremost amongst which was the wide variety of locomotives which had to be kept running. Rebuilding with standard components became the policy and where that was not possible the machine would be scrapped and a replacement constructed. George designed locomotives whenever the demand dictated and his designs were as good as any of the period. They showed the independent streak which was also in his character but the most noticeable feature was the colour. Locomotives were still green but it was a Wolverhampton green and not the shade favoured at Swindon. The dark blue-green would be lined in black and white whilst the red-brown framing and wheels were lined in black and vermilion.

During the Franco-Prussian war the French asked for assistance in building locomotives and the GWR volunteered George Armstrong. Considering his earlier experiences with the Gallic community he would have been justified in protesting but he did not and set about the task in Paris. Unfortunately defeat at Sedan put the French in retreat and all hands were required to defend Paris, even stout English hands. George did protest but a posse of gendarmes forcibly persuaded him to take up arms, which he did but only until they left him alone. He later went into hiding until the siege was lifted and he could return home.[35]

Unlike his brother Joseph, George Armstrong never married and his work seems to have been his prime interest, so much so that he remained in harness until the age of 75. He was a staunch

Methodist but, unlike his brother, not a passionate one. Both brothers did, however, share the same caring attitude towards their workers. George had a powerful bark and he could bite when necessary, but never without just cause. He retired in 1897 having built up the Northern Division to a powerful and respected force. During his term of office the workforce at Stafford Road doubled to 1,500 whilst in the Northern Division as a whole it almost trebled to 4,230. The years of retirement were spent happily visiting friends and the works using a horse-drawn carriage provided by the GWR. Whilst visiting the Wolverhampton Flower Fete on 11 July 1901 George Armstrong suffered a stroke and died before a doctor could be summoned. For his funeral the following Monday (15 July) the works were closed and many lined the route as they had done for his brother so many years earlier.[36] The death of George effectively saw the end of the Armstrong era and also the days of Wolverhampton as a major Great Western locomotive works.

A bright star in the Armstrong firmament had been Joseph Armstrong's fourth son, also called Joseph. To distinguish him from his father he was known as 'Young Joe' or just 'Joe'. He was a pupil of his father but was never in the best of health and at the end of his apprenticeship he was sent on a sea voyage to South Africa to recuperate. Whilst on that voyage his father died. He had a rare talent for originality and sound design which came out when William Dean set him working on a project to develop an automatic vacuum brake. Assisting Joe with the project was another bright lad a year younger, George Jackson Churchward. With the project successfully completed Joe was made Assistant Divisional Locomotive Superintendent for the Swindon division. In 1885 promotion followed with a move to Wolverhampton as Divisional Superintendent there and also as Works Manager under his uncle George. The moves indicated the possible future; 'Young Joe' was being groomed by Dean as the heir-apparent, just as he himself had been groomed by Joseph senior. Fate dealt a cruel blow.

Late in 1887 'Young Joe' went to spend a few days at Droitwich in order to recover from a bout of neuralgia. He told the works that he would be returning on New Year's Day 1888 and actually returned very late the previous evening, going straight to his office at the works. The night foreman of the locomotive department saw him and remarked that he appeared to be much improved and cheerful. 'Young Joe' went around the works to wish the men a happy New Year and then set off, walking along the line to his dwelling.

At 12.30 a.m. a shunting goods train hit him and he was decapitated.[37] A promising career had ended at the age of thirty-one and the Great Western had lost another well-loved Armstrong. The body of 'Young Joe' was taken to Swindon and placed in the family grave alongside that of his father. Years later Churchward remarked that if 'Young Joe' had lived he would have become Locomotive Superintendent of the GWR.[38] During the final years before the tragedy few would have argued with that.

3. William Dean

Upon the death of Joseph Armstrong the post of Locomotive, Carriage and Wagon Superintendent had fallen to William Dean, his assistant. He moved into the 'official' residence at Newburn House, Armstrong's widow, Sarah, and children making home at Woodlands not too far away. Sarah died eight years later and was buried alongside her husband at St Mark's.

The second son of Henry Dean, manager of the Hawes soap works at New Cross, London, William was born on 9 January 1840. The family, though not wealthy, did not suffer financial deprivation and William Dean could be sent to the Haberdasher's Company School for his early education. Dean remained a liveryman of the Haberdasher's Company until his death. With a keen interest in all matters technical he was apprenticed to Joseph Armstrong at Stafford Road works on 29 October 1855, being barely fifteen years old at the time. The apprenticeship lasted eight years during which time Dean proved himself to be a skilled and clever engineer. Though very much occupied with railway matters he still found time most evenings to visit the Wolverhampton Working Men's College in order to further his education. Whilst there he succeeded in winning a number of prizes for mathematics and engineering science offered by the Society of Arts.[39]

After completion of the apprenticeship, Armstrong took the extraordinary step of making Dean his chief assistant. The following year when Joseph Armstrong moved to Swindon, Dean became chief assistant to George Armstrong and also manager at Stafford Road works. He was then only twenty-four years old and had command of 850 men. Work at Wolverhampton was neither dull nor easy for at that time the works was producing an average of twenty new locomotives annually as well as attending to the repair of many more. During 1868 the call from Swindon came; Joseph Armstrong once again wanted Dean to be his chief assistant. The 'boss' at Swindon recognized the worth of the young engineer and that move pointed the way towards the future; Dean was destined to follow Armstrong as Chief Locomotive Superintendent.

Throughout the following years both men worked hard at developing the locomotive and carriage strategy of the Company, ensuring that

William Dean.

there was sufficient stock to meet changing demands. The experience which Dean obtained during the initial gauge conversions in South Wales played a vital part in ensuring that future conversions were well provided for in the way of locomotives and rolling stock. The tragic death of Joseph Armstrong in 1877 thrust William Dean into the position he must have desired but would have wished to achieve in happier circumstances. At the age of thirty-seven he became the supreme power at Swindon.

In many respects Dean was like Joseph Armstrong for he was also a quiet and retiring person, never seeking the limelight but being careful to ensure that justice was done. His charitable works were many but unostentatious, as is the case with any true philanthropist. Following the path of his predecessor, Dean became President of the Mechanics' Institute, devoting much time and effort to ensuring that the organization flourished. Many individuals had cause to be thankful for the help and encouragement offered by William Dean both technically and otherwise.[40] He did, however, have a sharp and abrupt manner with anybody who did not appear to commit himself fully to the task in hand.

Dean was instrumental in the founding of a branch of the St John Ambulance Association at Swindon works, becoming its President and remaining so until after his retirement. The class was one of the earliest in the movement and it gave him much pleasure later in life to know that he had helped form an organization which had so benefited the men at Swindon works.[41] Perhaps the only non-railway passion of William Dean was his involvement with the 2nd Volunteer Battalion, Duke of Edinburgh's Wiltshire Regiment, in which he participated eagerly. He became a Captain on 4 June 1869 and received the rank of honorary Major in 1889.[42] Though his position at the works will have given him considerable standing in the community, affection does not stem from any rank or job, and Dean was well respected and liked by the townspeople as well as the workforce. For many years he served the community as a County Magistrate. He married twice, his first wife having died before he took up the reins at Swindon. Only one of his three children, all by his first wife, outlived him.

Though he had undoubted talent himself, Dean was always willing to praise others for their efforts and allow his subordinates to take much of the credit. He could pick out the bright engineers, thereby gathering a staff upon whom he could rely. The selection of 'Young Joe' Armstrong and George Jackson Churchward are but two cases of

No. 3024, a convertible of the '3021' class, in broad gauge form.

that ability. In his retirement speech he commented on that fact but, typically, shied away from giving himself any credit. He referred to a speech by Andrew Carnegie who said that he wished his epitaph to read, 'Here lies a man who knew how to get round him a great many men who were much cleverer than he was himself.' Dean added that he felt his own position was not far away from that of Carnegie, but did not mean to say he had gathered those people by his own exertions, rather that they had been available.[43] Clearly such was not the case; good engineers need to be encouraged and developed. Talent requires directing in engineering just as in any other profession.

Work at Swindon and throughout the system required careful attention as the broad gauge was finally eliminated and the team gathered by the Locomotive Superintendent enabled the change to take place without a hitch. All coaching stock had been produced either as convertible for narrow gauge by removal of a middle section or to narrow gauge proportions but on broad gauge bogies. Likewise, locomotive building concentrated on the narrow gauge, with new designs being adapted to run on the broad gauge as 'convertibles' where necessary.[44] A number of new locomotives were built to the old Gooch design though they were, in fact, classed as rebuilds. To what extent old parts were retained is uncertain. The final trio in the 'Iron Duke' or 'Rover' class were not taken into stock until 1888, by which time the originals would have been well worn out. New building must have been very expensive but considered necessary for

some uncertain reason. Due to Armstrong's death, Dean was faced with the task of maintaining, or renewing, the stock from the recently absorbed Bristol & Exeter, South Devon and Cornish Railways. The amalgamations produced a locomotive fleet with a great many different classes which seriously tried resources to the limit. From the stock lists available it can be seen that a policy of scrap and build was eventually adopted, with many of the new machines being Armstrong-designed 'convertibles'.

To meet the demand for locomotives and rolling stock, Swindon works had to be expanded and during the Dean era the workforce and population of New Swindon increased at a dramatic rate. The workforce peak of the Dean period was probably reached following the final gauge conversion in 1892. Many locomotives and much rolling stock would have required conversion or scrapping and many hands would have been needed for the work. Earlier periods of conversion work allowed a team of skilled men to be assembled, but that work was intermittent and the retention of the men could not be justified during the slack periods. Adoption of 'creative' accounting in the provision of funds for 'locomotive renewals' allowed money from the revenue account to be drawn in excess of that actually needed for replacements. Factory activities extended beyond purely railway matters including the manufacture of machine tools for internal use and brickmaking.[45] No good manager would wish the dissolution of his team of skilled workers and no well intentioned or kind spirited person would like to see many people put out of work, particularly if alternative employment was not available. Swindon had no other employer of any size able to soak up redundant skilled men. Dean was a good manager—the way in which he kept the railway working during periods of major upheaval proved that,—and he was also dedicated to his workforce, as the actions mentioned above show.

Dean was a keen experimenter and his searching mind pursued knowledge about the materials used for locomotive construction. Metallurgy became a passion and, in 1882, he established a chemical laboratory at the works in order to carry out tests on materials. Tests were carried out on iron, steel and copper as well as on the water to be used in locomotive boilers.[46] Initially no space was available at the works and so the tests would be carried out in the back parlour of W.H. Stanier's home. Stanier, father of the famous W.A. Stanier who was later to be CME on the London, Midland & Scottish Railway, was Dean's confidential clerk and to a great extent his personal assistant. It was he, probably with Dean's encouragement, who inaugurated the system of evening technical classes for the apprentices at the works.[47] William Dean, as a result of the work carried out at the laboratory, presented a paper to the Institution of Mechanical Engineers in 1893. The paper, 'Tensile Tests and Chemical Analysis of Copper Plates from Fireboxes on the Great Western Railway', was the first, and for many years the only, paper concerned with metallurgical investigations into materials used for locomotive construction.

On the locomotive front Dean adopted an experimental view in his design policy. In 1886 he tried compounding with two locomotives, Nos. 7 and 8 of the 2-4-0 arrangement, but they were not a

Dean's broad gauge compound locomotive No. 8.

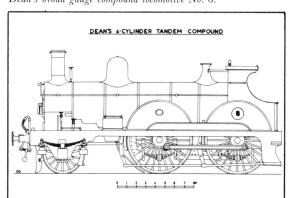

success mechanically; however, he did gain the experience of compounding. A tandem compounding arrangement was used with both HP and LP pistons being connected to the same rod. This differed from the generally accepted arrangement for compounding which had the HP and LP cylinders driving separate cranks. A notoriously unsuccessful, and for many years unacknowledged, 4-2-4 tank locomotive was tried. It had single 7 ft 8 in driving wheels, and the bogies were supported by rigid pins which probably accounted for its propensity for not running on the rails.[48] The design possibly originated as a trial machine to investigate the characteristics of the 4-2-4 wheel arrangement, which was used in the Pearson locomotives for the Bristol & Exeter Railway.

Over the years a number of 'one-off' locomotives were produced, allowing practical experience to be gained. Different types of boiler were tried, the flush topped domeless arrangement being much in favour. A centreless bogie was developed and used successfully for locomotives and carriages. Dean was very receptive to new ideas and does not appear to have been dogmatic in his approach to design. For that reason he probably encouraged Churchward to develop his locomotive designs. Churchward did not become Dean's chief assistant until September 1897, having been Locomotive Works Manager since 1896, and so any influence on design should have been noticeable after that period. It is doubtful if any other 'boss' would have allowed Churchward such freedom to experiment, but then Dean himself could not resist trying something different.

It has generally been accepted, without any proof, that Churchward took over the Locomotive Department during the final years of Dean's superintendence, leaving the 'senile old man' as titular head. People have perpetuated the story that Dean suffered from mental illness and could remember little of what was going on thus allowing Churchward to have his own way. That does no justice to the memory of Dean nor to the undoubted abilities of Churchward. Dean would have welcomed the new ideas which Churchward brought to the design team and would have encouraged them; he was that sort of person. Unlike the gregarious Churchward he was very retiring and would not have sought public appearances; he made very few before Churchward arrived except when they involved his own particular interests.

Without doubt Dean became ill during the final years of his period in office and willingly allowed his young assistant more control, but the suggestion that he knew nothing of what was going on

*Broad gauge scrap lines at Swindon, 1892 (*courtesy of GWR Museum, Swindon*).*

and was quietly shuffled into retirement is not true. He may have been ill but he knew what was going on and knew when he would be retiring, probably even organizing the date himself. As President, William Dean attended the annual meeting of the Swindon St John Ambulance Association at the Mechanics' Institute on Friday 17 February 1902. His speech was very well received and, as reported, was extremely lucid and humorous. Whilst acknowledging the vote of thanks and acclamation at the end of the proceedings, Dean stated that he was pleased to accept the post of President for a further year, adding, 'It was common knowledge that his connection with Swindon was drawing to a close.'[49] Hardly a statement from a man being nudged quietly into oblivion.

A few days following his retirement a presentation was made to the former chief by his successor. A collection throughout the engineering staff of the railway realized nearly £400 and it was decided to purchase a chiming grandfather clock. The Mechanics' Institute was crowded to capacity on the afternoon of Saturday 5 June 1902 when the Swindon staff showed their respects to the man who had headed the Locomotive Department for twenty-five years. Following Churchward's speech which outlined the career of the man they were honouring, Dean responded in some detail and at length. Even though the speech would have been written down he must have had his wits about him, particularly at one instant. Shortly after his response began the clock struck the quarter hour and amid applause and laughter Dean remarked that, '. . .it did not mean its existence to be overlooked.'[50] The remainder of the money raised from the collection was used for providing beds at a sanatorium near Winsley.

William Dean took his clock to retirement at Folkestone where a house, 10 Terlingham Gardens, had been purchased for him. He died there on 24 September 1905. The small funeral (he only had one surviving child) was attended by a number of officers from the GWR, the organization he had served with such distinction. In many respects Dean's life had been a sad one and possibly that brought about his illness. His first wife, whom he married in 1865, died soon after their third child was born. He married again in 1878 but his second wife died in 1889. Both daughters died before him, leaving just one son to attend his funeral.[51]

3. The twentieth-century men

1. George Jackson Churchward

Deep in the heart of former broad gauge territory is the sleepy little Devon Village of Stoke Gabriel. There on 31 January 1857 was born a man destined to have a profound influence on the development of railway engineering, not just on the Great Western but throughout Britain in general. The Churchward family had long resided in that part of the country, and George Jackson Churchward was the son of two cousins with the same surname, his father being called George and his mother, Adelina Mary. The middle name, Jackson, came from his paternal grandmother. There were two brothers, John and James, as well as two sisters, Mary and Adelina, resulting in the family of seven having to share a rather small house at Rowes Farm. An uncle, Frederick, the elder brother of George senior, occupied the manor house; that branch of the family had most of the money. George's upbringing encouraged an interest in the pursuits of fishing and shooting together with a general affection for the country-side.

George Jackson Churchward (courtesy of the National Railway Museum, York).

George Jackson Churchward received his education at Totnes Grammar School only a few miles away and soon developed an interest in engineering matters. Earnest in the choice of future career, he must have persuaded his father to utilize some of the little capital available to finance a period of training as pupil to John Wright, Locomotive Superintendent of the South Devon and Cornwall Railways.[1] Originally the South Devon Railway had been operated by locomotives provided by the GWR but, in 1851, the agreement was terminated and, as a private venture, Daniel Gooch, together with several partners, obtained a contract to provide motive power. When that agreement ended John Wright, who had been Gooch's works manager at Newton Abbot, became Locomotive Superintendent of the South Devon Railway and also the Cornwall and West Cornwall Railways.

Churchward went to Newton Abbot in 1873 and there met another pupil by the name of Richard Neville Grenville who also had a passion for engineering. The pair designed and built a steam-powered car using the boiler from a Merryweather fire engine to supply the steam.[2] In 1876, following the takeover of the South Devon Railway by the GWR, Churchward made an enforced move to Swindon in order to complete his apprenticeship. Conditions there were totally different. Not only was the works much bigger but the gauge of many of the locomotives was smaller. He had entered a world of narrow gauge machines. Naturally, Swindon offered greater variety and at the end of his pupilage, in 1877, Churchward moved to the drawing office. It was there that he first encountered that other potential engineering genius, 'Young Joe' Armstrong. William Dean directed Churchward to assist Armstrong on the development of a vacuum brake system and, undoubtedly, the two worked well together. Churchward later paid tribute to the talent of the young Armstrong. Such work was valuable experience for the Devonian.

Following that task Dean evidently recognized Churchward's talent and, in June 1882, made him Inspecting Engineer for materials. The post did not last long, for six months later he became assistant to James Holden, the Carriage Works Manager who was also assistant to William Dean. When Holden left to become Locomotive Superintendent of the Great Eastern Railway, it seemed a natural progression for Churchward to take over at the carriage works, and in 1885 he did. Very quickly he became aware that inspectors always blamed dirty bearings for axle-boxes running hot; that he did not believe. The story is related that to prove his point he modified a brake van bearing by having powdered emery fed into it whilst on a run from Swindon to Paddington. Upon arrival the bearing showed no trace of overheating but the journal had worn like an hour glass. From his studies of the theory of lubrication he well understood that a lubricant film was always needed to keep bearing and journal separate. The result was the O.K. axle-box for carriages which presented fewer problems for future inspectors and fitters.[3]

The departure of Holden and the death of 'Young Joe' Armstrong left Churchward as the only obvious successor to Dean. After ten years in charge of the carriage works he moved to the locomotive side as Assistant Works Manager and within months, on the retirement of Samuel Carlton, became Manager. The succession was firmly established when Churchward became chief assistant to Dean in September 1897. Over the next five years Churchward was able to indulge his ideas and experiment as Dean gave him his head. In the final year or two in office there is no doubt that Dean was ailing but, as mentioned in the preceding chapter, he was still capable of understanding what was going on at the works and design office. It must then be presumed that he encouraged Churchward in his new plans, for Dean himself was an inveterate experimenter. By 1902 Dean had decided (or been persuaded) to retire and Churchward assumed the mantle of Gooch. At the half-yearly shareholders' meeting held at Paddington in August 1902 the GWR Chairman remarked,

I am sure many proprietors will hear with regret that Mr. William Dean, who has held the post of superintendent of the Locomotive and Carriage Department since 1877, has had to retire on the ground of ill health. I am glad to be able to say that we had as Mr. Dean's chief assistant, Mr. Churchward, with whom we are perfectly satisfied, and to whom we can trust the arduous duties which that office entails. . . .I am sure that in appointing Mr. Churchward we have done the best we could in their interests.[4]

The chairman could not have realized how right he was.

Following the tradition set by Armstrong, Churchward devoted much of his time to public service. Upon the New Swindon Urban District Council being established in 1894 he was elected a member and became chairman in 1897. With the incorporation of old and new towns in 1900 Churchward became the first Mayor of the new

Churchward's desk. Now at the Great Western Museum, Swindon.

borough, a role in which he showed great pride even though the town possessed no mayoral robes or chain. Service on the board of the Water Company lasted for many years, as did duties with the Technical Education Committee, of which he was the first chairman when it was set up in 1898.[5] Education of the apprentices always found an important place in the Churchward scheme of things and in 1907 he persuaded the GWR directors to institute a plan for day release. Apprentices were allowed to attend technical classes on certain days of the week without loss of pay, the Company paying the fees. For the more distinguished students periods of training in the drawing office and chemical laboratory were held out as an extra inducement.[6] Those establishments did not normally form part of the training routine.

Churchward was an impressive figure, both in stature and personality, but he also had an autocratic nature; he was the boss and everybody had to be aware of the fact. A bowler hat, the traditional symbol of authority, found no favour with him; a trilby covered his balding head and matched the tweedy suits he habitually wore. Despite the engineering surroundings he retained the aura of a country squire. Like Dean he had the ability to select good young engineers and was thus able to form a valuable team which could assist him with his future plans. Unlike Dean, however, he was approachable, at least when he wanted to be. Junior drawing office staff would be consulted and allowed to offer suggestions, and it was not unknown for Churchward to sit beside one of the

draughtsmen and ask him directly to explain the project with which he was involved. In effect there was a team dealing with the project and he was team leader. Whenever necessary the foreman from a particular section of the works would be called in to clarify matters relating to the practicalities of manufacture.[7] The method worked, producing effective designs and good public relations which did much to promote a family atmosphere in the drawing office and Swindon works generally.

In 1916 the title of Locomotive, Carriage and Wagon Superintendent was changed to the shorter, and more impressive, Chief Mechanical Engineer (CME), no doubt at Churchward's suggestion. He was proud of the position he held and opposed anybody who tried to interfere in his department or reduce his authority. A notable 'adversary' was Sir James Inglis, who had been Chief (Civil) Engineer until 1903 when he became General Manager and had probably crossed swords with Churchward on more than one occasion, even before the latter took over from Dean. Due to loading gauge and bridge restrictions, the (Civil) Engineer was the only person effectively able to impose limits on the Mechanical Engineer. Overall the two departments tended to ignore each other, which did lead to unusual situations, one of which came forcibly to light during Collett's time. The CME reported directly to the board and not the General Manager, similar provileges being afforded to the Secretary, Solicitor and Chief Accountant.

When Inglis became General Manager he considered that the situation must be changed so that all access to the board went through him. None of the men affected by the proposal was in favour of the idea, Churchward least of all, and he

became leader of 'this little band of malcontent chief officers', as Sir Felix Pole called them. Churchward had the character, personality and reputation to back up his actions and he seems to have made life very rough for Inglis. According to Pole, a later General Manager, 'Mr. Churchward had a great standing, not only in railway circles but in the world of mechanical engineering at large— indeed as great as that of Mr. Inglis in civil engineering. They were both men of dominating personality.'[8] Inglis did get the board's agreement for his proposals but implementation was a different matter and it was not until after Churchward left the scene that any effective change came about.

Churchward, with the assistance of the Chief Accountant, was also instrumental in Inglis being severely criticized by the board for the high costs involved in running the Locomotive and Carriage Department. At that time the accounting procedure, in being since 1869, made no allowance for depreciation of stock and the Chief Accountant felt that there should be some provision for renewals and not just maintenance. It was usual for the Locomotive Superintendent to agree, with the Accountant, a certain figure to be held in reserve against the cost of future stock replacement. Naturally, there was a tendency to make that figure higher than it needed to be, in case more items of stock had to be renewed than actually were. Churchward jealously guarded the reserve he had built up, its value rising by over £1.5 million to £2,699,534 during the first eight years of his stewardship. It is not surprising that he should look upon high reserves as a necessity because his department had no revenue itself, and its supply of money could be restricted at any time. When asked by Pole why he did not tell Inglis of the reserves, Churchward characteristically replied, 'He was mad; had I told him, he would have spent the money.'[9] Nobody was allowed to interfere in his domain.

Though Churchward consulted many other railway engineers he would not allow any of them to dictate matters to him, either directly or through the board. Suggestions and criticism were welcomed whenever he presented a paper at one of the learned societies to which he belonged and he was not above offering such criticism himself. At times he took obvious delight in springing some surprise on a gathered audience. A meeting of the Association of Railway Locomotive Engineers on 28 November 1902 developed into a discussion about the de Glehn compounds on the Nord Railway in France. Churchward waited until most of the eminent engineers present had had their say and then silenced the meeting by calmly announcing that he had ordered one for trial on the GWR.[10] It was a stroke of audacity and marked his arrival in the top rank of railway engineers. When the pronouncement was made Churchward had been in his post officially for less than six months. Other engineers present, including H.A. Ivatt, S.W. Johnson and Wilson Worsdell, were men with many years' service in high office.

An incident of outside interference came about due to the joint control of the Shrewsbury and Hereford line with the London & North Western Railway. William Stanier relates that certain people from the L&NWR objected to the planned 4-6-0 'Saint' class engine being used on the line and so Churchward, rather tongue in cheek, set about designing the 4-4-0 'County' class. He was aware that the cylinders were much too powerful for the wheel base but 'was not going to be told what to do by Webb'[11], F.W. Webb being Locomotive Superintendent of the L&NWR. Only ten 'County' class locomotives were built and they proved notoriously rough riders as Churchward must have expected. 'Counties' could not be considered as part of a standard class, they simply made use of standard parts for a specific purpose. It does seem strange and expensive behaviour, however, merely to have one's own way regarding locomotive power. But then that was his way. If he had decided upon a policy there would be no changing it and heaven help anybody who tried.

During the First World War Churchward made every effort to ensure that the works could undertake the manufacture of munitions and weapons demanded by Government. In addition, locomotives and rolling stock had to be provided

for the transport of troops and munitions within this country and overseas. The works were very much under pressure and interference from Government departments did not help, but supplies of materials could be obtained officially, and unofficially, allowing contracts to be completed. Not everybody was happy about the situation, Collett in particular remembering how he had been treated when called upon to provide similar services during the later conflict. In the Birthday Honours List for 1918 Churchward was awarded a CBE, whilst OBEs went to C.B. Collett, Locomotive Works Manager, and F.W. Marillier, Carriage Works Manager.[12]

Another honour from which he derived considerable pleasure was conferred on him by the Borough of Swindon. For his services to the community George Jackson Churchward was made its first honorary freeman. A special council meeting on 12 October 1920 unanimously passed the resolution;

> In recognition of his valuable services to the town as the first Mayor of the Borough and in other public offices; the distinguished position which he holds in the engineering profession and the long and eminent services which he has rendered as head of the Great Western Railway Works, Swindon, having attained success in all these spheres by the conspicuous ability and diligence at all times displayed by him.[13]

Sixteen days later the Town Hall was packed to capacity for the ceremonial presentation of the casket containing the parchment conferring the freedom.

The war changed many things including the attitude of the shop floor workers to their employers and the Government to the way in which shop floor workers should be represented. It became common practice for workers to seek discussion with their superiors regarding matters of working conditions. That did not suit the autocratic Churchward who was unwilling, or unable, to adjust to the changing world. After the war a deputation from the works visited him in order to make known their wishes. The leader of the group, a district organizer, voiced the general feeling when he said, 'You know, the time has come when we wish to be asked to do a thing and not ordered to do it.' That was too much to stand and, according to Stanier, Churchward replied, 'D. . .it all, it is time the "old man" retired.'[14] Changing attitudes, not age or engineering difficulties, had beaten him.

Retirement came at the end of December 1921 when he handed over to his former deputy, Charles Benjamin Collett. Still only sixty-three years old, there must have been many useful years left in him but the future did not appear to be to his liking and he felt that the task he had set himself had been completed. Certainly the locomotive and rolling stock situation on the railway was far better than when he arrived and generally superior to that of any other British railway. Staff and workforce insisted upon a presentation of some sort but the 'old man' was adamant that he wanted nothing. When pressed he said that a fishing rod would be very much appreciated. The collection raised over £500, very much in excess of the amount needed to purchase even the most expensive of rods, and it was decided to devote the remainder of the money to a prize fund for apprentices at the works. The Churchward Testimonial Fund made awards to mechanical engineering apprentices throughout the railway on the basis of good academic work at local technical colleges.[15]

The large hall at the Mechanics' Institute was filled to capacity on the evening of 22 April 1922 when managers and shop floor workers gathered to say goodbye. As with all similar events it was a jovial occasion tinged with some sadness at the passing of an era. Collett could not be present as he was in Europe on business but all of the remaining engineering hierarchy attended. The chairman of the Works Committee concluded his speech of praise with the hope that 'every hair on his head will be a candle to light him to glory.' Churchward, who was almost completely bald, quickly reacted with the comment, 'There won't be many of them, Watkins.'[16]

Following retirement, the unmarried Churchward continued to live at Newburn House, Collett having no desire to move into the official residence. Domestic responsibilities lay in the hands of a housekeeper, so time could be spent enjoying

hobbies. Car maintenance came within that category, as did other engineering interests. A small workshop had been built up over the years and practical skills on the lathe could still be practised. There was also now more time for the leisurely country pursuits of fishing and shooting, from which he derived great satisfaction.[17] The works was only across the track from Newburn and he went back at regular intervals, though it is not recorded how Collett felt about the former 'chief' still paying visits.

Churchward's personality and manner generated feelings of affection in those with whom he regularly came into contact. He could be abrasive and was autocratic but his manner enabled him to get away with things which a less personable individual would be criticized for. Harold Holcroft, who worked for many years under Churchward, considered that, 'All those high qualities which distinguished the true English gentleman were inherent in him.' He also considered him to be a tactful administrator and first class leader of men with the ability to inspire people and draw the best from them.[18] Overall he could probably be classed as a benevolent dictator, loved by more people as he grew older.

Experimenting became a passion and something new always attracted him provided it was sufficiently stimulating. In his early years the American influence was great but that later gave way to an interest in French locomotive practice. Churchward cannot really be classed as an innovator as few of his ideas were really new in a general context, but they were usually new to British practice. He could adapt the best overseas ideas to the requirements of the GWR, modifying them to suit the conditions. His planning was bold and he had definite objectives which he knew could be achieved with effort. Following the building of test locomotives during the latter years of Dean's superintendence and the early years of his own, Churchward knew what was required in the way of locomotive classes for the entire system. Standardization was to be the byword both in terms of boilers and mechanical parts. By 1911 all the necessary types had been constructed and, except for special purposes, no new design should need to be introduced for another fifteen or twenty years.[19] That turned out to be the case although the timescale was not quite so long for certain classes. The resultant stagnation in design development did mean that a number of bright engineers, including Holcroft, sought adventure on other railways.

A stationary test plant, the first in Britain, was built at Swindon during 1904, mainly due to the influence of Professor Goss of Purdue University in America. A new dynamometer car was constructed in order to allow road test comparisons, but the stationary plant had little use in experimental terms as its maximum power capacity was a meagre 400 hp. Road testing became the normal way of determining locomotive capabilities. Boiler development ideas came from America and the French provided stimulation in the form of compounding. A valuable technical library built up at Swindon where technical journals from far and wide could be consulted in the search for useful ideas.

Churchward had a number of preferences and he allowed these to influence design even though there might be sound engineering reason against the course of action he adopted. Inclined outside cylinders just did not look right as far as he was concerned and were not allowed. That caused one problem with the early 2-8-0 locomotives where the cylinder centres had to be raised $2\frac{1}{2}$ in above the wheel centres in order to clear the loading gauge. Outside valve gear was prohibited, Churchward preferring an uncluttered outline. He also believed that better balance could be achieved with the valve gear inside.[20] That may or may not have been the case but inside gear caused considerable difficulties regarding access for maintenance. So far as aesthetics were concerned the 'old man' did not worry unduly; his task was to see that the machine functioned efficiently.

Excessive criticism did, however, have an effect upon him. Following his paper on Large Locomotive Boilers, presented at the Institution of Mechanical Engineers during February 1906, James Stirling criticized Churchward for the shape of his boilers. Churchward replied that he felt hurt at being accused of despoiling the appearance of the British locomotive, but added that '. . .the time has gone by for studying appearances in the construction of the locomotive boiler at any rate.'[21] He did, however, attempt to make concessions and had Holcroft smooth the appearance of some locomotives by extending the cab downwards and providing curves at the front and rear ends of the platform above the frames.[22]

Few people would argue that Churchward advanced the standard of GWR and British locomotives considerably during his term of office, even though some might consider that most machines looked very much the same and lacked style. That he was an engineering genius, as some would claim, is open to dispute. Certainly he was a leader who could adapt the work of others to suit the job in hand, namely to produce a standard range of locomotives having power and operational

efficiency. Engineering works will be discussed in later chapters and it will be for the reader to make a decision on that point.

One matter upon which most railway enthusiasts agree is that Churchward showed a complete lack of sensitivity and feel for railway history when he requested that the old broad gauge locomotives *North Star* and *Lord of the Isles* be destroyed. To be fair, he needed the room in the Swindon shops and had tried to find an alternative home at various institutions including the South Kensington Museum, but the vandalism in actually cutting up the remaining locomotive relics of a major part of GWR history is beyond belief. His letter to the board dated 16 December 1905 illustrates a disregard for sentiment which must have formed a strong part of his character and will have coloured the way in which he dealt with people. The autocratic nature shone through in all matters. 'These engines are occupying valuable space in our Shops at Swindon. They have been offered to several Institutions without success, and I beg to recommend that authority be given for them to be destroyed.'[23] That the board complied shows an even greater collective disregard for history. With a little effort a solution could have been found. Twenty years later, enthusiasm for a replica *North Star* showed no bounds and that model was found space on a perch in the locomotive shop.

Following retirement, Churchward remained part of the Swindon landscape and was frequently seen about the town. Death came tragically on the misty morning of 19 December 1933 and ironically was brought about by a steam locomotive in a similar way to that of his old friend 'Young Joe' Armstrong. Newburn House had a private access to the line and it was his habit to use that gate when going across to the shops or whenever he wanted a private walk along the line. At about 10.20 a.m. that day he was observed to leave the private entrance and walk along the pathway near the track. Nothing else was seen until the 'down' Fishguard express had passed. His lifeless body lay next to the track. The speeding engine, No.4085 *Berkeley Castle*, had hit him, extinguishing life instantly. The 'old man' was slightly deaf and had suffered from glaucoma for several years, having undergone a number of operations for the complaint. The eye trouble had also brought on attacks of vertigo on various occasions. Because of the nature of the accident a coroner's court with jury had to be convened. Its verdict was accidental death.[24]

As had been the case with Joseph Armstrong, the funeral brought Swindon to a halt on Friday 22 December. Workmen were given leave to attend and the mourners included Gresley from the LNER, Stanier from the LMS, Maunsell from the Southern, Collett from the GWR and an assortment of engineers and officers from the railway. In a quiet corner of Swindon Parish Church they laid the 'old man' to rest.[25]

2. Charles Collett

The retirement of Churchward did not produce many immediate changes, his deputy, Collett, assuming command on 1 January 1922. The two men were as different as chalk and cheese but they had proved a valuable team. Charles Benjamin Collett, the son of William, a journalist, and Mary Helen was born on 10 September 1871. The family lived at 33 Tavistock Crescent, Westbourne Park, which is close to Paddington Station and it is likely that GWR trains in close proximity had an influence upon young Charles.[26] He received his early education at Merchant Taylors School, Charterhouse Square, in London, before studying at The London University, City & Guilds College. Following that period of education he became a pupil at the works of Maudslay, Sons and Field, Lambeth, the famous marine engine builders. Several references, probably taken from the same source, indicate that Collett was a pupil of Joshua Field one of the firm's founders, but that cannot have been the case as Field died during 1863. May 1893 saw Collett obtain a position with the GWR when he entered the Swindon drawing office as a junior draughtsman. Within four years he was given charge of the section responsible for buildings and a year later, in 1898, the post of assistant to the Chief Draughtsman came his way.

The hard-working Collett soon made his mark and other promotions quickly followed. In June

Above *Charles Benjamin Collett.*
Below *Proposed design for a compound 'Castle'.*
Below right *The Engineering Offices at Swindon Works.*

1900 he was made Technical Inspector at the Swindon Locomotive Works and a few months later became Assistant Manager at the same place. Another twelve years elapsed before the mana-

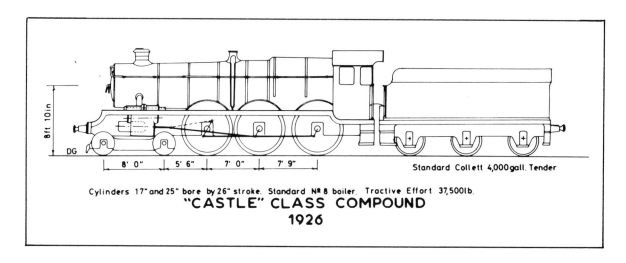

Cylinders 17" and 25" bore by 26" stroke. Standard Nº 8 boiler. Tractive Effort 37,500 lb.

"CASTLE" CLASS COMPOUND
1926

gership of the works became his. During that intervening period and the succeeding seven years in the manager's chair he developed an attitude towards the manufacturing side which was to play an important part in future GWR locomotive production. Appointment to the post of Deputy Chief Mechanical Engineer in May 1919 paved the way for him to follow Churchward.[27]

It has been suggested that Churchward and Collett did not get on too well but that is now difficult to prove or dispute. Certainly the men had different personalities but the 'old man' must have recognized the talent and potential in Collett or he would not have promoted him or designated him as successor. Churchward loved Swindon and the GWR and would have wished to ensure that the future was secure. Seniority did not necessarily play a major part in promotion and so Collett's potential must have been considered greater than that of Stanier. The Churchward standard designs met the foreseeable needs and so a locomotive designer was not required. A good works man would bring production facilities into the twentieth century just as Churchward had brought design. With his training and experience Collett had to be the obvious choice.

In January 1922 Collett took over the position of Chief Mechanical Engineer. It cannot have been easy following a man with the charisma of Churchward, particularly as that man only lived across the track from the works, in the 'official' CME's residence, and took frequent walks over the line to visit his former domain. Collett bore the burden well and never appears to have passed comment or wished to restrict access. His attitude was milder than that of Churchward and he was much less domineering though he still insisted upon high quality work and loyalty.

Trades union and other worker representatives certainly found it much easier to communicate with Collett than with his predecessor. That does not mean he could be duped but indicates he had feelings for the position and justifiable aspirations of others. Conditions of service and problems regarding hours or rates of pay would be dealt with in a careful and considerate manner.

> The quiet and helpful way in which he dealt with such matters will be kindly remembered by those who from time to time sat round the table with him. Difficulties were overcome with little trouble, and the quiet confidence and respect in which he was held by the men has remained unbroken. It was this feeling of co-operation that helped to create a spirit of loyalty as between the trades union representatives and the Chief Mechanical Engineer.[28]

That was the sentiment of one commentator writing a brief biography upon Collett's retirement. The occasion may have coloured the text slightly but it does show the nature of the man as being distinct from that of Churchward. Collett may not have been 'loved' but his fairness earned respect.

After three years in the Swindon drawing office Collett considered himself financially secure enough to support a wife. In 1896 he married a vicar's daughter by the name of Ethelwyn May Simon.[29] They had no children and were passionately devoted to each other. Apart from a weekly visit to the cinema the couple were not seen much about the town, though Mrs Collett did become involved in a number of charitable groups. Collett himself had very few outside interests, being satisfied with the company of his wife. Her

premature death in 1923, following a short illness, devastated Collett and, in the view of K.J. Cook, then an assistant manager at the Locomotive Works, nearly killed him.[30] He never fully recovered from the trauma and became even more isolated from other people. His appearance changed dramatically and he lost a considerable amount of weight, though Cook considers that he may have been ill himself. In later years Collett claimed that his cancer had been cured by careful attention to a vegetarian diet and abstention from alcohol. Certainly he had an extensive knowledge of medicine and was very critical of certain aspects of the medical profession.[31] That knowledge may have resulted from a desire to fight his own cancer after orthodox medicine had failed him or it may have resulted from a desire to understand more about his wife's illness. Whatever the reason, it does show a determination of character which must also have been part of his work ethic. This desire for greater knowledge led him to become a member of the Institute of Experimental Metaphysics and the London Metaphysical Group.[32]

His rather aloof nature did not attract many friends but then he did not seek them. Even when his wife was alive public social appearances were few and far between, and following her death he adopted a hermit-like existence as far as activities away from work were concerned. His deputy, W.A. Stanier, performed the usual social functions expected of the CME and took an active part in organizations such as the Medical Fund Society, Mechanics' Institution and GWR Athletic Association. Collett avoided activities of that nature and could only rarely be persuaded to attend any

social event. One such occasion happened in February 1927 when he agreed to be chairman of the fourth annual music festival of the GWR Social and Educational Union. Sir Felix Pole, the General Manager, expressed delight at seeing Collett in the chair and the sentiment received extended applause, obviously indicating some affection. Collett himself expressed pleasure at being able to attend.[33]

After the event he took trouble to write to the GWR Magazine with his views on a phrase chosen for one of the public speaking competitions. That phrase, 'Procrastination is the thief of time', drew a detailed analysis from him indicating aspirations, and even talent, in the realms of philosophy.

> . . .We are each allotted a portion of time—our life time—every moment of which we have to live and are responsible for. We can employ our time usefully or otherwise, but we can neither lose nor find nor give time, and it certainly cannot be taken from us. . . .Our time, however, comes to an end and this occurs when our soul departs from our mortal body, and we are then faced with the great eternity, from whence we came at birth. Therefore, I say, that Procrastination cannot be a Thief and Time cannot be stolen.[34]

Unlike his predecessors Collett took very little interest in the affairs of the town and his only public post was that of magistrate from 1921 to 1928. He received the OBE for his efforts at producing munitions during the First World War, but the troubles he had to endure, and the perfidious behaviour of the Ministry of Labour whilst he was Locomotive Works Manager, influenced his later attitude. K.J. Cook, Works

Manager during World War II, suffered similar problems. Collett's long memory did not allow him to forget the earlier treatment and when the second conflict broke out he was very reluctant to allow the GWR workshops to undertake any munitions work. Eventually, under pressure from Paddington, he agreed to work being done but made his despleasure known so that if the GWR rolling stock fell into disrepair due to lack of facilities or materials, he could point the finger at others.[35] In view of the appalling state of the railways at the end of the war his cautious attitude would appear to have been correct.

After Churchward's departure the General Manager got his way in being able to exercise control over the CME in non-technical matters. Collett did not concern himself too much with that as Sir Felix Pole was an amiable sort of person. What he could not stand was pomposity from certain of the directors. A number of individuals in that group had expressed, quietly or otherwise, a desire that locomotives should bear their names. At about that time, 1936-37, it was decided to combine parts of the old 'Duke' and 'Bulldog' classes to form a renewed class, the 'Earls' or 'Dukedogs', which could work over the Cambrian coast line. Though nominally a new group of locomotives they were distinctly nineteenth-century in appearance. Collett decided that these 'new' engines should be given the titles of those directors who were so keen on the idea. The class was named after Earls in order to indicate the 'respect' the CME had for those directors and the titled fraternity in general. When one of the batch arrived at Paddington the directors were not amused.[36] Later, the plates were put on 'Castle' class engines but Collett had had his joke.

Collett had hoped to be able to complete Churchward's standardization of locomotives early in his stewardship but other factors got in the way, not least the desire of those at Paddington for publicity. There was a need during the early years of the 1920s for a more powerful locomotive than the 'Star' class and so Collett set about designing an updated version to the weight limit allowed on the West of England line. An enlarged boiler with greater evaporative rate and increased diameter cylinders brought the nominal tractive effort to 31,625 lb, making the 'Castle' the most powerful British locomotive. Paddington was delighted and made the most of the coup when *Caerphilly Castle* was displayed alongside Gresley's *Flying Scotsman* at the British Empire Exhibition at Wembley in 1924.

A few years later came the 'King' class, though there was no real need for such a machine. The 'Castles' had been designed to the maximum permitted axle loading of 19½ tons and Collett considered such a limit to be a disadvantage, indicating to Pole that if the limit had been 22½ tons a much more powerful machine could have been produced. The Civil Engineer later made it known that all new bridges were designed for an axle loading of 22 tons and would take 22½ tons. He added that only a few on the main London to Plymouth line remained to be strengthened. The outcome was that Pole informed Collett he could build his bigger locomotive though he had never really expressed a desire to do so.[37]

In 1933 the idea of streamlining was much in vogue and some people felt that the GWR should

Left *Collett-designed* Manton Grange *and* King Edward III *at Dawlish on 28 August 1952* (D. K. Jones Collection).

Right *No. 7029,* Clun Castle, *and No. 4930,* Hagley Hall, *two Collett-designed classes hauling an enthusiasts' special during 1985.*

join in the mania. Collett was informed of this and, though he did not feel that any useful purpose would be served, he agreed to a trial. The story is that he sent an office boy to obtain some plasticine, then proceeded to smear it over a paperweight model of a 'King' on his desk until the desired effect was produced. Retelling the tale is often a means of deriding the engineer but, in truth, as an initial step that would be the best means of approach. There was absolutely no need for a completely new class and so any steamlining would have to be applied to an existing engine. No British streamlined engine then existed and so no information was available. The approach was the only one possible. In wind tunnel testing an initial basic wax model is always made and that is what Collett was attempting. No real wind tunnel tests were carried out and from the start he must have realized the major limitations in steamlining a locomotive for use on a British railway. Subsequent events indicate that he was corect in not pursuing the exercise.

Collett made full use of the testing facilities available, employing the dynamometer car to road test many newly designed or modified engines. Analysis was thorough and his paper, 'Locomotive Testing on the Great Western Railway', presented to the World Power Conference in 1924, is a model on the subject. He also modernized the Swindon test plant through the provision of better drawbar arrangements and more powerful brakes, allowing it to absorb at least 2,000 hp and accommodate locomotives running at a line speed of 70 mph.[38] The plant could deal with any engine then available and was a major improvement on the 'home trainer' which Churchward had produced. More sophisticated instrumentation turned it into a piece of scientific apparatus.

The criticism is always levelled at Collett's locomotive designs that they were generally extensions of the Churchward standard machines. That is true in most cases but, as mentioned earlier, the standard series had been produced to cover expectations for fifteen or twenty years and they did so admirably. Collett, in fact, made the designs better. He introduced good workshop practices which cut down manufacturing costs and through techniques such as optical alignment he turned the Churchward engines into precision machines. Comparative running and maintenance costs for locomotives belonging to the 'Big Four' companies show that, in 1938, the GWR was the most economical. Repairs and renewal costs per engine amounted to £484, whilst on the LNER it was £568. The costs per engine mile were also much lower. GWR engines burned less coal and used less water than those of any other company.[39] There is no reason to doubt that similar figures could be produced for other years.

Collett was an engineer, not just a designer. It is easy, or convenient, to forget that it was the job of the Chief Mechanical Engineer to oversee all aspects of engine and rolling stock design, construction, maintenance and performance. An effective maintenance policy is helped by having a minimum number of standard engines to suit the traffic demands. In 1921 the GWR stock included seventeen types comprising fifty-two classes of locomotive; by 1941 there were thirteen types and thirty-seven classes. Grouping brought a variety of different machines into stock and during the same period the types were reduced from eighteen to eight and the classes from 184 to 57.[40] The fact that the GWR was able to fulfil all engineering demands upon it during the 1920s and 1930s proves that Collett was well able to do his job.

The carriage side was not neglected and many innovative features were incorporated. Bogies greatly influence the smoothness with which a carriage will ride and Collett was particularly aware of that fact. When he took office there were seven different types of bogie in common use and he decided to test the riding of each type before designing a standard bogie. A train of seven coaches, each with a different type of bogie, was formed and run along different sections of track. This was known as the whitewash train because the lavatory tank in each coach had been filled with

'6100' class No. 6118 at Swan Village on 3 March 1962. The '6100' class was a Collett update of Churchward's '3100' class (D. K. Jones Collection).

whitewash of a different colour. An observer in each lavatory was instructed to release some wash whenever a bad lurch was felt. It was later possible, from the rainbow colour of the ballast, to see if particular bogies reacted better to particular defects in the track. If all colours had been released at one spot the track itself was considered to be in need of rectification.[41] This was an effective solution to the very difficult problem of testing bogies and track.

William Stanier was Collett's right-hand man at Swindon but he also had aspirations of his own, namely to be CME. Stanier was only five years younger than Collett and as the years went by it looked less likely that the latter would resign soon enough to allow Stanier many years in the Swindon hot seat. When an approach was made to Stanier by the LMS he, naturally, discussed the matter with his chief who indicated that the GWR chairman had requested him to stay in the post as long as possible. There would then be no chance of Stanier becoming CME at Swindon.[42] Stanier went to the LMS and Collett became even more insular.

Though Collett had a less autocratic manner than Churchward he could be very domineering if the situation dictated, particularly when he considered the matter important for efficient operations. Precision in boiler manufacture was a passion and he felt that the boilermakers did not work to close enough tolerances. Accordingly Collett appointed a fitter as Boiler Shop Foreman, a step which did not find favour with the boilermakers. He was, however, determined and informed them that, if necessary, he would designate the fitter, F.R. Higgs, as Boiler Shop Manager. Collett got his way and boiler manufacture became more precise, causing fewer problems with interchangeability.[43]

Another instance of the domineering side of his character came about in relation to membership of one of the professional institutions. Collett was a member of both the 'Mechanicals' and the 'Civils', encouraging staff members to join. He would, however, have nothing to do with, and forbade staff from joining, the Institution of Locomotive Engineers, considering the members to be little more than 'b. . . commercial travellers'.[44] Certainly the organization consisted of men from the private locomotive builders and maybe he did not take kindly to salesmanship, but this attitude does appear to contain some elitist sentiments.

People have criticized Collett's decision to rebuild Churchward's *Great Bear* as a 'Castle', considering it to be pique and a desire to erase the work of the 'old man' which might detract from the praise being heaped on his 'Castles'.[45] By 1924 'The Bear' had been in service for sixteen years and

its boiler was worn out. Replacement for a 'one-off' would have entailed unnecessary and unjustifiable expense, particularly as the locomotive had very restricted route availability. From an economic and engineering point Collett had little choice but to rebuild, but from a publicity angle the GWR lost out. It has been said that Churchward was fond of the *Great Bear* and its destruction greatly upset him.[46] Such sentiment towards a locomotive would appear to have been out of character for a man who destroyed the last two remaining broad gauge locomotives.

Collett did not finally retire until July 1941 and then only because the matter seems to have been forced upon him. With few friends or family and little interest in other matters, his work was his life and he clung to it as long as possible, though during his last few years in office he spent a lot of time in London, leaving John Auld, his deputy, to deal with day-to-day matters at Swindon. Auld, six months older than his chief, had been persuaded to stay on so it could not be said that Collett was the oldest at Swindon. Eventually Auld decided to go and Collett went at the same time.[47] That is the explanation given by K.J. Cook, then Locomotive Works Manager, and it is probably as near to the truth as any second-hand report is likely to be. The departure of Auld meant that the deputy could not be promoted and so Frederick William Hawksworth, who had been Assistant to the CME, became the new power at Swindon.

Collett severed all links with Swindon and moved to Wimbledon. He already owned a house there and had done for some years, though only one person at Swindon knew the address.[48] He was always a very private person. After eleven years in retirement he died, aged eighty-one, on 5 April 1952. The funeral was attended by a small gathering which included Hawksworth, Stanier and Pole.[49]

3. F.W. Hawksworth

F.W. Hawksworth was a real product of the Great Western Railway and of Swindon. Born in that town on 20 February 1884, he joined the GWR as an apprentice at the Locomotive Works in August 1898. Following a period of service in the test house he moved to the drawing office in 1905 and soon showed that his talents lay in that field. Whilst he was an apprentice he received the Gooch prize for machine drawing at the Swindon Technical Institute and also the GWR chairman's prize for the best aggregate results. A subsequent course at the Royal College of Science produced an award with first-class honours in machine design.[50]

Hawksworth, due to his exceptional talents, was

Frederick William Hawksworth (courtesy of the National Railway Museum, York).

Modified 'Hall' No. 7919, Runter Hall, *at Bristol Barrow Road shed on 17 October 1965* (Chris Surridge).

given the task of drawing out the general arrangements for Churchward's *Great Bear*,[51] and it is likely that the experience did much to fire his enthusiasm for building a 'Pacific' later in his career. Following a spell as a senior he was appointed Assistant Chief Draughtsman in 1923 and two years later occupied the Chief Draughtsman's chair. His interest in the subject prompted him to teach machine drawing and design at Swindon Technical Institute. He was later responsible for the organization of these classes and became technical representative on the advisory committee appointed by the board of the Institute. Hawksworth was always a firm believe in technical education and occupied a number of posts concerned with the subject both locally and nationally. Being born and bred in Swindon he felt a great affinity for the place and played an important role in local matters including that of town councillor and magistrate.[52]

For his work in education Hawksworth became the second Chief Mechanical Engineer of the GWR to be specially honoured by the town of Swindon when, at the end of 1960, he was given the Freedom of the Borough. The award restored the title of 'Freeman' to to town as all previous recipients had by that time died.[53] Like Churchward, Hawksworth never married and he threw himself wholeheartedly into the service of the railway and borough. His hobbies mainly consisted of golf and

music, with a keen interest in St Mark's church choir.[54] But overall he was a railwayman and proud to be in the service of the Great Western.

Whilst occupying the position of Chief Draughtsman Hawksworth had responsibility for design of the 'Kings' and worked closely with Stanier on a number of other projects. One of these was a plan for a compound 'Castle'. The machine had 17 in diameter high pressure cylinders and 25 in diameter low pressure ones producing a tractive effort of some 35,700 lb. They took the design to Collett who listened for five minutes and then dismissed the idea.[55] Compounding was still out of favour and remained so even with the two advocates when they eventually reached high office. The rebuke did not stifle the Hawksworth flair and when he finally did have the power, GWR locomotive design turned another corner.

Departure of Stanier to the LMS left the deputy's position vacant: it went to John Auld who had been the CME's Personal Assistant with particular responsibility for docks. Auld was older than Collett and not likely to succeed him but Hawksworth, who was appointed Assistant to the Chief Mechanical Engineer at the same time, had the right qualifications and attributes. Unfortunately Collett stayed on too long and stagnation began to set in. It was not until July 1941 that the Great Western got its first, and only, Swindon born and trained chief.

Chill~Out Sunday

23 September 2007
3:00pm–7:00pm

You are invited to enjoy an afternoon of pampering at Grove House, Sunday 23rd September from 3:00 pm to 7:00 pm.

£5 entry per person, ta include refreshments.

Chill-Out
with our therapies on offer including: aromatherapy, indian head massage, reiki, reflexology, manicure, hair consultation, makeovers, pedicure, facial relaxation, and more at £5 each.

Shop
while you relax. There will be a selection of exclusive gift stalls, and you could win fabulous raffle prizes!

Tickets available from:
Liz Hizli - tel: 01727 731010 email: lizh@grove-house.org.uk
Maria Mauro - tel: 07932 020115 email:m.1.mauro@herts.ac.uk

GROVE HOUSE

Reg Charity No: 1003462

The time could not have been less auspicious with the country engaged in all-out war and the works at Swindon concentrating on munitions production. New passenger designs were out of the question, unless your name was Oliver Bulleid and you could dress your new 'Pacific' in the guise of a mixed-traffic locomotive. Hawksworth did not have such good fortune or, maybe, he just did not try hard enough. However, within the restrictions then in force he did wonders and stamped his own name on GWR engineering practice. Many Churchward ideas which Collett had considered amost sacrosanct were discarded. GWR locomotive practice would enter a new era and shine bright again, though unfortunately political involvement dimmed the lamp.

Throughout the war years Hawksworth kept the locomotive and carriage departments functioning as well as conditions allowed and also maintained munitions production. Ambulance trains were fitted out, fully equipped with six ward carriages, a sitting-up carriage and even an operating theatre. The first of these trains was handed over by Hawksworth on 23 March 1943. New locomotive designs did come about, and a scheme for modifying some existing classes was put in hand. Whereas Collett made no attempt to overturn the Churchward doctrine, Hawksworth did. He returned to the two-cylinder concept for his 4-6-0 'County' class design, diverting from the accepted American pattern of cylinder block which incorporated the smokebox saddle. That arrangement had introduced problems regarding the main framing and Hawksworth wished to employ traditional British plate frames. His cylinder and valve case

castings bolted onto the sides of the plate frames and a separate smokebox saddle had to be employed. A similar arrangement was used for the 'Modified Hall' class with great success.

Outside cylinders and Walschaert's valve gear even found their way onto a group of 0-6-0 tank engines, the '1500' class, considerably changing the GWR style. Increased superheat temperature was adopted. Again Hawksworth had the mark of originality about him. He also introduced a high side tender, which gave improved weather protection, and lockers were provided at each side; at last somebody seemed to be concerned for the driver and fireman. Following the end of hostilities coal supplies remained scarce and of poor quality. That hit GWR locomotives badly as firebox design had been based upon the use of good Welsh steam coal. Hawksworth sought, and was granted, permission to experiment with oil firing. A number of locomotives, including examples from 'Castle', 'Hall' and '2800' classes, were converted to burn oil. In general the experiment was a success and plans were drawn up to make Cornwall, eventually, an oil fired areas.[56]

Seeing advantages in the scheme the Government decided that it should be adopted nationally, thereby saving coal which might go for export in order to earn valuable foreign exchange. Hawksworth was requested to provide details of the oil firing system to other railways. That he did, and several million pounds were spent in arranging for other conversions. However, the scheme came to an abrupt end when it was pointed out that scarce foreign exchange would be required to purchase the oil.

Hawksworth was a designer and he appears to have been consumed by one abiding passion, the production of a 'Pacific'. His early association with

Proposed Hawksworth 'Pacific' design.

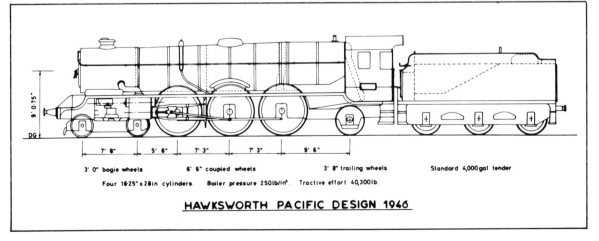

HAWKSWORTH PACIFIC DESIGN 1946

the *Great Bear* must have stimulated him and as soon as he became CME the drawing office was set to work. The original plan called for a large boiler operating at 280 psi and 6 ft 3 in driving wheels connected to 'King' class sized cylinders 16¼ in diameter by 28 in stroke. That combination would produce a massive 47,000 lb tractive effort.[57] However, government bodies would not sanction the production of new express passenger locomotives during the war and nothing came of the design.

At the end of hostilities the plan was revived with a boiler pressure of 250 psi, experience with the 'County' class having shown that a pressure of 280 psi caused certain problems. The same sized cylinders were retained but the driving wheel diameter was increased to 6 ft 6 in giving a tractive effort of 40,300 lb, the same as a 'King'.[58] The external appearance of both 'Pacific' designs was very much the same, looking more like a Stanier 'Princess Royal' then a Swindon machine.

Again Hawksworth was out of luck as the post-war austerity conditions were not considered suitable for the sanctioning of passenger-only classes. If, like Bulleid on the Southern, he had dressed his 'Pacific' in the guise of a mixed-traffic locomotive, matters might have turned out differently, but he didn't and design work on the 'Pacific' ceased. An embittered Hawksworth never raised the matter again. It has been suggested by no less an authority than O.S. Nock, who had close

associations with Swindon during the post-war period, that Hawksworth destroyed all drawings of the locomotive in order to avoid any public comment.[59] Such action may appear extreme but is understandable. Hawksworth had waited in the wings for Collett to retire and when his chance came wartime conditions thwarted his undoubted design talents. Cessation of hostilities did not improve matters and forthcoming nationalization would remove any prospect for him to stamp his individualism on locomotive design. Hawksworth must have been the most misused of all GWR Chief Mechanical Engineers.

Although he was a steam locomotive designer Hawksworth did not consider himself rigidly tied to that form of motive power. The coal situation promoted a search for alternative means of traction and the 1946 International Railway Congress, held in Switzerland, provided an opportunity to view such a machine. Brown Boveri Ltd had, in 1939, supplied a gas turbine locomotive to the Swiss Federal Railways, the machine performing regularly and satisfactorily throughout the war years. It was basically an electric locomotive with its own generator driven by a gas turbine engine. Hawksworth and Sir James Milne, the General Manager, attended the congress and were both impressed by the locomotive, which was then running on the French railway system. That 2,500 hp prototype satisfied requirements for hauling the 'Cornish Riviera Express', and Hawksworth decided to recommend that the board purchase such a machine for trial use on the GWR.

Delivery of No. 1800 did not take place until after nationalization so it cannot be considered as a Great Western locomotive, but it was part of the Hawksworth plan and indicates his attitudes. He also ordered a second gas turbine locomotive, No. 1810, from Metropolitan Vickers Electrical Co., and this was taken into stock in 1951, a year after the Swiss machine. That Hawksworth should be interested in a gas turbine is not surprising as in 1907, whilst in the drawing office, he spent some time working on steam turbine design and even presented a paper concerning steam turbines to the Swindon Engineering Society.[60]

Efficiency of a gas turbine is lower than that for a diesel but the use of lower grade fuel oils and reduced lubricating oil consumption were considered by Hawksworth to be an advantage. In practice that did not turn out to be the case and fuel consumption was extravagant due to the fact that maximum efficiency had been arranged at maximum power and, apart from climbing banks, the machine was not required to develop full power. Hawksworth, though brilliant with steam, did not appear to be able to grasp the problems relating to other forms of motive power, or maybe he was just playing out the years, leaving the problems to those in charge of the nationalized railways. His attitude regarding the 'Pacific' drawings gives some indication as to his feelings

towards outside interference in railway matters. Whilst the LMS enthused about diesels and electrification found favour with the LNER and Southern, it is appropriate that at the end of its independent existence the GWR should be different and choose to 'play' with gas turbines. After all, it was different at the beginning by way of its broad gauge and, like the broad gauge, the gas turbine became a defunct part of railway history.

Upon nationalization R. A. Riddles assumed power in the railway land as far as mechanical engineering was concerned and Hawksworth remained in charge at Swindon. Effectively his power had gone and all major decisions were taken by the Railway Executive; he even had to seek permission to ride in his own dynamometer car during the interchange trials of 1948.[61] By the end of 1949 he had had enough and retired from Railway life. His going brought to an end the Swindon era as British Railways Western Region then really took control from the former GWR regime.

Hawksworth continued his public life, serving the community of Swindon in the offices mentioned earlier, but he appears to have had little contact with the railways and when the preservation movement took hold at the beginning of the 1970s he offered no support. Retiring from public life in 1959 he spent the remaining years in relative solitude until his death, on 13 July 1976, at the age of 92.[62]

Above left *Hawksworth's* County of Hants *in Sonning Cutting on 12 August 1952 (*D. K. Jones Collection*).

Right *Hawksworth's '9400' class No. 9457, one of the last Swindon Works steam shunters. At Swindon 14 September 1965 (Chris Surridge).*

4. Chain of command

At the outset Brunel was given complete responsibility for all Great Western engineering work but the situation soon changed with the appointment of Daniel Gooch. Brunel could not attend to locomotive and carriage matters as well as his other duties, thus it was essential that an officer be appointed to supervise routine maintenance. It would also appear from Gooch's letter of application that the railway intended to set up a locomotive manufactory and hence, at some future date, construct its own locomotives. No facilities of any sort existed when Gooch took up his post and an initial task was the preparation of plans for the engine houses to be erected at Paddington.[1] He also had to inspect the engines being built by contractors and arrange for the employment of mechanics, drivers and firemen.

Gooch worked under the direction of Brunel and, it would appear, took his orders from the 'little giant', not the company directors, though they must have been in overall command. Gooch organized the working of locomotives as well as

Isambard Kingdom Brunel in later years.

their repair, thereby setting a precedent which remained with the GWR throughout; the Locomotive Department had control over the Running Department and could direct the use or removal from service of locomotives provided that the needs of the Traffic Department were met.

Gooch worked long hours with his men ensuring that the Brunel 'freaks' were capable of doing some work and that some semblance of a schedule might be maintained. The failure of many engines prompted the directors to seek a report from Gooch. He, naturally, felt himself to be in a difficult position, as up until then he had '. . .reported to Mr. Brunel alone, as my chief'.[2] Although the matter initially caused a certain amount of ill-feeling, it did clarify the situation to some extent and Gooch became more independent and freer from Brunel's overall control. Shortly afterwards the directors instructed the young Locomotive Superintendent to prepare designs for future stock. Although Brunel still had overall engineering control it was waning as far as the Locomotive Department was concerned.

During 1840 the first of the Gooch locomotives were delivered and further sections of the GWR main line opened for traffic. An already massive workload increased further when the directors agreed to provide motive power for two other railways, the Bristol & Exeter and the Cheltenham & Great Western Union. Gooch required help and was granted permission to appoint an Assistant Superintendent. From his days at the East Foundry, Dundee he remembered a former colleague and recruited Archibald Sturrock to fill the post.[3]

At that time all of the main design and repair work was undertaken at Paddington with small depots at other points along the line, particularly Bristol. In order to carry out design work Gooch had organized a small team under the direction of Thomas Crampton, the Chief Draughtsman.[4] The size of that embryo drawing office staff is uncertain but it fulfilled the immediate design requirements of the GWR and formed a basis for future development. It appears that the Company was still uncertain about manufacturing its own locomotives or rolling stock at that stage.

With agreements for leasing the two railways already mentioned it became obvious that facilities closer to the two lines would be essential for reasonable services to be maintained. Gooch was called upon to recommend a possible site and reported that Swindon, then only a small town, would be ideal. In 1840 he visited the place with Brunel and both agreed that there could be no better position. That, in fact, was true for Swindon was at the junction with the Cheltenham branch and located almost at the end of the easily graded section of line from London and before the more heavily graded section to Bristol. Changing engines would, therefore, be convenient.

On 25 February 1841 the directors agreed 'to provide an engine establishment at Swindon commensurate with the wants of the Company, where a change of engines may advantageously be made and the trains stopped for the purpose of the passengers taking refreshments. . . . The establishment there would also comprehend the large repairing shops for the Locomotive Department.'[5] That statement by the board mentions the Locomotive Department in isolation, indicating that it was already considered to be a separate entity and implying that Gooch was in command of his own department. Brunel, however, as the founding engineer would have taken an interest and it will only have been his death which truly separated mechanical and civil engineering sections.

The statement also introduced a famous section of Great Western history, that of the Swindon refreshment rooms. The refreshment rooms have no part in the subject material of this book apart from the fact that the GWR was short of money at the time and entered into an agreement over them with J. & C. Rigby. That concern had already constructed several GWR stations and undertook to build the one at Swindon, together with refreshment rooms and 300 workmen's cottages. Cottages were essential to the proposed works as most skilled labour would have to be imported from other parts of the country. In return for the buildings a 99-year lease on the rooms was agreed with Messrs Rigby for the annual rental of one penny. That was not all: the Company agreed to halt every train at Swindon for a period of ten minutes in order that the passengers might take refreshments. It was that ten-minute halt which restricted an acceleration in train timings and it was not removed until 1895 when the Company bought out the remainder of the lease.[6]

Erection of the workshops commenced immediately approval was granted and they were fully operational in January 1843. Gooch remained at Paddington with his design team and Sturrock became manager of the Locomotive Works at Swindon. The works were still only intended for locomotive repair and maintenance and the labour force would have reflected that requirement. Gooch was in overall control, visiting Swindon

Sir Daniel Gooch, chairman of the Great Western Railway.

whenever necessity dictated and supervising the design work for new locomotives. He would also have had dealings with contractors regarding tenders for, and the construction of, new locomotives.

During 1845 Gooch was extensively engaged in locomotive testing for his appearances before the Gauge Commissioners. The results of those experiments convinced him that larger and more powerful locomotives should be constructed. He, in turn, convinced the directors and early in 1846 they instructed him to build a 'colossal locomotive working with all speed'.[7] Speed was essential in order that test results from the more powerful machine might be available before the next session of Parliament, and hence the next session with the Gauge Commissioners.

Time was not on his side as manufacturers would need to be informed of the specification, tenders requested and then contracts arranged. The only solution was for the Company to construct its own locomotive at the Swindon works. Working day and night the engine, *Great Western*, was completed in thirteen weeks from the day on which the directors sanctioned construction.[8] *Great*

Western became the first engine to be completely built at Swindon works but locomotive construction was already in progress at the beginning of 1846. The first engine actually to emerge from the works, in February of that year, was *Premier*, an 0-6-0 goods locomotive which gave its name to that class of Gooch standard machines. Boilers for the entire class of twelve engines were constructed by an outside contractor.[9]

It is uncertain exactly when the decision was made that the GWR would construct some, or all, of its own locomotives, but it must have been towards the latter part of 1845 as a number of 'Prince' class engines were also built during 1846. Manufacture of locomotives necessitated an increase in the Swindon workforce from the 423 men of January 1843 to some 1,800 in 1848. Sturrock had overall control of the works but shop managers will have been provided in such places as the boilermakers', erecting and turning shops. At Paddington the design staff must have increased in order to deal with the additional work entailed in producing standard designs, a Chief Draughtsman being already in charge under the direction of Gooch.

As the GWR expanded, and with responsibility for the Bristol & Exeter line still continuing, Gooch arranged for a number of repair and maintenance depots to be built at various locations. Each will have had a supervisor and a number of fitters. Drivers and firemen, who came under the control of the Locomotive Superintendent, had to be trained and located at each depot. Though the increase was gradual it laid the foundation upon which the GWR Locomotive Department functioned throughout its independent existence.

A major development came during 1854 with the absorption of the Shrewsbury & Birmingham and Shrewsbury & Chester Railways. That brought additional rolling stock and engineering facilities within the control of Gooch. The gauge was also different. At the same time the main repair facilities for both railways were centred on Stafford Road works at Wolverhampton with a smaller depot at Saltney, both under the control of Joseph Armstrong. Lines to the north were of the 4 ft 8½ in or narrow gauge and it seemed prudent to keep the two systems separate, Gooch being in command but leaving Armstrong to run the narrow gauge division based upon Stafford Road.

Gooch's new policy of building locomotives had to be extended to the Northern Division with the Stafford Road works being reorganized for that purpose. Whilst facilities were made available at Wolverhampton it was necessary for Swindon to construct a number of narrow gauge locomotives,

the first of these appearing in 1856. Private builders Beyer, Peacock & Co. also constructed some narrow gauge engines for the GWR during 1855 to a Gooch design.[10]

With Stafford Road works extended it was possible for Joseph Armstrong to design and construct locomotives himself. Gooch left him very much to his own devices and Wolverhampton became almost independent. It says a great deal for the ability of Armstrong that Gooch had so much confidence in him, and illustrates the strength of Gooch's character in that he was willing to allow part of his domain to be controlled by somebody else. Both men possessed such unique qualities of leadership, engineering skill and management that they were able to conduct the locomotive affairs of the GWR in a manner which must have been the envy of every other contemporary industrial venture. Without both men the relationship which grew up, and remained for nearly fifty years, between Swindon and Wolverhampton could not have existed. There appears to have been neither animosity nor conflict.

Most of the early locomotive construction was carried out on the 'contract' system. A 'contractor' (many went to Swindon from Wales or northern England) would specialize in a particular branch of the manufacture such as steam hammer work or foundry work. As each 'lot' of engines was authorized the works manager would negotiate a price with a contractor for particular parts, the theory being that the contractor would then arrange the work with his men, sharing any profits amongst them. The workmen received a low basic rate and their earnings would be made up from any profits. In practice that was not always the situation and many contractors rarely made any profit for their men, though a number amassed considerable fortunes. The system did not last long and then a piecework arrangement was introduced with a chargeman distributing the gross balance for any job between his gang.[11] It is unknown if the 'contractor' system definitely extended to Wolverhampton but as it was part of the GWR any method adopted for Swindon is likely to have been used throughout the Company.

Archibald Sturrock gave up his post as Locomotive Works Manager at Swindon during 1850 and took up the position of Locomotive Superintendent on the Great Northern Railway. He was replaced by Minard C. Rea who held the post until 1857 when William F. Gooch, Daniel's younger brother, took over. Throughout those years the works expanded with output of new locomotives increasing. In 1860 a rolling mill was built so that worn or damaged rails might be reconditioned. The town

A Gooch 'Firefly' class locomotive in the original engine house at Swindon.

and works grew together.

Absorption of the West Midland Railway during 1863 introduced a complicating factor due to the formation of a Worcester Division. Edward Wilson was placed in charge of all narrow gauge lines. That situation did not last long and need not be covered.

Carriages and wagons for the broad gauge were initially constructed by outside contractors though in certain cases iron underframes and iron wagons were made at the locomotive works. On the Northern Division a similar situation existed with Saltney being the main carriage and wagon depot. Although it was intimately connected with the locomotive side of the railway, the Carriage and Wagon Department was separate and had its own superintendent, James Gibson. This department was based at Paddington and had managers at various depots.

The resignation of Daniel Gooch in 1864 allowed for rationalization of the situation to take place, for Wilson and Gibson retired at the same time. Joseph Armstrong became responsible for the entire locomotive, carriage and wagon fleet whilst the outpost at Stafford Road remained a more or less autonomous unit though still under his control. Reasons for its independence were basically the need to maintain a narrow gauge manufacture and repair facility in the north and, perhaps just as important, the presence of George Armstrong in command.

Joseph Armstrong took up his position at Swindon, all design and management facilities being relocated from Paddington. Samuel Carlton became manager at the Locomotive Works in 1864 and remained there for thirty-two years, thus guaranteeing a period of stability. A final format for the GWR mechanical engineering structure was beginning to take place. Locomotive manufacture, repair and maintenance, together with carriage and wagon repair, came under a central control which functioned effectively. There only remained the manufacture of carriages and wagons and the empire would be complete.

In 1865 plans were made for the erection of a carriage works at Oxford, the position being ideal as broad and narrow gauge tracks to the town already existed. Oxford Corporation was delighted but university dons were not at all amused by the thought of 'mere mechanics' invading the town. The row continued throughout the summer with *The Times* strongly attacking the railway authorities. Potter, the chairman, put forward a very strong case as to why the works had to be positioned at Oxford and the shareholders supported him. Potter resigned the following year and Gooch replaced him. Without referring to the shareholders Gooch abandoned the plan for a carriage works at Oxford and got rid of the agreement with the Corporation. In March 1868 the board voted the sum of £26,000 for constructing new carriage shops at Swindon. At the same meeting Gooch pointed out that the board had originally planned to spend between £60,000 and

£70,000 on the Oxford scheme, of which he had never approved.[12]

Why Gooch did not agree to the carriage works being built at Oxford is unknown. Certainly it seemed to fit every criterion at the time, Swindon being out of favour as there was no narrow gauge track leading there. He may have come under pressure from masonic friends in the Oxford University circle but, on the whole, Swindon was the better choice in the long term due to the spread of the narrow gauge as well as the centralized engineering facilities and skilled workforce it offered. That farsightedness of Gooch saved the Great Western from many disasters and set it well on the road to financial security.

Construction of the carriage works at Swindon occupied a number of years, with T.G. Clayton being in charge at the time. In 1873 James Holden was transferred from the Saltney Works to be the first Carriage and Wagon Works Manager. Reorganization was complete, all major repair, manufacturing and design facilities were grouped at Swindon with the Locomotive, Carriage and Wagon Superintendent also being located there. The situation remained that way until the end of the Great Western Railway.

The fact that Daniel Gooch, a former Locomotive Superintendent, occupied the seat of power as company chairman certainly helped the mechanical engineering side of the railway. Swindon works, and the town itself, were financially more secure under his direction than they would have been under any other personage. A relationship developed between the Locomotive, Carriage and Wagon Superintendent and the board due to the fact that Gooch was chairman. It was a matter which Gooch seemed actively to encourage and which others, at a later date, appeared to think disintegrated the management structure. Felix Pole, General Manager between 1921 and 1929, held firmly to that view.[13] It would have been natural for Gooch to take an interest in the locomotive side of the railway, but the special relationship which built up was due in no small part to the personality and ability of Joseph Armstrong. The close and confidential nature of the rapport which existed between Armstrong and the board, as well as the influence of Gooch, resulted in future Chief Mechanical Engineers having direct access to the board rather than going through the General Manager. That irritated Pole.

Joseph Armstrong stamped his authority upon the locomotive and carriage departments, ensuring that the changing needs of the railway were always met. Conversion of some broad gauge lines to narrow gauge imposed a considerable burden but the works was able to cope. As mentioned in chapter 2, Joseph Armstrong was a strict disciplinarian but he was also scrupulously fair. The general affection felt for the man certainly helped produce a good atmosphere within the works and management/worker relations were at a high level for that time.

At Stafford Road, George Armstrong ruled his domain well but was always subordinate to his elder brother. Wolverhampton designed locomotives possessed a styling similar to that produced by Joseph, but that might have been because both brothers had been subject to the same early influences and not because Swindon was dictating design. Joseph did move people about in order that they might gain experience, and a spell at Stafford Road was considered to be useful training; William Dean certainly benefited from the experience. At that time all communications were hand written and each senior engineer would have required at least one clerk to deal with his correspondence. Dean was so impressed with his clerk, W.H. Stanier, that he took Stanier with him to Swindon when he became chief assistant to Joseph Armstrong.

A major change came about during 1876 when the Bristol & Exeter, South Devon, Cornwall and West Cornwall Railways merged with the Great Western. Armstrong had a bigger empire to deal with. It was natural that all major work would be centred upon Swindon and the larger facilities of the other lines, such as the Bristol & Exeter's works at Bristol, were downgraded to repair depots. John Wright, Locomotive Superintendent of the South Devon, and James Pearson, of the Bristol & Exeter, both retired when the GWR took over, thus making Armstrong's task somewhat easier.[14]

Unfortunately Armstrong died the following year before he could stabilize the Locomotive, Carriage and Wagon Department. That task fell to William Dean who was able to mould an extensive system into one which functioned most effectively. Engineering tasks like the final gauge conversion were dealt with admirably, but the organization which went into ensuring the availability of sufficient narrow gauge stock was formidable. Only by having an efficient management structure, with department heads knowing the exact requirements, was the task able to be completed without major disruption to services. That structure had been organized by Joseph Armstrong and it served the Company well.

Naturally the works at Swindon, and to a lesser extent at Wolverhampton, expanded throughout the Dean period, with new machinery being installed to suit specific functions or to replace that which was worn out. Works managers, generally reporting to an assistant superintendent, had the supervision of the workmen by means of foremen and individual plant managers. Additionally there was the drawing office, controlled by a Chief Draughtsman, and the stores department. A chemical laboratory was also developed under the direct control of Dean himself, and by the time Dean retired a number of chemists were employed. Through various managers Dean also controlled the brick works and gas works within the Swindon complex.

Outside Swindon a major item of plant requiring constant maintenance and supervision was the pumping equipment needed to keep the Severn Tunnel dry. Add to that the Stafford Road works, the repair depots throughout the system, numerous running sheds, locomotive testing together with the supervision and training of footplate personnel, and it can be seen that the Locomotive, Carriage and Wagon Superintendent of the Great Western Railway was faced with a formidable task. The Outside Assistant dealt with all matters appertaining to locomotive running and footplate crew training. Dean, it has been alleged, was notoriously difficult to see and left day-to-day affairs in the hands of his assistant.[15] That may well have been the case, but his management structure seems to have functioned very well and the senior personnel must have had ready access. It is in that context that he should be judged rather than compared with later officers like Churchward who, apparently, maintained more of an 'open door' policy, at least for those he wanted to see.

James Holden, the Carriage Works Manager, became Dean's assistant in 1878 but remained in control at the carriage works. Churchward became assistant at the carriage works in 1883 but probably dealt with all day-to-day matters as Holden, being assistant to Dean, would have been fully occupied. When, in 1885, Holden left to become Locomotive Superintendent at the Great Eastern Railway, the senior post at the carriage works fell to Churchward.

By the time Churchward took over from Dean in June 1902 a very effective management structure was in place. Changes were made to suit the new 'chief' but they tended to be in personnel not in actual posts. Younger blood found its way into many of the important positions, one in particular, C.B. Collett, becoming Assistant Locomotive Works Manager. Churchward had a keen interest in experiment and development with the result that two supernumary assistants were appointed at the locomotive works in order to investigate the possibilities of new ideas and carry out necessary

G. J. Churchward during his final years in office.

testing. G.H. Pearson and J.W. Cross were both young men and fitted in well with the Churchward team.[16]

Locomotive testing, both on the stationary test plant and on the road using a dynamometer car, played a major role in the Churchward scheme, at least during the early years of his stewardship. Both types of testing, apart from running-in, fell under the control of the Chief Draughtsman and a valuable team of skilled engineers built up. Churchward did play a more open role and was more willing to deal with his engineering team directly than was his predecessor, so maybe it was that aspect of his character which endeared him to so many. He was still, however, very autocratic and that showed up particularly when dealing with people from other departments. His relationships with Inglis, the Chief (Civil) Engineer, and with various General Managers have already been covered in chapter 3.

Direct access to the board was important to Churchward as, like Dean and Armstrong before him, he was able to put his case for more money or works expansion to those who controlled the purse strings and not go through some intermediary. The problem regarding bridge weight restrictions, again already dealt with, highlights a major failing in the overall GWR management structure, that being the lack of any suitable interdepartmental communication. Matters improved somewhat when Pole took over as General Manager and developed that post into one having a true management role. Views were, however, very entrenched and each department still tended to think of itself in isolation for many years afterwards.

From the early years of Gooch until the final days under Hawksworth, all new locomotive building had to be approved by a Locomotive Committee of the board. Apart from Hawksworth's failure to get his 'Pacific' sanctioned, there appear to have been no major cases of approval being withheld for the building of a locomotive class, but persuasion to modify designs must have been exerted. Following World War II Hawksworth proposed the construction of a further batch of '57xx' tank engines but Sir James Milne, then General Manager and probably influential with the Building Committee, expressed the view that a steam dome had no place on a modern locomotive.[17] The CME took the hint and produced his '94xx' class. Churchward with his style and forcefulness had no problem getting his major building programme approved by the Committee.

Design of new or replacement classes required considerable thought and many people must have been involved in the process. Collett, who has frequently, and wrongly, been criticized for rigidly following the Churchward plan and not having any ideas of his own, spent a great deal of time with his assistants discussing proposals.[18] All aspects of operations would be discussed before any final decisions were made and everybody would be able to offer suggestions in the light of his own experience and knowledge. That was a sensible way of dealing with the design process.

Spending money on land purchase also came within the remit of the CME if that land was required for future plant extension either at the main works or at some outpost. In 1873 Joseph Armstrong arranged the purchase of some sixteen acres of land between the then existing sheds at Swindon and the North Wilts Canal.[19] George Armstrong at Wolverhampton also negotiated the purchase of land when the situation dictated. Naturally, any purchase had to be approved by the board.

Not only did Churchward extend the works and replace worn out machinery with newer equipment, he also introduced electrically driven plant.

That required a power supply and as one was not available he arranged for the building of a power station at the works. Actually a number of small power stations were constructed to serve particular shops within the works. Gas powered internal combustion engines provided the drive for dc generators in each of the power houses.[20] As the use of electrical equipment increased there was need to employ qualified electricians and supervisors, responsibility for those remaining with the Chief Mechanical Engineer.

The retirement of George Armstrong in 1897 marked the end of an era and the beginning of the end for Stafford Road Works as an independent centre. W.H. Waister replaced Armstrong but he was quickly called to Swindon as Locomotive Running Superintendent. He was replaced by J.A. Robinson, but Churchward's influence was beginning to be felt and as soon as the standard range of locomotives had been settled no new designs were produced at Wolverhampton. Several '45xx class 2-6-2 side tanks of the standard range were constructed during the first decade of the twentieth century but after that all locomotive building ceased.[21]

Churchward did not have to contend with any independent thinking by those in charge at the northern outpost; everything was centred on Swindon. That certainly eased the management task but the Great Western lost something with the demise of Stafford Road. Joseph Armstrong and William Dean, together with a number of other engineers who served the railway well, spent many years at Wolverhampton and its independence must have encouraged a spirit of originality. Though centralization may have helped the command network it played a part in stifling imagination. The Swindon mould worked well and produced good machines, but the appearance of those machines has often been criticized for lacking imagination and being 'typically Swindon'. Maybe a spell at Stafford Road would have been beneficial to Churchward, Collett and Hawksworth.

When Churchward retired at the end of 1921 it was possible for Felix Pole to introduce his radical change in management organization, so that the Divisional Officers would not have direct access to the board but would all report through the General Manager. Inglis had proposed such a structure many years earlier but opposition from Churchward and others had prevented implementation. The diplomatic Felix Pole was content to introduce the scheme slowly as the older chief officers retired.[22] Neither Collett nor Hawksworth seems to have been restricted by the arrangement, in fact Pole appears to have been instrumental in

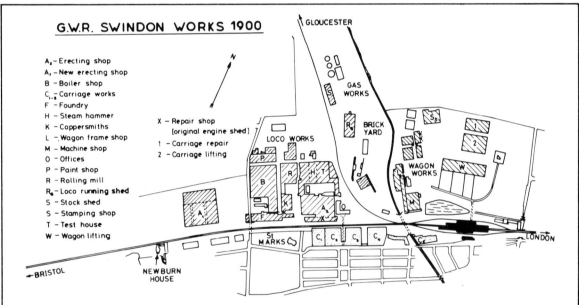

G.W.R. SWINDON WORKS 1900

A$_e$ – Erecting shop
A$_r$ – New erecting shop
B – Boiler shop
C$_{1-5}$ – Carriage works
F – Foundry
H – Steam hammer
K – Coppersmiths
L – Wagon frame shop
M – Machine shop
O – Offices
P – Paint shop
R – Rolling mill
R$_s$ – Loco running shed
S – Stock shed
S – Stamping shop
T – Test house
W – Wagon lifting

X – Repair shop
[original engine shed]
1 – Carriage repair
2 – Carriage lifting

Top *The end of the line for No. 5322 of the '4300' class. At Barry scrap-yard 13 November 1965* (Chris Surridge).

Above *Swindon Works layout circa 1900.*

Right *No. 6414 of Collett's '6400' class designed for light passenger duties. At Exmouth Junction shed 23 April 1966* (Chris Surridge).

Above far left *Sir Felix Pole, General Manager.*
Above left *C. B. Collett.*

Left *Swindon Works hierarchy in 1935.*
Back row (left to right): S. J. Smith, Chief Draughtsman;
R. G. Hannington, Loco Works Manager; J. Kelynack, Chief
Clerk; E. T. J. Evans, Carriage & Wagon Works Manager.
Front row (left to right): J. R. W. Grainge, Electrical Assistant
to CME; J. Auld, Principal Assistant to CME; C. B. Collett,
CME; F. W. Hawksworth, Assistant to CME; F. C. Hall,
Outside Assistant to CME (courtesy GWR Museum,
Swindon).

Above *Collett-designed and Pole-inspired 'King' and 'Castle'*
classes: No. 6000 King George V *and* Clun Castle.

promoting a number of locomotive projects,
namely the 'Castles' and 'Kings', as will be
considered in a later chapter. The monthly chief
officers' conference, organized as part of the
scheme, produced some degree of centralized
control and resulted in greater efficiency. However,
the standing of the Chief Mechanical Engineer and
other chief officers was considerably reduced.[23]

Unlike the situation existing on other railways
the Great Western CME had complete control over
footplate staff as well as locomotives, and that
presented problems in rostering drivers and
firemen with other train staff. Throughout Church-

ward's period in office the system was separated
into seven divisions for ease of operation, each
division having a Locomotive Divisional Superintendent responsible for both men and machines. In
charge of those superintendents was the Outdoor
Assistant to the CME. By 1922 the situation had to
be changed and the title became Locomotive
Running Superintendent & Outdoor Assistant to
the CME. In the former of the roles the holder of
the post was responsible to the Superintendent of
the Line, as a principal assistant, for all matters
regarding the running of trains. In the other part of
his role he was responsible to the CME for routine
maintenance of the rolling stock.[24]

Railway grouping in 1923 brought a number of
smaller lines into the GWR system but it did not
materially change matters regarding management
or operation. Two more divisions were added,
Cardiff Valleys and Central Wales, and the
opportunity was taken to tidy up the boundaries of
the other divisions. Divisional Superintendents
were apointed and the system functioned in much
the same way as it had before grouping. The influx
of senior staff from the absorbed railways caused
certain problems as not all wished to retire. In
many cases the men remained in their old areas as
Superintendents or assistants but some went to

Swindon. One such was John Auld, formerly CME of the Barry Railway, who became docks assistant to Collett. That post possessed great importance as many of the smaller railways had extensive port facilities on the South Wales coast. Auld later became Assistant CME when Stanier moved to the LMS.

That basic structure of control lasted until the demise of the Great Western Railway. The CME had overall control with his assistant supervising day-to-day matters regarding the works and divisional operations. Locomotive and carriage works each had its own manager and Divisional Superintendents controlled matters locally via District or Depot Superintendents. At the works and depots there would be foremen in charge of the fitters, drivers, *etc.*

Control over the footplate staff by the CME started with Gooch, as he was responsible not only for maintenance of the locomotives but also procurement of the drivers and firemen. Gooch supervised their training and exercised discipline over the wrongdoer. He kept a 'Black Book' in which details of offences and fines were religiously recorded. In 1910 *The Engineer* reproduced a number of extracts from the book, using only initials and not full names, presumably to protect the 'guilty', or their familes, from adverse comment. An entry dated 4 September 1840 with the initials J.H., which must be Jim Hurst, the friend of Gooch mentioned in chapter 2, reads: 'For running his engine in a careless manner when pumping water upon the main line, and striking the "Wild Fire" engine so as to break her frame end, and considerably injured his own tender.— Fined 10s.' Early locomotives employed crank driven pumps to put water in the boiler, so it was necessary to drive the engine along the line in order to keep up the level.

In February 1841, Engineman R. . . was ordered to pay restitution of £4.4s. to a passenger whose flute he had retained over Christmas 1840. On 5 May 1842, Engineman T. . . was 'Reported by a passenger for walking along the steps of the carriages to the guards during the time the train was in motion, and drinking some beer with them. The case was brought before the directors, who fined the conductor very heavily, dismissed the guards and fined T. . . 20s.' The fact that the driver got off comparatively lightly indicates their importance at the time. Good, or even bad, drivers were not easily come by. Three years later the situation had changed somewhat as Engineman B. . . found out. 'On two occasions within the last fortnight he has stopped the mail train by neglecting his pumps, and having his fire to pull out in both

cases. When the pumps were examined they were found in good order. He has become generally careless and I fear getting into drunken habits.— Discharged.'[25]

In later years charges such as theft generally went before the courts, but sometimes the matter remained within the railway to be dealt with by the CME. Churchward, a good engineer, had a direct manner and, although popular with the men, appears to have been rather insensitive regarding personal matters, possibly due to the lack of a close family. In April 1908 a sixty-nine year old driver was brought before him accused of stealing a small bag of coal from a locomotive. Almost twenty years earlier the old driver had refused promotion to express work as it would have meant moving to Bristol and he considered himself too old to move. The Company's insistence that he go resulted in a breakdown followed by a spell in the County Asylum. On five shillings per day the depressed old chap returned to Swindon as an engine turner, incurring fines for negligence due to his state of health. Theft of small portions of coal eked out his meagre pay.

Churchward reduced the man's wages to three shillings per day and ordered that he retire at the end of the year. In effect the fine amounted to nearly £17 and next day the old man was found drowned in the canal.[26] The inability of Churchward, and others, to recognize problems outside the engineering domain made them unsuitable to make decisions of a personal nature. Not all engineers were, or are, blessed with the caring social attitude of Joseph Armstrong.

The drawing office came under the direct control of the CME with a Chief Draughtsman being responsible for a number of senior and junior draughtsmen as well as the locomotive test team. Churchward and Hawksworth were keenly interested in design and would spend many hours discussing a particular project with the drawing office staff. Collett was not so inclined and merely outlined proposals, leaving the Chief Draughtsman to produce a final design. Collett, however, had an enquiring mind, being interested in production techniques and machinery failure analysis. He was prepared to spend time with subordinates investigating the reasons for particular problems.[27] The depth of talent within the Chief Mechanical Engineer's Department allowed each CME to concentrate upon his own special interests with the assurance that the Department as a whole would function effectively. From Gooch to Hawksworth each holder of the office provided facilities to meet the needs of the railway and only a good manager is able to do that.

5. Design influences and construction

Brunel laid out his line between London and Bristol so that it would be as straight and flat as possible; that was his primary design criterion. Speed was important to Brunel and, as locomotive matters stood during the early years of the 1830s, only a level line with the minimum of sharp curves could allow the velocities envisaged. The same considerations applied between Bristol and Exeter although that line belonged to another concern. Even in South Devon speed was important but there it depended on the atmospheric system. Had that system not turned out to be such a mechanical failure, high speeds could have been consistently attained. It is certain that a more level, though less direct, route would have been chosen had he initially set out to construct for locomotive operations. However, in arranging for atmospheric propulsion Brunel adopted much steeper gradients (1 in 40 at times) than on any of his other lines and the South Devon banks became a governing factor for future locomotive designs.[1]

Failure of the atmospheric system prompted the Great Western to help its offspring, the South Devon Railway, with Daniel Gooch designing the powerful *Corsair* and *Brigand*. Various other standard Gooch engines were also transferred to work the railway but the two specially designed bogie saddle tanks found full employment on the steep banks.[2] In later years contractors provided the Railway's locomotives, though these were still of Gooch design as Daniel Gooch was one of the contractors. For the final ten years of its independent existence the SDR itself took control of the locomotive department, obtaining machines from a variety of sources. All SDR broad gauge locomotives were tank engines. With absorption of main line railways in Devon and Cornwall by the GReat Western during 1876 a single company had control of through trains between London and Penzance. Gooch 'Iron Duke' class engines had proved themselves and took on the duty as far west as Exeter. The end of the broad gauge was, however, in sight and it would have been pointless to design a new class to undertake the arduous work of climbing the banks, so the old South Devon engines struggled on.

The banks were not, however, steady but undulating and so a banking system, as used on Shap or Beattock, could not be employed. Trains had to be hauled by one or more locomotives. Only when the narrow gauge was in place and the line had been upgraded did the call go out for a more powerful locomotive. William Dean designed the '3252' or 'Duke' class especially to work the heavy gradients in Devon and Cornwall, the first of the class appearing in 1895. Already Brunel's atmospheric failure was having its influence on narrow gauge locomotive design.

That main line to the west was also constructed to Brunel's 7 ft gauge which allowed for increased stability and the high velocities planned. The 'little giant' argued that his gauge did not require much more land than a narrow gauge and that the increased excavation for tunnels and cuttings was minimal.[3] That claim could be disputed, but as this is not a discussion concerning early GWR finances its accuracy does not really matter; what is important is that extra space was allowed. Broad gauge locomotives and rolling stock could be wider than their narrow gauge counterparts with all the

No. 3267, Cornishman, *of the 'Duke' class, designed for work on the gradients in Devon and Cornwall* (courtesy GWR Museum, Swindon).

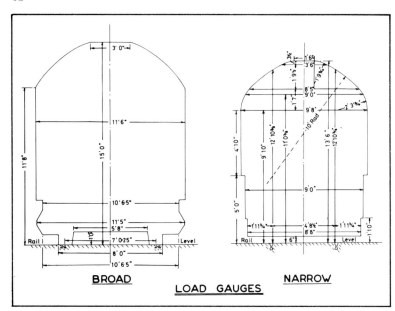

BROAD   LOAD GAUGES   NARROW

advantages that offered. Following conversion to narrow gauge the GWR found itself with increased available width where it mattered, in tunnels and cuttings. Platforms and similar constructions can be fairly readily altered but holes in the ground are a more expensive proposition. Brunel's courage provided an ample loading gauge for the Great Western, though later narrow gauge rolling stock designers did not fully exploit it. That is, perhaps, just as well, for the movement of GWR stock would have been even more restricted than it later was, other concerns not being so generous with clearances. *The Engineer* for 1910 lamented that fact in presenting profiles of the broad and narrow load gauges; '. . .one cannot help expressing regret that the load gauge of the year 1840 does not exist in 1910. The possibilities it would present by allowing increased cross-sectional dimensions would relieve every railway engineer of much anxiety in dealing with modern heavy traffic.'[4]

GWR locomotive designers did make some use of the increased width available to them, as the present-day enthusiast knows. Steam-hauled rail tours using former Great Western locomotives are confined to tracks within the old GWR system due to clearance problems. Even then there are speed restrictions under certain bridges where height limitations may exist due to repacking of the track. The problem of reduced headroom became obvious during the evening of 6 September 1974 when *King George V*, whilst travelling at speed, hit road overbridge with its safety valves. The valves were torn off, resulting in rapid release of steam, and

hence water, from the boiler, Only prompt attention by the fire brigade avoided more serious damage.[5]

Early coaching stock did not make full use of the loading gauge as there was never any particular demand for more spacious accommodation from the Victorians or Edwardians. In any case locomotives were not powerful enough to cope with massive trains. Churchward provided a number of coaches 70 ft long and 9 ft 6 in wide, known as the 'Dreadnoughts', some of them seating eighty third class passengers in a fair degree of discomfort. These long and wide vehicles were mainly limited to former broad gauge lines where space existed for them to negotiate curves with safety. Collett, however, did not consider such long coaches to be safe even on former broad gauge lines, despite the fact that enlarged buffers were fitted in order to prevent them from becoming locked. He convinced Felix Pole, the General Manager, that all new coaches should be less than 70 ft long.[6]

In 1929 Collett built the 'Ocean Liner Saloons' to serve the transatlantic passenger ships. They were luxurious and though constructed to the then standard 61 ft 4½ in length were of the maximum width permitted, 9 ft 7 in. During 1935 the special 'Centenary Stock' was introduced which also had a 9 ft 7 in width. Such wide stock had to be limited to particular routes and was not allowed over other companies' lines. The ample loading gauge could, therefore, be used to effect, particularly for passenger luxury, but the stock was imprisoned on the Great Western. Whilst that was satisfactory for a few trains it did not suit the majority as the rail system became more integrated with increased numbers of through workings. Designers on the GWR were, in effect, constrained due to limitations imposed by other railways, not their own.

Brunel's baulk road presented certain problems because it did not yield to the same extent as a transverse sleepered track employing bullhead rail carried in chairs. The situation existed even after gauge conversion, which merely involved cutting the transoms and moving the longitudinal sleepers closer together. Sandwich frames, employed with all early locomotives, were found to give better running on the baulk road and continued to be used for many GWR engines long after they had ceased to be employed elsewhere. The Great Western had many miles of serviceable mixed gauge and converted track so the step was an obvious one. Continuous and unyielding support provided by the bridge rail and longitudinal sleepers also required more flexible springing. Flexibility was achieved by employing open leaf springs, the individual leaves being kept apart at the buckle by thin distance pieces in order to reduce internal friction.[7]

Over the years sandwich plates differed slightly but they followed the basic construction, comprising thick planks of hardwood between thin flitch plates of iron or, later, mild steel. In some instances distance pieces might be used alongside the timber planks; in other cases only timber kept the flitch plates apart. Horns and spring hanger sockets had to be located between the flitch plates before they were tightened together. Oak was preferred, but the acid in it would eventually corrode the bolts. Other wood was used, but charring of the oak prevented acid attack, a red hot bar pushed

through the bolt holes in the oak achieving the effect.[8]

Though sandwich frames had advantages usage was spasmodic, none of the nineteenth-century engineers appearing to have a consistent policy. The same might be said about the use of double frames, though to a lesser extent. A prime factor in the continued use of double frames on the Great Western long after the practice had been abandoned by other railways was the continued presence of the broad gauge. For the convertible engines of Armstrong and Dean it was a very suitable arrangement, allowing broad gauge wheels to be positioned outside the outermost frames or narrow gauge wheels to be placed between the frames. Both men appeared to vary the use though Dean applied double frames to all of his large tender engines whilst using inside frames for tank engines. It might be supposed that Dean had in mind the conversion of a number of engines for broad gauge work. That, however, cannot have been the case as the 'City' and some other classes did not appear until after the turn of the century. Obviously the merits of double frames impressed the ailing engineer and he continued to use them long after the essential need had ceased.

Double frames gave greater weight and had a higher initial cost but they did produce advantages. Axle bearings at each of the frames provided a much greater bearing surface area than was the case with inside frames, whilst shorter inside bearings meant that less of the crankshaft length was taken by the journals. Longer crank pins and wider webs could, therefore, be provided together with increased distance between inside cylinder centre lines. That allowed a larger steam chest or bigger cylinders if the steam chest was placed below them. Holcroft observed that double framed engines had a greater tendency to break crank axles than was the case with single framed engines though the reason remained rather doubtful.[9]

Increased engine power usually required increased weight and there was always a limit to the axle loading which might be applied, particularly on bridges. The Civil Engineer would dictate maximum permitted loading and it remained the duty of the Mechanical Engineer to keep within given limits. During the nineteenth century there appears to have been no difficulty in complying with the restrictions as earthwork and bridge structures were adequate for the small locomotives then existing. As Churchward developed his more powerful engines, route availability became more of a problem. The incident concerning Collett's building of the 'King' class has already been considered but it illustrates the problem. Even then

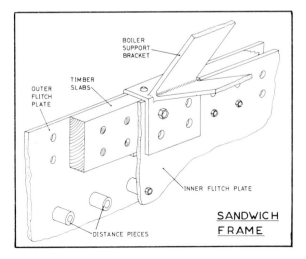

SANDWICH FRAME

BOILER SUPPORT BRACKET

OUTER FLITCH PLATE

TIMBER SLABS

INNER FLITCH PLATE

DISTANCE PIECES

the 'Kings' were confined to certain major routes. The situation was even more restrictive for Churchward's 'Pacific', *The Great Bear*, which could only operate on the line between London and Bristol.

Bridge loading not only comes from the static weight of the engine but also from the hammer blow effect caused by the balance weights fitted to the wheels as the wheels rotate. Force of the blow actually increases with speed. Such weights are essential in order to balance the piston and crosshead reciprocating masses and so some hammer blow cannot be avoided. It can, however, be reduced by using a smaller balance weight but that is only possible if the reciprocating masses have a tendency to balance themselves. For a two-cylinder engine having cranks at 90° the disturbing forces are large, requiring two thirds of the reciprocating masses to be balanced. Weights are fitted almost diametrically opposite the crank pins on the wheels concerned, resulting in large hammer blows. The extra crank on a three-cylinder engine enables a reduction in the mass of balance weights but these must be placed opposite each other on right and left wheels, which tends to produce a slight rocking motion.

A much better situation exists with a four-cylinder engine which has the inside cylinders connected to the front coupled wheels and the

Diagram showing the balance weight positioning requirements and resultant hammer blow forces for two-, three- and four-cylinder locomotives.

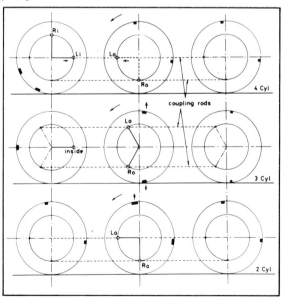

outside cylinders driving the middle coupled wheels. The left inside and left outside cranks are positioned diametrically opposite, thus the reciprocating masses tend automatically to balance each other, dramatically reducing the size of any balance weights. A similar situation exists on the right-hand side of the engine. With smaller balance weight the hammer blow effect on the rails is reduced. A four-cylinder engine is also able to provide a higher starting force.[10]

Churchward was probably not greatly influenced by the reduced hammer blow effect when designing his four-cylinder 'Star' class as the axle loading was below 19 tons and within the limits then in force. During 1923 the four grouped railway companies set up the Bridge Stress Committee in order to investigate stresses set up in bridges by various loadings, wheel spacing and hammer blows. As a result of tests it was decided that higher static axle loadings could be allowed with multi-cylinder engines than was permitted for those having two cylinders.[11] That fact, and the continuing scheme of bridge strengthening, allowed Collett to construct the 'Castle' and later 'King' classes. Hawksworth, in designing the 'County' class, adopted a two-cylinder configuration for ease of maintenance and simplicity in construction. The price paid, however, was in route restriction and, on certain routes, speed restriction because of heavy hammer blows.

Any locomotive consists of two separate but essentially linked systems, namely the boiler and propulsion mechanism. Efficient steam generation requires correct combustion of the fuel. All early locomotives consumed coke as that burned readily without producing clouds of black smoke which was considered objectionable from moving machines but not, apparently, from factory chimneys. As firebox design improved with the introduction of the brick arch it became possible to burn coal rather than coke, that fuel being preferred because of its higher calorific value and availability. Unfortunately, coal quality varies considerably, whilst combustion produces ash and clinker which have a tendency to restrict the flow of air through the fire. Good quality coal burns well, releasing its heat readily and leaving a minimum of problematic waste. For poor quality fuel the opposite is true and a relatively wide firebox is needed to ensure correct combustion.[12] Other factors influence firebox design but type of fuel is of major importance.

The Great Western had easy access to good quality Welsh steam coal and its Swindon boilers were designed for burning that only. Narrow fireboxes, high ratio of heat transfer surface area to grate area and draughting were all arranged to suit lively Welsh coal. When running on other lines during interchange trials the local coal had to be used and performance generally suffered. To be fair, performance depends not only upon coal quality but also on firing rate and the ability of the footplate crew. An optimum firebed varies in bulk with evaporation rate and fuel characteristics such as carbon content and swelling index.[13] Any fireman must, therefore, arrange his fire to suit the coal if the boiler is to steam well but greatest efficiency can only be expected if the boiler is burning fuel for which it has been designed.

Following World War II shortage of Welsh steam coal prompted trials with oil firing and, after nationalization, modifications to draughting were required before former GWR engines could operate satisfactorily on indifferent coal. These were arranged by S.O. E11 following extensive tests during the early 1950s. Although his work came after the GWR ceased to exist, brief mention is warranted, if only to emphasize that Swindon boilers were designed for good steam coal and not the inferior material provided later. Following many tests E11 recorded;

> In narrow firebox boilers, draught and discharge limits may approach and sometimes equal the grate limit. A good front end is a vital necessity; many otherwise good boilers have been condemned by an inferior front end. In many cases, improvements may be carried out at little cost, even for a single orifice design and can place the boiler limit of continuous evaporation over 30% higher than its normal working rate, and in doing so can also improve the combustion efficiency and ability to burn inferior coal.[14]

Modified draughting on the 'King' class improved performance overall and particularly when using lower grade fuel, for which it was not originally designed.

Type of duty influences the style of a locomotive, whether for Great Western or other railway. Goods engines are required to provide a high starting force with sustained pull, particularly on banks, and GWR mineral traffic was extensive especially in the Welsh valleys. That requirement called for smaller diameter wheels which, ideally, would all be coupled, thereby making most of the locomotive weight available for traction. An extensive system of branch lines for both passenger and freight traffic produced a need for many small but powerful locomotives capable of negotiating tight curves. Tank engines are ideal on short runs, for lines without turning facilities and where the adhesive weight of water in the tanks can usefully be employed. Many locomotives were designed to

suit particular traffic needs as will be discussed in a later chapter.

In every sphere of design work personal preference plays an important part with regard to final appearance and construction. There may be no logical reason why a particular feature is incorporated or omitted, it is just that the designer considers certain aspects more important than others. Chief Mechanical Engineers of the Great Western Railway were no different from other people in holding preconceived views on locomotive and carriage design. The directors also had some influence, though to a lesser extent.

Daniel Gooch was a fervent supporter of the broad gauge but he was also a shrewd businessman. It cannot be doubted that he derived pleasure from the fact that the 7 ft gauge lasted until the end of his life and so played an important part in locomotive affairs on the GWR. Some people have considered that Brunel's gauge was only retained out of respect for him whilst he remained chairman. Such a situation is unlikely as the businessman in Gooch would have prevented him from acceding to the arrangement if financial factors had dictated otherwise. Earlier gauge conversions had gone ahead for commercial reasons and Gooch would have recognized that final elimination of the broad gauge was just a matter of time. By the end of 1876 the only broad gauge lines were in Devon and Cornwall on the recently absorbed railways, mixed gauge on the line from Paddington being retained in order to allow through trains. Fifteen years were to elapse before final abolition. That abolition came three years after the death of Gooch might imply deliberate retention for his lifetime, but conversion cost the Great Western money both in the actual process and in new rolling stock. At the time available finance was directed towards constructing the Severn Tunnel and conversion of a relatively small region of the Company's domain could wait. Repercussions of that decision were to be seen in the convertible locomotives and carriages.

Financial restraint due to the general economic situation and the chaos left by Potter imposed severe restrictions on Gooch's ability to improve train services. The compulsory refreshment stop at Swindon also had its detrimental influence in that it was unnecessary to design locomotives or carriages for long non-stop journeys. Gooch had no desire to increase train speeds above what they were when he became chairman, nor was there a real economic demand. However, Armstrong and Dean were faced with the need to produce higher powered engines for heavier trains; the demands of

Left *Joseph Armstrong's first design with inside bearings on the driving wheels and outside bearings on leading and trailing wheels, after the fashion of George Gray.*

Right *Early form of wheel construction.*

Below right *French compound No. 103,* President *(courtesy GWR Museum, Swindon).*

fast running could be ignored.

Armstrong locomotives, from Joseph and George, are characterized by their lack of cabs, the only form of weather protection for footplate crew being weatherboards with circular windows. At a later date wings were added but it was not until the 1880s, following Joseph's death, that cabs came into normal use on the GWR. Even then facilities lagged far behind those offered by other railways where tank engines, required to run bunker first, would be fitted with enclosed cabs. Both Armstrongs had been drivers and knew the rigours of footplate work, so they were asking no more of the men than they had suffered themselves. Coke firing had been the norm during their time on the footplate and it was considered that noxious carbon monoxide and sulphurous fumes could build up in an enclosed cab when the regulator was closed.[15] With coal firing and thinner fires this was less likely, but the view persisted, with the result that cabs remained out of favour even during the early years of the Dean era. The tradition continued with GWR cabs and other footplate amenities such as seats and lockers always falling well below the standard set by other railways. There is no logical reason as to why that should have been.

Joseph Armstrong was greatly influenced by the work of his early mentor, George Gray, and he adopted some of the design ideas Gray employed on the Hull & Selby Railway. Two of Armstrong's first narrow gauge engines employed the novel feature of bearings for the driving wheels being attached to the inside frame only whilst the leading and trailing wheels had bearings in single plate outside frames. Armstrong adopted Stephenson link motion for valve gear rather than the Gooch arrangement which then predominated.[16] That system remained standard until Churchward

modified Walschaert's gear for use on his four-cylinder engines.

Apart from Dean's predilection for double frames there seem to have been few things which he considered to be sacrosanct. In fact Dean was an avid experimenter and produced more 'one-offs' than any other engineer, including Churchward. Some showed immediate advantage whilst others, such as the 4-2-4 No. 9, appeared to be doomed to failure from the start. Knowledge was gained even from the disasters and put to good use either in development or avoidance of similar mistakes. His mind jumped about trying new ideas whenever something promising manifested itself but the apparent lack of a cohesive plan gave the impression that he was erratic and incapable, particularly towards the end. Such a conclusion is unfair as Dean produced some extremely useful machines despite being hampered by financial restraint due to the Severn Tunnel and the upheaval of final gauge conversion. Without his willingness to experiment it is doubtful whether Churchward could have introduced his changes so quickly.

Dean maintained the GWR preference for single wheelers even when that arrangement fell from favour on other railways. Apart from those in the west, GWR main lines were moderately graded allowing for high speed running, whilst the single wheeler also offered advantages in ease of maintenance, lower coal consumption and smoother running than for coupled wheels.[17] In beauty and grace few locomotives have been able to match the Dean single wheelers. They had style and an elegance which no balance sheet or engineering report could convey.

Locomotive wheels are critical and must be soundly manufactured with precision. Before the advent of high quality casting techniques large driving wheels had to be constructed from a number of individual sections hammer welded together. The method remained very much the same from the early Stephenson engines to the final batch of broad gauge 'Rover' class and some of Dean's narrow gauge single wheelers. Each spoke consisted of two pieces, the head including a segment of the rim and the tail including a portion of the nave, each piece having been forged using a steam hammer. (Spokes for 8 ft wheels of the 'Rover' class were in three pieces.) A head and a tail were then welded together using the steam hammer in order to form a single spoke. Eventually the wheel would be built up in sections by hammer welding to form the nave and rim, filler pieces being employed as necessary. Coupled wheels required a forged block known as the 'use' to be introduced in order to take the crank pin. Daniel Gooch used steel tyres held onto the wheel by a dovetail joint filled up with zinc. In the case of the Stephenson engines riveting was employed and at a later date tyres were shrunk on. Many large broad gauge wheels comprised well in excess of 100 pieces; from them the smith had to create a wheel capable of withstanding the stress of high speed rotation whilst the locomotive travelled at speeds above 60 mph. Those who made the wheels earned the right to be called craftsmen.[18]

Churchward changed the Great Western locomotive scene. A number of his ideas came from abroad, though he would modify them to suit British practice. American and French influences were strong at certain times but they did not predominate. Impressed though he was with the performance of de Glehn compounds running in France, Churchward was not willing to jump on the compound bandwagon until it had been given a trial. In the end the system did not suit and was not

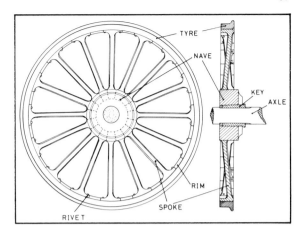

adopted. The de Glehn bogie did, however, find favour and, suitably westernized, became the standard.

American influence was felt in boiler design and semi-plug piston valves. The idea of a taper boiler having a long narrow firebox appears to have been borrowed from the Illinois Central Railroad.[19] Whilst others avoided the use of piston valves because of wear problems, Churchward jumped at the chance of using the American semi-plug type. Though a high degree of skill was needed in its fitting the benefits were many. An effective piston valve formation allowed the use of a single casting which contained cylinder, valve chest and all steam passageways. Two identical castings bolted together along the engine centre line formed a saddle to carry the smokebox. The arrangement was simple, cut out many steam joints and allowed for the use of a single casting pattern. With but minor changes from the initial fitting to No. 99 in 1903 the design was adopted for all Churchward

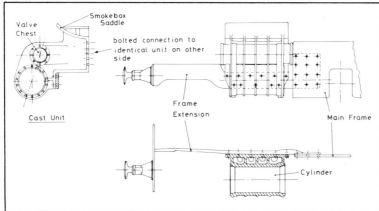

Above *'4500' class No. 4538 at Bristol on 12 August 1950, Churchward's larger wheeled development of his '4400' class for branch line duty. The horizontal cylinders are evident* (D. K. Jones Collection).

Left *The cylinder casting units and bar extension frames as introduced for the two-cylinder Churchward standard designs.*

Below *2-8-0 heavy freight locomotive No. 3822, a development of the '2800' class.*

Valve Chest

Smokebox Saddle

bolted connection to identical unit on other side

Cast Unit

Frame Extension

Main Frame

Cylinder

and Collett standard two-cylinder locomotives. Because the castings did not allow plate frames to extend as far as the buffer beam, an adjustment at the front end was necessary. Following American practice, a thick rectangular slab connected with the buffer beam at its front and was splayed out at its rear to connect with the main frames just behind the cylinder castings. On smaller wheeled engines extension frames had a downward set in order to pass below the cylinders resulting in heavy buffing shocks. Support stays connected to the smokebox saddle had to be employed.[20]

For some unknown reason the 'old man' had an aversion to inclined cylinders, even those close to him such as Harold Holcroft being unable to discover why. Slight inclination would have reduced the need for downward set on the extension frames. It would also have avoided the necessity for raising the cylinder centre line 2½ in above the driving wheel centres so that cylinders cleared the loading gauge when tyre wear was near maximum.[21] A similar inexplicable dislike for outside valve gear also existed. Churchward preferred a clear-cut outline and it has been stated that he wanted to have as little motion as possible outside in order to reduce out-of-balance forces.[22] The balance problem cannot have been a major one and no other railway company designer followed the style. Aesthetics must have been the prime factor but maintenance inaccessibility was a high price to pay. Apart from one digression by Hawksworth, the '1500' class with outside valve gear, both practices were perpetuated until the end of Great Western steam.

Churchward also came under the spell of Professor Goss with regard to locomotive testing. Road testing provided valuable data but his hurried decision to construct a stationary test plant at Swindon does appear to have been ill-conceived. Until Collett updated the plant it was a costly monument to American influence.

The brilliance of Churchward in deriving a standard range of boilers set the pattern for GWR locomotive appearance until the railway ceased to exist. A boiler is the most imposing part of any locomotive and its shape provides the engine's outline. Churchward's taper boilers, with their unchanging brass safety valve covers, were, and are, distinctive. A locomotive with such a boiler is obviously Great Western no matter what it looks like below the frames. That fact is evident from the appearance of reboilered French Compounds. With little need for future CMEs to change the basic boiler styling, a pattern had been set which made later locomotives appear rather antiquated, though they were, in fact, very much up to date. It

is not unknown for the latter-day enthusiast to comment that 'all Great Western engines look the same'.

Boilers require water as well as coal, and the quality of that fluid is critical to future performance. Scale formation in the boiler impairs heat transfer and frequent boiler wash-out is required to remove sludge which forms. Corrosion can easily result from poor quality water and the life of a boiler is drastically reduced. Brunel and Gooch were conscious of the low quality of water in the Swindon area but did not consider it a problem as locomotives could pick up better supplies elsewhere. However, it would be fair to say that the operating lives of all early locomotive boilers were restricted by indifferent water. Dean became concerned about the problem and introduced regular testing of water from all parts of the railway system. As a result of the tests carried out at the Swindon chemical laboratory he organized water-softening treatment for difficult supplies.[23]

Churchward was a firm supporter of water treatment, considering it to be essential for higher pressures.[24] He continued the treatment policy, extending and modifying where necessary. He also made changes in the boiler feed supply system through the introduction of top feed whereby the incoming feed water discharged onto trays and not directly into the water. Scale would form on the tray and not the boiler shell or tubes which remained in a better condition than was the case with normal bottom feed. Trays could be removed periodically for cleaning or replacement.[25] This arrangement produced a degree of feed water heating which supplemented the heat input of the exhaust steam injector when the engine was running or the live steam injector when stationary. Such heating resulted in a feed temperature only about 40°F below the boiler water temperature. Churchward offered that contribution as part of a discussion at an Institution of Mechanical Engineers meeting in 1913, adding that 'experience showed that the wear and tear on the boiler were very considerably reduced by this means, and it was well worth heating the feed-water to obtain the economy in boiler repairs even if no saving resulted in steam consumption.'[26]

K.J. Cook, a later Locomotive Works Manager at Swindon, agreed and considered that combined with water treatment the effect was to more than double the life of a boiler from 400,000 miles to nearly 1,000,000 miles before it was likely to be condemned. During the early period of the twentieth century it was necessary to provide two boilers to cover an engine's life but by the 1930s the average was reduced to about one and a quarter.[27]

The implications for repair costs and engine availability were dramatic as, up until the 1920s, boiler condition was the limiting factor. Easy interchangeability of boilers was built into design because a heavy boiler repair might take much longer than repairs to the remainder of the locomotive. A new or repaired boiler would be allocated to the rest of the engine which could return to traffic long before repairs to the original boiler had been completed. The system was costly in spare boilers but reduced the time a locomotive spent in the shop.[28] Naturally all parts had to fit and careful construction was required; standardization ruled. Even with the extended boiler life due to improved water supplies and better treatment, designs allowing easy removal and replacement of boilers were considered essential in order to progress a repair through the shops. What Churchward started, no man put asunder.

Collett continued his predecessor's policy with regard to locomotive design and appears to have been influenced only by him. Churchward dogma was followed almost to the letter in many cases even though there had been developments which rendered certain practices outdated. Austere lines remained, cylinders were horizontal and valve gear stayed hidden between the frames even with the advanced 'Castle' and 'King' classes. Without doubt the Churchward designs were functional and effective but Collett appeared unwilling to show publicly any signs of individuality. However a number of changes in design and construction were made without accompanying fanfare. In one major aspect he stuck rigidly to the doctrine and failed to

take any notice of improvements made by others: low temperature superheating remained a Great Western feature.

Superheating is basically the raising of steam temperature above that at which it generates from water at boiler pressure. In order to achieve that condition the steam must be removed from the water region and passed through a separate heater element. Two major advantages of superheating are the storage of an increased amount of heat energy per unit mass of steam, thus allowing more work to be obtained without a need to increase steam pressure, and the avoidance of condensation whilst steam is in the cylinder. A disadvantage of superheating lies in the fact that lubricating oil has to be supplied to the cylinder in order to minimize wear. Superheated steam is 'dry' and so does not contain any water droplets which act as a lubricant; high degrees of superheating prevent water droplets forming during expansion in the cylinder and so it is of prime importance that cylinder lubrication is provided.

Locomotive superheating had been employed in Germany and America around the turn of the century, but Churchward is given credit for introducing the practice to Britain although other engineers were developing systems at the same time. Two arrangements were tried initially, the German Schmidt type superheater on a 'Saint' class engine in 1906, with an American Cole type being fitted to a 'Star' class locomotive the following year. This is not a discourse on superheating and so it is unnecessary to give design details. Both were effective but Churchward was

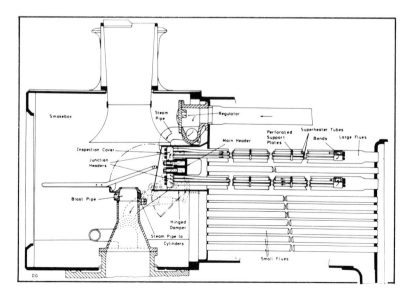

Left *Swindon standard superheater showing damper doors which were later removed.*

Right *Front view of the Swindon standard superheater.*

not satisfied and set about designing his own arrangement. The third attempt fulfilled his requirements and became the standard Swindon superheater.

Each superheater element consisted of a nest containing six small tubes, one end of each tube being connected to a header junction. At the opposite ends pairs of tubes were connected by a bend in order to provide a return steam flow. Each nest of tubes was inserted into a large flue in the boiler and the header junctions connected to the main header which was supplied with steam from the regulator. Early superheaters were encased in damper boxes, the damper being opened by a steam cylinder whenever the regulator was opened. The idea of this was to prevent gas from flowing through the flues whenever the superheater tubes were empty but it was later found to be unnecessary. The Swindon system provided a low degree of superheat as Churchward did not favour high superheat; he was only interested in avoiding cylinder condensation.[29]

High and low superheat are relative terms and Churchward became embroiled with fellow locomotive engineers regarding temperature. Following a lecture by Henry Fowler on superheating he disputed the claim that a Swindon superheater only gave a low degree of superheat, arguing that the positioning of pyrometers influenced the temperature indicated and that his superheaters were as effective as any others in achieving high temperature. The argument was not convincing, Gresley and Fowler, amongst others, weighing in with counter-claims. Fowler quoted figures which

Churchward could not dispute.[30] It must have been one of the few occasions on which the 'old man' lost an engineering argument. Swindon continued to use a lower superheat temperature despite the fact that clear evidence existed to prove the link between higher superheat and increased efficiency. Any superheat was, however, beneficial and as early as 1910 it could be claimed by the Great Western that a superheater paid for itself within a year by the fuel it saved.[31] As Churchward said at the Fowler lecture, 'It is the coal pile that talks.'

High superheat caused lubrication difficulties during the early years of the twentieth century because oil technology had not attained the degree of perfection it was later to achieve. Carbonizing of the cylinder oil resulted in problems as piston and valve rings became stuck in their grooves causing blow-past. A low degree of superheat minimized this risk. Whilst others employed mechanical pumps for the supply of lubricating oil to the cylinders, Churchward went his own way and developed a hydrostatic lubricator. There was no real problem with the pump arrangement: he just wanted a Swindon system. A small supply of steam was used to inject a quantity of atomized oil into the main steam path between regulator and steam chest. Built into the system, which operated by movement of the regulator handle, was a mechanism whereby the oil supply rate varied with the regulator valve opening. The regulator system was so arranged that when the locomotive drifted, a small supply of steam and oil always passed to the steam chest. That not only provided for lubrication but also maintained a low steam pressure in the valve chest in order to prevent exhaust gas and ash from being drawn in through the blast pipe. Without such provision excessive wear could have resulted.[32]

An outstanding engineer such as Churchward could have cajoled the oil companies into developing better lubricants, thus allowing the adoption of higher superheat, if that had been his intention. However, he never did consider higher temperature to be beneficial, as evidenced by his contribution to the discussion of Fowler's paper. 'It was incorrect to say that the maximum degree of superheat should be aimed at. Any given engine requires a certain degree of superheat for maximum economy. . . .a great deal of the advantage obtained from superheating was due to reduction of the cylinder losses.'[33] He also mentioned that metallic packing quickly melted and that copper pipes could not be used when high degrees of superheat were employed. Apart from the lubrication problem such matters did not appear materially to effect other railways. His avoidance of the

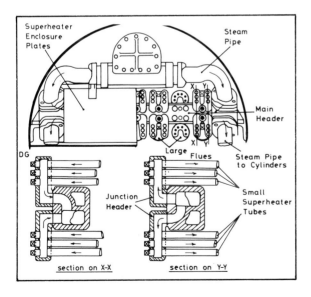

superheat levels being used by contemporaries indicates a certain conservatism not shown elsewhere in his designs.

The amazing thing is that Collett perpetuated his predecessor's policy on superheating even when better quality lubricants and materials were available. Adherence to outmoded practice resulted in advanced locomotives of the 'King' and 'Castle' classes being less advanced than they might have been.

For many locomotive engineers superheating was a means of obtaining increased steam energy, and hence engine power, without the need to increase boiler pressure. Higher pressure caused design problems and the need to employ thicker plate. Churchward knew boilers and saw no difficulty in constructing them for increased pressure. The use of 225 lb per sq in was considered by many to be excessive when applied to the first of the standard range in 1903. For Churchward it was reasonable and provided the right balance with his low superheat. Collett extended the policy and increased the pressure by 25 lb when it suited with the 'Kings'.

Whilst Churchward's fundamental design concept remained in force throughout the 1920s and 1930s, construction and maintenance techniques improved dramatically. Collett may have followed the 'master's' plan in many respects but when it came to the workshops he was his own man. Modernization of the locomotive fleets belonging to the grouped companies became a priority and if the engines could not be adapted for standard boilers they were replaced by newly constructed standard machines. Collett had little time for fiddling with designs; they had to follow the Churchward pattern.[34]

In the workshops there was major reorganization. Optical alignment and the new horn grinding machines allowed streamlining of locomotive repairs to be put in hand. Instead of an engine being allocated to a particular gang, which took it through all stages from stripping to final reassembly and testing, a form of production line was introduced. All locomotives had to be inspected using the Zeiss optical apparatus before they were dismantled; that equipment required specialist operators. It was an opportune moment to introduce a repair circuit with the locomotive, or its constituent parts, passing through a number of distinct sections in the erecting shop where certain tasks would be performed. Section A entailed stripping and cleaning with parts being distributed to fitting and machining shops. Section B dealt with cylinders and frames including a Zeiss survey, whilst Section C covered replacement of a repaired boiler, if it had been removed, and reassembly of wheels and axle boxes. Eventually the locomotive reached Section D where final assembly took place.[35]

Including painting and varnishing a locomotive would be returned to traffic in seventeen days, as good as new.[36] Closer tolerancing during construction and maintenance and improved boiler management resulted in extended operating intervals for all locomotives. These factors together with improved reporting arrangements for defects resulted in better locomotive availability as fewer were kept at the shops awaiting repair. It became possible to scrap a number of the more run-down engines without need for replacement as those remaining were well able to meet all traffic requirements.[37] Collett may not have set the locomotive design world alight but he ensured that locomotives under his control, even sacred Churchward engines, were able to perform a full day's work.

His apprenticeship at Maudslay, Sons and Field must have had a major influence on Collett as that concern was a leader in marine engine building at the time with a reputation to match any engineering company in the land. Henry Maudslay and Joshua Field were both brilliant engineers who sought perfection in all of their products, and the company which they founded followed the same admirable traditions. That concern was linked with Brunel in a number of his schemes, including the supply of boilers and engines for his original steamship *Great Western* and some of the pumping plant for his atmospheric railway. Maudslay's were not operators, they only produced and Collett's training would have been biased towards production engineering. That training served the Great Western well.

Hawksworth was a product of Swindon. He was a designer from the start and his formative years were served in the drawing office whilst Churchward was in command. The surprising thing is that upon taking charge he tended to move away from accepted practice and adopted ideas of his own. No doubt some of these ideas had been developed many years before but others resulted from wartime conditions prevailing when he came into office. Reverting to a two-cylinder design with his 'County' class reintroduced problems but easier access for maintenance was the order of the day. Outside valve gear on the '1500' class allowed the little engines to be serviced without the need for a pit, and servicing was easier. More than any of his predecessors Hawksworth was shackled by outside influences but he made the best of things and saw the Great Western out in style.

6. Nineteenth-century locomotives

The history of nineteenth-century GWR locomotives concerns both broad and narrow gauges. Broad gauge operations ceased before the end of the nineteenth century and discussion of the locomotives will, therefore, be confined to this chapter. Locomotives for both gauges were designed and constructed under Gooch, Armstrong and Dean, making it convenient to deal with the topic in sections rather than chronologically. Because the Great Western began solely as a 7 ft gauge line the broad gauge will be considered first.

As mentioned in chapter 1, the early locomotives were designed to Brunel's very loose specification which resulted in a mixed bag of mechanical specimens. Apart from a limited number of examples the collection was not a success and resulted in many problems for the young Locomotive Superintendent. Initial contracts were agreed with manufacturers but it became evident that insufficient locomotives would be available to operate services when the line eventually opened. The rapid development of the railways in Britain resulted in a shortage of locomotive building capacity and Great Western engines were to be of non-standard gauge, thereby causing additional problems.

Brunel became desperate to ensure that his engines would be available when the railway opened and in sufficient numbers. A letter to Mather, Dixon & Co., dated 12 November 1836, illustrates his problem. He begged for details regarding delivery of the two engines already ordered and expressed a willingness to increase the order to six or eight engines if the GWR was given priority.[1] It would appear that his request met with approval as that builder did construct six locomotives, two, *Premier* and *Ariel*, in the first 'lot', with *Ajax*, *Mars*, *Planet* and *Mercury* in the second. It is highly probable that Brunel regretted his decision for five of the engines had been withdrawn by December 1840 and the sixth, *Mercury*, lasted but three years more. Only the Hawthorn engines, *Thunderer* and *Hurricane*, were less successful. Though some boilers found use in stationary applications all eight engines could be classed as costly examples of Brunel's mechanical inexperience.

Six engines from Vulcan, three from Sharp Roberts and two by the Haigh Foundry all performed somewhat better, though not to the degree of perfection which had been desired. Rebuilding extended their lives but none could be classed as a success and they had no influence upon

future locomotive policy apart from ensuring that 'real' engines were constructed quickly. Robert Stephenson's works were too busy to tender for construction of GWR locomotives but financial problems at the New Orleans Railway resulted in two 5 ft 6 in gauge engines becoming available. Brunel quickly accepted them and they were converted for 7 ft gauge with the first, *North Star*, being fitted with 7 ft diameter driving wheels whilst the somewhat smaller *Morning Star* had 6 ft 6 in drivers. Delivery of a second batch comprising ten 'Stars' commenced in 1839. The machines were perfection itself and on 16 January 1840 Brunel wrote to Robert Stephenson asking for another 'Star'.[2] Whether that was delivered and increased the second batch to eleven is unknown but it clearly illustrates that the 'little giant' had found a product to his liking.

Daniel Gooch had been employed at the works of Robert Stephenson and later in his life claimed that the first engines, *North Star* and *Morning Star* had been designed by him as part of a Russian 6 ft gauge contract which failed. *The Engineer* for May 1892 reproduced, from the Swindon collection, a drawing of a 'Star' type engine upon which Gooch had appended a statement indicating his part in the design.[3] Robert Stephenson contended that the Russian order had actually been delivered and that the first two 'Stars' were engines originally destined for America.[4] The project upon which Gooch was engaged may or may not have been the future *North Star*, but for the purposes of this work it does not matter; what is important is the fact that Gooch had a hand in the design of 'Star' type locomotives. That involvement, and his operating experience with the class, became vitally important and shaped future GWR broad gauge design.

With the railway in operation it became apparent that Brunel's machines were not up to the mark and the directors instructed Gooch to prepare designs for future locomotives. That gave the young 'Geordie' an opportunity to show what he could really do. Some people have expressed the opinion that the early Gooch-designed engines were but extended copies of the Stephenson 'Stars'. Had they been different it would have very surprising as the 'Stars' were a major success and Gooch had been so intimately involved in their design. Outside manufacturers had to construct the engines and so it was essential that they received as much information as possible. Drawings were lithographed, specifications printed and iron templates made for parts needing to be

interchangeable.[5] Such measures avoided any confusion regarding dimensions or construction and ensured that an entire class would be identical. Standardization was important to Gooch who appears to have learned quickly from the folly of Brunel.

First of the standard locomotives to be delivered was *Firefly*, which gave its name to the entire class of sixty-two 2-2-2 engines delivered between March 1840 and December 1842. Apart from the twenty engines constructed by Fenton, Murray and Jackson, all were identical, the only difference in the Fenton engines being a 1 in increase on the wheelbase of 6 ft 7 in + 6 ft 7 in. Gooch considered the Fenton engines to be the best but they all performed well and were extremely durable.[6] In his memoirs Gooch makes the statement, 'When I had completed the drawings. . .', which might imply that he personally did all of the design work. That is extremely unlikely as he would have been busily engaged in other matters and had a drawing office staff supervised by 'a clever fellow', Thomas Crampton. There can be little doubt that Gooch provided the driving force and main ideas for design but, like later Chief Draughtsmen, Crampton will have been responsible for implementation and detail work.

'Fireflies' were fitted with 7 ft diameter flanged driving wheels, 4 ft carriers and 15 in × 18 in cylinders. A 'haycock' style domed firebox gave the boiler, and hence the locomotive, a distinctive shape. In that feature Gooch was obviously expressing some dissatisfaction with the fairly flush fireboxes of the 'Stars', though no evidence exists to indicate the reasoning. Some 'Stars' were later

rebuilt and given enlarged firebox boilers which does illustrate a desire for increased steam space. Boilers originally worked at 50 psi pressure but that was later raised slightly. Sandwich frames were employed for the engine and tender, the latter having an iron water tank sitting on the frames, not built into them.

Valve gear is very important for the proper operation of a steam engine and Gooch paid particular attention to that item. He had not, at that stage, developed his own form of valve gear and the 'Gab' arrangement, as employed on the 'Stars', was used. Only high quality materials could be used, the specification being very rigid. Eccentrics were to be of cast iron, straps of wrought iron and connecting bolts of steel. In order to minimize wear, rubbing faces and bushes on items such as the operating lever fork ends had to be given a layer of steel and then hardened.[7] Gooch appears to have been a firm believer in 'steeling' which was, basically, the welding of a bar of steel upon the wearing surface of an iron component. His patent of 1840, already mentioned in chapter 2, concerned the steeling of rails and tyres.

In order to avoid disputes with manufacturers, as had occurred between Brunel and Mather, Dixon & Co., Gooch insisted that some form of Company safeguard be written into the specification. That was done and manufacturers agreed to deliver locomotives in full working order at either London or Bristol as directed by the Company. Additionally the manufacturers had to provide an unconditional guarantee for the first 1,000 miles of normal operational service.[8] Testing of locomotives following manufacture presented problems as only

Left Tiger, *from the second lot of* 'Fireflies', *as later modified.*

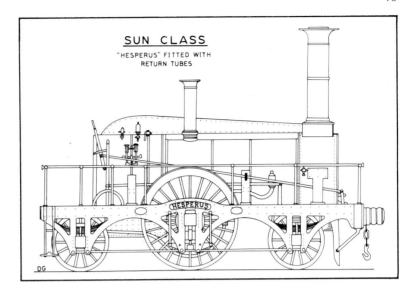

SUN CLASS
"HESPERUS" FITTED WITH
RETURN TUBES

HESPERUS

Right *The 'Sun' class* Hesperus *as fitted with Hawthorn's return tubes.*

the Great Western had broad gauge track. The insistence upon a 1,000 mile warranty was, therefore, reasonable and something upon which Brunel should have insisted. At a later date when narrow gauge engines were first built at Swindon similar problems arose as they had to be transported to Wolverhampton before any real running was possible.

The engines worked well, being capable of hauling 80 ton loads at speeds up to 60 mph; the 'Stars' pulled all express trains during the early years. A number of 'Fireflies' were rebuilt as tank engines whilst others received round top boilers during working lives which, on average, lasted thirty years.

For less demanding passenger duties between Swindon and Bristol the 'Sun' class was designed and delivered concurrently with the 'Fireflies' of which they were, in effect, smaller versions. Driving wheels were only 6 ft diameter and carrying wheels 3 ft 6 in but the wheelbase, at 6 ft 10 in + 6 ft 10 in, was longer than on the express engines. They lacked adhesive weight and all were rebuilt as tank engines between 1849 and 1850, but not before some had been used in South Devon pending the opening of the Atmospheric Railway. Twelve of the original twenty-one engines were withdrawn in 1870 and the remainder in 1879, though they had all ceased work a number of years prior to withdrawal from stock.

One interesting variation occurred with *Hesperus*, from the works of R. & W. Hawthorn, Newcastle. An experimental system of return flues was employed to promote better use of the energy developed during combustion. Most of the com-

bustion products passed through the boiler twice before escaping up the chimney, thus allowing more time for heat transfer. *Hesperus* was provided with a total heat transfer surface area of 804 sq ft compared with 608 sq ft for the remainder of the 'Sun' class and 699 sq ft for the 'Firefly' class. Tests carried out during 1842 showed that the return flue arrangement was very economical. *Hesperus* evaporated 10.3 lb of water per pound of coke whilst *Royal Star*, the best of the 'Sun', 'Firefly', 'Leo' and 'Star' classes tested, could only manage 7.4 lb. Though train loads differed slightly for each engine tested, the coke consumption per mile for *Hesperus* was significantly better than that for any of the other engines.[9] Despite obvious economic advantages the system must have posed problems concerning maintenance and the engine was later altered to conform with the rest of the class.

Gooch catered for increasing goods traffic with eighteen engines of the 'Leo' class, delivered during 1841 and 1842 by three builders. These 2-4-0 engines had 5 ft diameter coupled and 3 ft 6 in leading wheels. Outside sandwich frames were used and, like the 'Fireflies', 15 in×18 in cylinders provided the power. Three members of the 'Sun' class used the same sized cylinders but the majority had bores 1 in smaller at 14 in. Obviously Gooch had standardization in mind at a very early stage. The 'haycock' boiler had the usual length of 8 ft 6 in, but at 3 ft 6 in diameter the barrel was 6 in smaller than the 'Firefly' and 3 in smaller than the 'Sun' classes. Most of the 'Leo' engines lasted until 1870 and then joined the other early Gooch classes in mass withdrawal.

In common with some members of the 'Firefly'

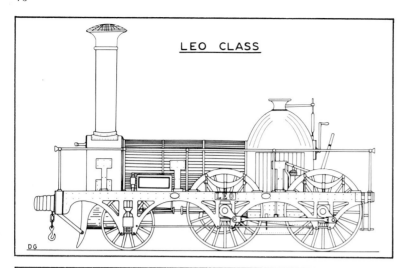

The 'Leo' class goods engine.

'Hercules' class, an 0-6-0 based on the 'Fireflies'.

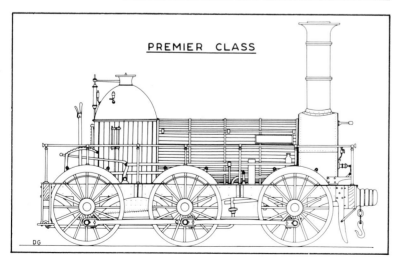

'Premier' class, the first class turned out by Swindon works.

and 'Sun' classes, all 'Leo' class locomotives were later rebuilt as saddle tanks. As well as the fitting of tanks, frames had to be extended at the rear in order to accommodate the bunker. Engines were designed to deal with the size of train operated at the time, but they were soon shown to lack adhesive weight for hauling larger trains. The provision of saddle tanks was an expedient solution to the problem of adhesion.

A group of four 0-6-0 engines, the 'Hercules' class, completed Gooch's initial GWR design venture. Above the outside sandwich frames and in cylinder dimensions they were identical to the 'Fireflies', whilst the coupled wheels were of the same 5 ft diameter as employed with the 'Leo' class. The reasoning behind the design is unknown, but they originally formed part of an order from Naysmyth, Gaskell & Co. for twenty 'Fireflies'. It could well be that Gooch decided to experiment with an 0-6-0 arrangement following early operating experience with the 2-2-2 and 2-4-0 engines. Using standard boilers, cylinders and wheels from other classes the design change was not as major as the alteration in wheel arrangement might indicate. 'Hercules' class engines were delivered between July and October 1842 and because of the use of standard components the final format may not have been decided until the early part of that year. Gooch will have had plenty of time to assess the performances of his early 2-2-2 engines, the first of which was delivered during 1840, and the 2-4-0 locomotives, which began to enter service in January 1841.

Through his adoption of standardized parts and strict specifications with full drawings, Gooch was able to obtain exactly the engines he wanted. The advantages were readily apparent not only in procurement but also in repair and the ability to obtain, quickly, a class not originally specified. Obviously the 0-6-0s were a success as none was rebuilt and that wheel arrangement became popular with Gooch and his successors.

By 1843 the Gooch form of valve gear had been developed and that was fitted to several machines as they came up for major overhaul.[10] As with the Stephenson link motion it allowed a locomotive to be worked expansively, thereby saving on steam and hence fuel. Records show that some twenty-six engines had been so treated up to 1849 and the likelihood is that most others were converted during later years. It is uncertain which of the Gooch brothers, Daniel or John, actually developed the gear. The first locomotive recorded to have been fitted with Gooch valve gear was *Snake*, on the London & South Western Railway, where John Gooch was Locomotive Superintendent.[11] As

no patent was lodged it would be fair to credit both brothers with the invention.

With completion of orders for the classes mentioned, deliveries of locomotives ceased until 1846. In the intervening period Gooch was able to rebuild some of the existing stock at the recently constructed Swindon works. Most of the Brunel machines were so treated and subsequently used for branch line work. All GWR designed engines originally worked with a boiler pressure of 50 psi, but this was later amended to 75 psi, giving a higher efficiency. The early classes, though generally successful, were modified to suit changing patterns of traffic and technology. Gooch's first designs can, to a great extent, be treated as experimental. Lessons were well learned and later designs served the railway for many years without major modification.

Increasing traffic called for more 0-6-0 freight engines and twelve 'Premier' class engines were laid down at Swindon. 'Haycock' boilers came from outside contractors but Swindon manufactured the remaining parts and erected the engines. *Premier* was the first engine actually to emerge from the Swindon works but, because of the boiler, cannot be considered as having been completely built there. Delivery of the class took place from February 1846 to May 1847 and they were the last GWR engines to have 'haycock' boilers. A further six engines, the 'Pyracmon' class, took goods engine development a stage further. The same 16 in × 24 in cylinders and 5 ft coupled wheels were employed but larger wheelbase and bigger boilers provided for increased power and stability.

As a result of experiments carried out for the Gauge Commissioners it was evident that more powerful express engines could be built and Gooch proposed 8 ft diameter driving wheels and 18 in cylinders. Impressed by such a prospect, the directors instructed Gooch to proceed with construction of a single trial locomotive. In just thirteen weeks the engine was ready for running. *Great Western* emerged from Swindon works during April 1846 and introduced a new phase in GWR locomotive history. In its original form the engine was a 2-2-2 with a large 'haycock' firebox, slotted sandwich frames and an 8 ft + 8 ft wheelbase. It was also powerful and fast, hauling a test load of 100 tons over 77 miles at an average of 62 mph.[12] Similar good results were obtained during other tests.

A major fault soon became evident when the leading axle broke during a test run near Shrivenham. Excessive loading was considered to be the cause and Gooch quickly set about rectification. His corrective action was to lengthen

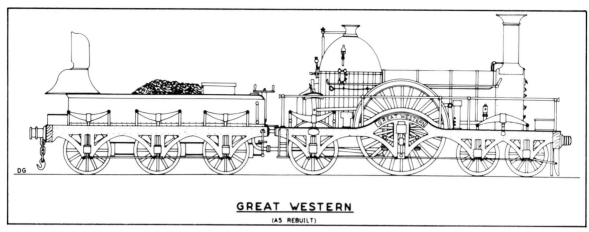

GREAT WESTERN
(AS REBUILT)

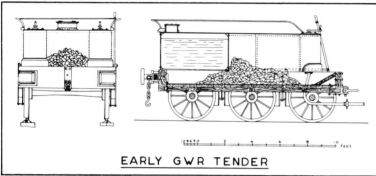

EARLY GWR TENDER

Above Great Western *as modified to a 2+2-2-2 wheel arrangement.*

Left *An early standard form of GWR tender.*

Below Corsair, *the Gooch bogie design showing sledge type brakes.*

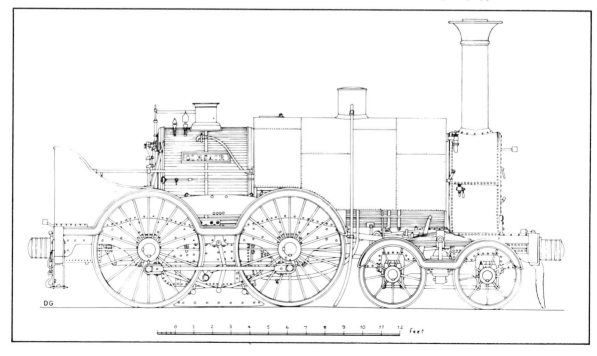

the frames and fit a second leading axle which increased the rigid wheelbase by nearly 3 ft. Although a 16 ft wheelbase (8 ft + 8 ft) might have been satisfactory for the narrow gauge it was short for the 7 ft gauge. A longer wheelbase reduced the side to side movement which occurred due to imbalance of the reciprocating masses. Loading on the front carrying wheels was, therefore, reduced and with two carrying axles the stress induced was relatively low. A single inverted laminated spring supported both leading axle-boxes on each side of the engine, thereby ensuring an even distribution of weight between the two axles.[13]

A modified 4-2-2, or rather 2+2-2-2, *Great Western* set the pattern for an express engine design which lasted until the end of the broad gauge. Most noticeable difference between *Iron Duke*, which appeared in April 1847, and its earlier sister was the boiler. Instead of a 'haycock' Gooch introduced a rount top raised firebox casing, a brass 'squashed bonnet-box' safety valve cover being the only interruption in the clean lines. The style became standard for all Gooch engines and remained with the 8 ft singles until the end.

Over an eight-year period some twenty-nine 'Iron Duke' engines were constructed, twenty-two at Swindon and seven by Rothwell & Co. (At a later date the entire class, together with the later 'Rover' rebuilds, was covered by the collective title of 'Alma' class.) There were slight differences in detail between the earlier and later engines but nothing of major significance. All had 18 in × 24 in cylinders, 8 ft flangeless driving wheels and 4 ft 6 in carriers. The first six engines had a different wheelbase and slightly longer boilers. Later boilers operated at 120 psi pressure whilst the initial six worked at 100 psi, which was later increased to 115 psi. For most people these engines were the Great Western broad gauge and they hauled all principal trains between Paddington and Bristol, only venturing further west before 1849 and after 1876. (Throughout that intervening period the Bristol & Exeter ran its own trains.) Until conversion to narrow gauge the line from Paddington to Birmingham was also served by the 'Iron Duke' class.

Whilst results of tests with *Great Western* were being evaluated there was still a need for further engines and Gooch filled the gap with six 2-2-2 inside-framed 'Prince' class locomotives, employing as many standard parts as could be used. Only the boilers appear to have been radically different from earlier engines in that they were 1 ft 6 in longer than those fitted to the 'Fireflies' and contained more tubes. Frames were lengthened to suit the boiler. Items such as cylinders, wheel fittings and tender followed previous patterns. All

early tenders were of the same basic design as that applied to the 'Stars', comprising an iron water tank connected to a wooden platform with sandwich frames. Most were of six-wheel construction but some early photographs show that others had four wheels. It may well be that four-wheel tenders were transferred from early Brunel engines converted to saddle tanks. An 1849 report by Gooch mentions that surplus tenders would be used for goods engines and it seems reasonable that the practice began much earlier.[14]

'Iron Duke' class tenders were to a new design which employed iron frames. Wheels of 4 ft diameter and a wheelbase of 6 ft + 6 ft became standard even when the capacity was increased from 1,760 gal to 1,880 gal and fuel capacity from 79.3 cu ft to 102.8 cu ft. Original tenders for the 8 ft singles were all characterized by the hooded seat or 'iron coffin' at the back. It accommodated a travelling porter whose job it was to guard the train, signalling the driver to stop in the event of passenger distress, lost luggage or disconnected coach. The arrangement was not popular with those unfortunate enough to find themselves occupying the seat, particularly during winter months.

Operation on the steeply graded lines in South Devon presented problems which the early GWR locomotives could not completely overcome. In 1849 Gooch produced two machines of totally new styling. *Corsair* and *Brigand* were true bogie engines of the 4-4-0 saddle tank type. A ball and socket joint provided the pivot with the ball being connected to a double gusset riveted to the boiler barrel and steam chest. Inside sandwich frames extended only between the rear buffer beam and front driving wheels resulting in the boiler becoming a structural part of the locomotive thus transmitting force between cylinders and coupled wheels. A single centre stay did relieve some of that load but the use of a boiler as part of a locomotive's main structure was a radical departure from accepted practice.

Equalizing levers were provided between the coupled wheels allowing the locomotive's weight to be carried at three points rather than two. That was one of the first instances in which such an arrangement was used on railways in Britain. The front coupled wheels were flangeless, Gooch seeming to have a predilection for such a feature. He applied it to the 'Iron Duke' class drivers and some drawings appear to indicate that the 'Waverley' class was similarly fitted. There was no logical reason for flangeless wheels as the wheelbase of the engines was not excessive, nor could curves on broad gauge lines be classed as tight by any stretch of the imagination. The first four 'Stars' from Stephenson had flangeless driving wheels and Gooch probably found the idea useful, but later 'Stars' and all 'Fireflies' performed satisfactorily with flanged driving wheels. Later rebuilds of the 'Iron Dukes', the 'Rover' class, were provided with flanged wheels and it is likely that many of Gooch's flangeless wheels were given flanged tyres by Armstrong or Dean.

A further innovation with *Corsair* was its sledge brakes between the coupled wheels. Braking during the early years of railways was by no means an exact science but to fit such devices seems to have been a direct invitation to trouble. Sledges damaged rails, became entangled at crossings and tended to lift the rear of the engine whenever applied.[15] Needless to say, the sledge brake was not fitted to *Brigand* nor to any of the thirteen similar engines produced by Hawthorns during 1854 and 1855. The two prototypes returned to GWR when the South Devon took over operation of its own lines and, with the rest of the class, found employment on branch lines and in Wales.

Ten 'Waverley' 4-4-0 and eighteen 'Victoria' 2-4-0 engines completed the Gooch main line passenger designs. Known later as the 'Abbot' class, the 'Waverley' engines were all built by Robert Stephenson and delivered during 1855. Strictly speaking they were 2+2-4-0 engines

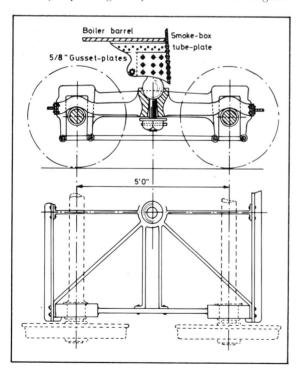

following the familiar pattern set by the 8 ft single wheelers. Boilers were of the standard Gooch type although slightly smaller in diameter than those fitted to the 'Iron Duke' class. Inside slotted sandwich frames provided axle bearings for the 7 ft drivers and 4 ft 3 in carrying wheels. Though differing in appearance from other engines they followed the proven Gooch design and put in valuable service on secondary passenger routes.

'Victoria' class engines looked similar to their 4-4-0 brothers but with somewhat smaller components. Two 'lots' were built at Swindon, the first during 1856 and the second in 1863 and 1864. The fact that a second lot of ten engines was produced leads to the conclusion that they must have been very useful performers. The only novel feature appears to have been the compensating levers which linked all three axles.

Freight locomotives were not neglected for there was an increasing goods traffic throughout the system. Six 'Caesar' class engines, similar to the 'Pyracmon' class, appeared during 1851 and the following year the first of 102 'Standard Goods' engines came out of Swindon. During the ten years that series was in production a number of modifications were made but the class, generally, followed the same pattern, the main variation being in boiler dimensions. The first sixty-six locomotives had boilers identical to those fitted to 'Waverley' engines, and the entire class had 17 in × 24 in cylinders. Boiler pressure of 120 psi was considered high for the time and exceeded, by a wide margin, that applied on most other railways. Gooch knew his boilers, designing them for strength and performance.

Many standard features applied to Gooch boilers, one of these being a transverse water-filled partition in the firebox known as a mid-feather. Without doubt the device increased the heat transfer surface area, but that was not its sole purpose. With long fireboxes a mid-feather provided some degree of internal transverse support, and it also kept the fire reasonably intact by dividing it into two parts; that also aided combustion. With the introduction of the brick arch effective coal burning became possible and, apart from a few isolated cases, the mid-feather fell into disuse. Another feature applied to Gooch boilers was a system of louvred dampers placed immediately in front of the smokebox tubeplate. These regulated gas flow through the tubes and could be controlled by the driver.

Daniel Gooch's final locomotive design was somewhat of a novelty though it served a very practical purpose. For operation in tunnels on the Metropolitan Railway a series of condensing

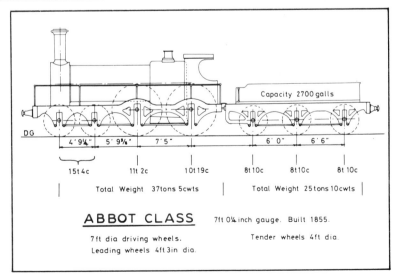

Left *Ball and socket bogie pivot on* Corsair.

Top Telford, *of the 'Victoria' class, showing the guard's 'iron coffin'.*

Above Liffey, *of the 'Caesar' class.*

Right *Diagram of the 'Abbot' or 'Waverley' class in final form.*

Capacity 2700 galls

DG

4' 9¼" 5' 9¼" 7' 5" 6' 0" 6' 6"

15t 4c 11t 2c 10t 19c 8t 10c 8t 10c 8t 10c

Total Weight 37 tons 5 cwts Total Weight 25 tons 10 cwts

ABBOT CLASS 7ft 0¼ inch gauge. Built 1855.

7ft dia driving wheels. Tender wheels 4ft dia.
Leading wheels 4ft 3in dia.

engines was constructed. The task was not undertaken lightly and some years before the need actually arose Gooch had carried out experiments to see how far a locomotive would run without a suitable blast on the fire.[16] It was his intention that a normal type of engine should be allowed to work in the tunnels but with its exhaust blast stopped and an ash pan damper destroying the draught. The idea worked and the 'Metropolitan' tanks were produced between 1862 and 1864, the first condensing locomotives in Britain.

A flap valve directed exhaust steam into the atmosphere when working in the open and to water tanks whilst operating in tunnels. Capacity of the tanks, one under the boiler holding 468 gal and the other under the footplate holding 250 gal, was not sufficient for prolonged tunnel operation as the water overheated resulting in the need for exhaust to be vented into the tunnel. Because of the tank under the boiler it was necessary to fit outside cylinders, which had to be inclined in order to clear

the leading wheels. Gooch incorporated many features not associated with other GWR locomotives but the class of twenty-two did the job for which they had been designed. Their lives were short, however, as the Great Western fell out with the Metropolitan Railway, and in 1869 the locomotives were placed on local London services with condensing apparatus removed.

Joseph Armstrong also produced a series of six condensing engines, the 'Sir Watkin' class, during 1865 and 1866: they were slightly more successful than Gooch's. The same concept was employed but large side tanks were fitted and boilers had domes. Under difficult conditons both designs functioned reasonably well considering the state of technology at the time.

With the 'Sir Watkin' class, broad gauge design came to an end. Apart from rebuilding and renewal of some 8 ft single wheelers there were no new broad gauge engines. Convertibles were designed for the narrow gauge and adapted to run on 7 ft

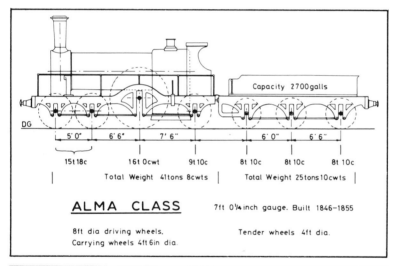

Diagram of the 'Alma', 'Rover' or 'Iron Duke' class.

Iron Duke, *at the end of the broad gauge* (courtesy of the National Railway Museum, York).

Final through broad gauge train departure from Paddington on 20 May 1892 (courtesy GWR Museum, Swindon).

Armstrong standard goods engine with wheels arranged for broad gauge use.

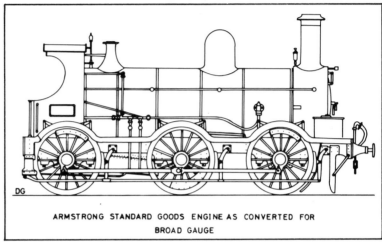

ARMSTRONG STANDARD GOODS ENGINE AS CONVERTED FOR BROAD GAUGE

track. Armstrong designed two other classes for broad gauge use prior to construction of his condensing engines but they were really only extensions to former Gooch designs. In effect, Daniel Gooch was the only broad gauge locomotive designer.

During 1865 and 1866 Armstrong produced twenty-six locomotives based upon the 'Victoria' class but with slightly smaller boilers and driving wheels. Engines were named after famous locomotive builders, the entire class being designated by the name of the first, 'Hawthorn'. Some later became saddle tanks with 5 ft diameter wheels instead of 6 ft and cylinders were enlarged to 17 in diameter. More than half of the class lasted until the broad gauge ceased to exist. One of them, *Hedley*, following service in a colliery and as a stationary boiler, was not cut up until 1929.

A variation on Gooch's standard goods came with fourteen engines of the 'Swindon' class. They were essentially the same design apart from a number of features which Armstrong applied to his three broad gauge classes. Most fundamental amongst these were inside solid plate frames and Stephenson link motion for operating the valves.

Armstrong and later Dean each produced 8 ft singles to the earlier Gooch design. Officially known as rebuilds or renewals they were completely new engines, though a number of orignal parts might have been used for the three turned out in 1871. Nine came out during Armstrong's term of office and fifteen during that of Dean. Flanged driving wheels, cabs and improved boilers operating at 140 psi were the main differences compared with the originals. Known as the 'Rover' class, it was these engines which saw out the broad gauge, the final three only operating for four years. It is difficult to see why they were actually sanctioned in view of the imminent demise of the broad gauge. Convertibles were, after all, available. Possibly Dean and the directors had them constructed out of respect for Gooch; there was no economic reason.

A number of Armstrong 0-6-0 narrow gauge saddle tanks were constructed with wheels suited for broad gauge operations and Dean later adapted several more in the same manner. Only in that respect did they differ from engines used on the narrow gauge, to which all were later converted. Joseph Armstrong was preoccupied with development at Swindon but early gauge conversion work proved to him that new broad gauge designs were not required. Brunel's 7 ft track would not last long enough to merit the effort. The idea of convertible

locomotives was a stroke of genius. They could be easily modified, did not take up vast amounts of design expertise and, perhaps most importantly, were cost-effective. By using longer axles, wheels could be placed outside the frames allowing operation on broad gauge lines. For use on narrow gauge track the wheels came inside the frames or between them if it was a double-framed engine. Longer axles and fitting of extension cranks for the coupling rods were the only changes necessary to suit broad gauge operation. Tenders were similarly arranged. Very few of the 111 engines modified to run on the broad gauge did not see later service on the narrow.

One locomotive which did not survive to a narrow gauge conversion was Dean's No.8 of 1886, an experimental 2-4-0 compound with a narrow gauge sister, No.7. Both pairs of cylinders were inside, connected in tandem with the low pressure cylinder to the front. Two low pressure cylinder extension piston rods passed outside the high pressure cylinder to connect with the high pressure piston rod at a single crosshead. Why such a cumbersome and obviously risky arrangement was tried is difficult to comprehend. Needless to say, the arrangement did not prove a success and both compounds ceased work very quickly. An important fact about both engines was the boiler pressure of 180 psi, which was very high for that period. Engines No. 14 and No.16 were larger 2-4-0s but not compounded. Both worked successfully throughout the four years until gauge conversion but as they were not from a large standard class conversion to narrow gauge was not a priority. Two years later they were rebuilt as 4-4-0 locomotives.

Without the convertible concept operations during the final years of the broad gauge would have been expensive and difficult. Construction of many more obsolete Gooch designs would have been essential or valuable design time wasted on new designs. In many respects it is a pity that broad gauge design did finish in the 1860s with the

last of the Gooch engines. A fairly modern, high-powered broad gauge locomotive never evolved.

Though Daniel Gooch is remembered for his broad gauge engines he did produce designs for the narrow gauge, even if they were rather forced upon him. Acquisition of other railways and restrictions imposed by the Gauge Commissioners necessitated the construction of such locomotives. His first design for the 'inferior' gauge, from now on to be called the standard gauge, was a 2-2-2 passenger type which had all the characteristics of his broad gauge engines, including outside sandwich frames, Gooch link motion and raised round top firebox. Eight of the engines were built by Beyer, Peacock & Co. and delivered during 1855-6. Simultaneously with that design he also developed an 0-6-0 goods engine of which twelve were constructed at Swindon during the same period, the first standard gauge engines built there. It has been said that the work was not to the men's liking as they considered anything other than broad gauge below their dignity. Possibly some of the managers or directors may have felt that way but workmen will have been glad of any work they could get; piecework and contract rates were not high. Again the 0-6-0s had many similar features to their 7 ft gauge counterparts but boilers, cylinders and motion were also common with the Beyer 2-2-2s.[17] Standardization and interchangeability had arrived on the Stephenson gauge.

During the next few years further Gooch-designed locomotives were constructed for standard gauge work, but most had to be built at Swindon as the Stafford Road works at Wolverhampton were preoccupied with maintaining those absorbed when the northern railways were taken over. Certain features not common to other Gooch locomotives began to appear and it is evident that Joseph Armstrong was making his presence felt even though, at the time, he had no connection with Swindon. Armstrong had to maintain standard gauge stock and it is reasonable that he should have had a say in design features. That provides another illustration of the close relationship which developed between the two men and their respect for each other. Gooch could have insisted upon his own ideas, which were tried and tested, and particularly upon the retention of the valve link motion which bore his name. The fact that he did not indicates modesty and a distinct absence of vanity. Such a character trait contradicts the belief held by many that Gooch encouraged retention of the broad gauge purely for his own self-gratification.

Two side tank engines with inside plate frames were provided in 1860 and further 0-6-0 heavy goods engines in 1861 to supplement those constructed four years earlier. With a batch of goods engines supplied in 1862, Stephenson gear became standard for future construction. Further 2-4-0 and 2-2-2 passenger designs were produced to the usual Gooch pattern except for the valve gear. Whilst most locomotives came from Swindon,

Joseph Armstrong did not remain idle for he introduced designs of his own. Only restricted construction facilities at Wolverhampton limited his output and dictated that Swindon help out.[18]

Two single driving wheel passenger locomotives, Nos. 7 and 8, appeared in 1859 and were built to replace two older machines of the Shrewsbury & Chester Railway. There was nothing of outstanding interest about them apart from the fact that they differed completely from Gooch-designed engines. As already mentioned in the previous chapter, Armstrong followed the practice of George Gray in providing outside bearings for the driving wheels but inside bearings for the carriers. Two further 2-4-0 passenger engines were built in the following years but of different dimensions. The designer seems to have been searching for an ideal combination of cylinders and boiler.

Early designs tended to be for one or two locomotives and it was not until 1863 that an Armstrong class, comprising six 2-4-0 locomotives,

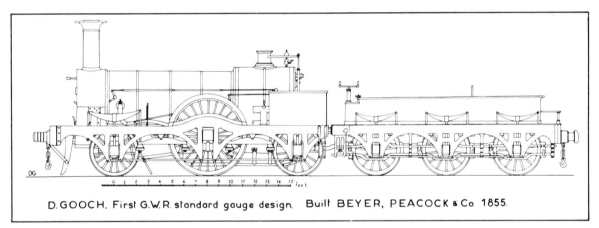

D. GOOCH. First G.W.R. standard gauge design. Built BEYER, PEACOCK & Co 1855.

Above left *Dean 'Convertible' No. 16 in broad gauge form. It was never actually converted for standard gauge use* (courtesy of the National Railway Museum, York).

Above *Daniel Gooch's first standard gauge design.*

Right *The first standard gauge locomotive actually constructed at Swindon.*

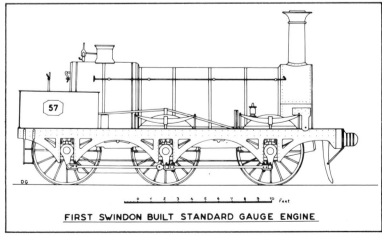

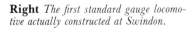

FIRST SWINDON BUILT STANDARD GAUGE ENGINE

began to leave Stafford Road. Outside bearings and double plate frames with platforms which curved smoothly over the coupled axles gave them a distinctive appearance, although the boiler was of Gooch form albeit with a different safety valve cover. At about the same time Armstrong designed some 2-4-0 and 0-6-0 saddle tanks. They introduced no new ideas nor did they advance the cause of standardization, but the foundation for locomotive production at Stafford Road had been laid and Joseph's brother would reap the rewards.

With Gooch's retirement in 1864 Joseph Armstrong moved to Swindon and became involved with broad gauge engines as mentioned earlier. Standard gauge engines were not neglected and a series of twelve 0-6-0s for freight traffic appeared in 1866. Many usual features were to be found in the '360' class including outside plate frames slotted, in a similar way to the 0-6-0 saddle tanks, so as to form stays between the horns. A more distinctive change was with the boiler which had a flush top firebox and a dome. The old order changed quickly as Armstrong stamped his authority on design.

There was nothing outstandingly remarkable about performance of the 0-6-0s, nor were they innovative in any design concept, but they pointed the way to the future. Over the succeeding ten years almost 300 Armstrong standard goods engines were built to a design based upon that initial arrangement. This '388' class used standard parts as applicable to another design upon which Armstrong was engaged at the time. Boilers, cylinders, motion and other assorted small parts were also common to the 2-2-2 'Sir Daniel' class constructed between 1866 and 1869.[19] Boiler pressure was 140 psi, slightly higher than used previously.

Standard goods engines operated throughout the standard gauge system, moving into new areas following gauge conversion. Many alterations took place over the years, particularly with regard to the boiler, and a number survived in service until 1930. For heavy coal traffic between South Wales and the Mersey twenty goods engines were constructed with 4 ft 6 in coupled wheels, 6 in smaller than the '388' class. These became 'Coal Engines' or the '927' class and, though they suffered similar boiler modifications to their larger wheeled brothers, six survived until 1925. The longevity of both classes is a testimony to the soundness of Armstrong's design.

In complete contrast to earlier engines, Armstrong designed a series of five 2-4-0 inside-framed locomotives which did not fit into any standard pattern. A year later, in 1869, further 2-4-0s were constructed but, although having similar dimensions to the earlier group, the framing was entirely different and there was no obvious design evolution. Construction of these engines appears to have been an attempt to fulfil an immediate need rather than develop a standard range. Such constraints were always on the designer whenever traffic changes occurred. Ten 2-4-0 engines of the '717' class appeared in 1872 and made use of some standard items in that boilers and cylinders as employed on the standard goods were used. Inside frames allowed inside bearings on the driving wheels, but a deep platform valance extended at the front end, producing the local effect of double framing and enabling the use of outside bearings on the leading axle.

Engines of the '717' class were the first capable of working through from Swindon to Wolverhampton. Track between Didcot and Swindon was made mixed gauge during 1872 using rail removed when the Didcot – Wolverhampton line became solely standard gauge. That year also saw conversion of the Milford – Gloucester and Swindon – Gloucester lines, thus increasing the need for standard gauge locomotives. Engines of the '806' class were almost identical to the '717' class save that they had slightly larger driving wheels, and Swindon built twenty in 1873. Saddle tank engines of the '1076' or 'Buffalo' class, almost identical to those built at Wolverhampton, had many parts interchangeable with the standard goods and large numbers were needed for shunting and short haulage. During 1872-3 Swindon built fifty of the class and over a twelve-year period a total of 266 were constructed.

With nearly 300 standard goods, twenty 'Coal Engines', thirty 'Sir Daniel' and 266 saddle tanks using many similar components, particularly boilers and cylinders, Armstrong firmly, if unspectacularly, extended the standardization policy of his predecessor.

Armstrong returned to the single wheeled concept with the production of No. 55, *Queen*, in 1873. It was much larger than engines of the 'Sir Daniel' class and included new features not used before on GWR locomotives. Driving wheel axle-box springs were underhung and a two-bar crosshead slide replaced the usual four-bar version, necessitating the use of a forked connecting rod end to connect with the crosshead pin. A mid-feather in the firebox indicated a return to earlier Gooch practice but it is difficult to understand the reasoning behind such a step, the use of a brick arch and coal firing by then being common practice.[20] *Queen*, as its name suggests, could be found in regular employment hauling Royal trains, brass dome cover, brass splasher beading and

gunmetal axle-box covers all highly polished for the occasion. Large cylinders 18 in × 24 in, 7 ft driving wheels and a boiler pressure of 140 psi resulted in a tractive effort of just over 11,000 lb.

Two years after the introduction of *Queen* a further twenty similar locomotives were produced though they had domeless boilers. The entire class exceeded the broad gauge single wheelers in tractive effort and adhesive weight though not in boiler power. Apart from Royal train duties for *Queen* the entire class found employment on the fastest passenger expresses from Paddington to Swindon and Gloucester as well as to Wolverhampton. Dean rebuilt the class about ten years after introduction, fitting domed boilers without firebox mid-feathers. Steam ports were reduced in area and exhaust ports enlarged, a step which improved steaming. High speed running was always steady due to the large wheelbase of 8 ft 6 in + 9 ft provided by Armstrong. The class was Joseph Armstrong's final new design. The promise of future developments remained unfulfilled but the class did, perhaps, form a fitting finale to the short career of an outstanding engineer.

At Wolverhampton, George Armstrong continued along his own course, meeting the needs as they arose. Much of his work involved rebuilding older engines as major repairs became necessary, introducing standard components such as cylinders, motion and boilers. Where suitable modifications could not be carried out the policy was one of scrap and renew.[21] The first new design of George Armstrong followed closely the '111' class of his brother. Twelve 2-4-0 tender engines of the type were constructed at Wolverhampton to the design though two earlier engines, Nos. 108 and 109, were similar, being renewals of two Birkenhead Railway locomotives.

Most famous of the Wolverhampton designs produced by George was the class of 0-4-2 tank engines originally developed during the 1860s. The first group of about fifty engines, constructed between 1868 and 1870, were saddle tanks and used for local passenger duties. Side tanks became popular from 1870 onwards and new construction to that pattern continued, the original group being rebuilt with side tanks and extended wheelbase to conform to later specification. Coupled wheels were 5 ft diameter and trailing wheels 3 ft 6 in

Above *Joseph Armstrong's 'Queen' class No. 1000 as originally built* (courtesy GWR Museum, Swindon).

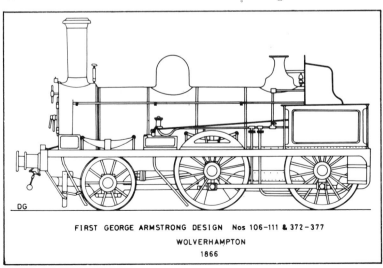

FIRST GEORGE ARMSTRONG DESIGN Nos 106-111 & 372-377
WOLVERHAMPTON
1866

Right *George Armstrong's first locomotive design.*

Collett's 0-4-2 '1400' tank class No. 1466, a design almost identical to George Armstrong's 0-4-2 of the 1860s.

though slight variations did occur. Numbered from 517 onwards, they became the '517' class, which found employment throughout the GWR system for local and branch line work. Their 15 in×24 in cylinders and 140 psi boiler pressure turned them into powerful little engines with a tractive effort of nearly 11,000 lb.

Over the years of construction, which lasted until 1885, small changes did take place in terms of boiler and cylinder sizes but the basic format remained the same. In subsequent years new boilers were fitted but George Armstrong's original design concept was fundamentally sound. Many had auto train apparatus fitted and most survived until the 1930s. Coal consumption was very low considering the type of stop-start working upon which they were engaged, averaging no more than 31.5 lb per mile.[22] The fact that Collett adopted an almost identical design for construction of the '14xx' class during the 1930s indicates how effective the design was.

George Armstrong produced other designs, though they tended to be of the tank variety for local and shunting duties as main line engine construction became centred at Swindon. He was also engaged in rebuilding earlier Gooch and Joseph Armstrong engines, the less glamorous though demanding and essential side of locomotive work. For that reason George Armstrong's work is often overlooked and even here it has not been possible to give a detailed analysis. Without George Armstrong at Stafford Road the GWR would have had difficulty in meeting the requirements of its standard gauge lines other than by major new construction. Rebuilding older stock

eased the burden and saved money. At the same time demands of the branch lines and shunting yards were met.

Although William Dean had been summoned to Swindon in 1868 as assistant to Joseph Armstrong, his elevation to the top position in 1877 was unexpected and he must have been somewhat unprepared for the enormity of the task facing him. Armstrong's death thrust him into a changing railway world. Gauge conversion and traffic growth resulted in a need for more locomotives, but many of the earlier standard gauge engines were reaching the end of their economic lives and replacements would be necessary. First to be so treated were ten Gooch-designed '157' class engines, built by Sharp, Stewart & Co. in 1862, which were replaced by locomotives similar to the 'Queen' class but with outside sandwich frames. Reversion to sandwich frames may appear to have been a retrograde step but Dean obviously considered it more suitable for running on the longitudinal baulk road which still existed on mixed gauge lines.[23]

Having been thrust into the post of Locomotive Superintendent after barely nine years as assistant, it is reasonable that Dean should have wanted experience before committing himself to major designs. Experimental locomotives were the obvious way of obtaining that experience and knowledge for the future. One facet of Dean's character appears to have been a thirst for engineering knowledge which was to be gained by experimentation. The large number of experimental engines he constructed bears witness to that point. In some cases it might have been classed as fiddling without sufficient ideas as to the full implications. During 1879 three 2-4-0 tender engines were constructed as side tanks for passenger work, but the axle loading proved too heavy for six wheels and they were soon converted back to tender engines.[24]

The message was not lost, nor was the partiality for tank engines, and a year later another side tank appeared, this time of the 4-4-0 type with tanks carried forward to the smokebox. A notable feature of the engine was its leading bogie which had no centre: its frame was attached to the main locomotive frame by sprung hangers connected to brackets. The arrangement permitted lateral movement of the bogie, control being exercised by inclination of the hangers when they were displaced from the vertical. Flexibility at the front end had been the aim but the system was too flexible and, in 1882, leading axles replaced the bogie. Again the exercise paid dividends though not just for locomotive purposes, as the bogie was subse-

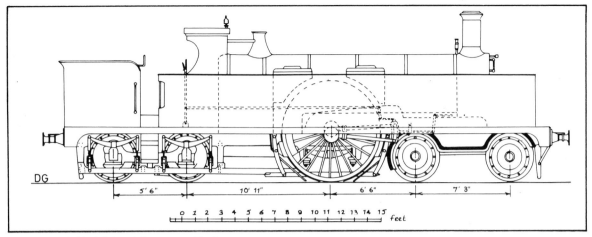

Dean's remarkable 4-2-4 tank locomotive, No. 9.

quently developed to become the famous Dean suspension or centreless bogie for carriages.

A more infamous, though less publicly acknowledged, experimental engine was the 4-2-4 side tank, No. 9. Something of a mystery shrouded the locomotive and Swindon appeared reluctant to admit that it ever existed. David Joy, the engineer, was with Dean at Swindon when No. 9 made its debut, an event notable for the fact that the engine proceeded to 'tumble over the turntable'.[25] Predisposed to wander from the tracks no matter how carefully driven, it was quickly laid aside. Churchward, when first queried about the engine, denied its existence but later, faced with evidence produced by correspondence in *The Railway Magazine*, admitted that it had been constructed.[26]

Information regarding the 4-2-4 is sketchy but E.W. Twinning in *The Locomotive* for January 1940 produced a reconstruction from known data. As with other Dean experimental engines several novel features were incorporated, a problem in itself as the real worth of any single innovation could then be difficult to analyse. Although experimentation is an essential part of any good engineer's work, Dean appears to have taken it to extremes in introducing several new features at the same time. With such a large stock of locomotives at his disposal there should have been plenty of scope for the trial of individual ideas.

The original order upon which No. 9 was built in 1881 had been for two engines, the second using Joy's valve gear, hence the presence of David Joy at Swindon. That second 4-2-4 was cancelled and an experimental goods engine subsequently constructed using Joy's valve gear. In designing the 4-2-4 Dean may have been attempting to improve

on the Bristol & Exeter Railway's 4-2-4 tanks of 1868, which had recently been reconstructed as 4-2-2 tender engines following a fatal derailment by one of their number. Possibly the wheel arrangement or bogie types then available did not suit the permanent way. No. 9 had 18 in×26 in cylinders driving 7 ft 8 in wheels and 3 ft 9 in carrying wheels. The very long tanks held 2,535 gal of water and the overall wheelbase was 30 ft. In September 1884, three years after its initial construction, No.9 appeared in revised form as a 2-2-2 tender engine. Cylinders, driving wheels, outside motion and parts of the frame seem to have been retained from the original. A similar locomotive, No. 10, was constructed and both performed satisfactorily over many years.

The experimental goods engine No. 1833 previously alluded to was originally constructed in 1882 as an 0-6-0 side tank, but variation in the quantity of water in the tanks affected operation of the valve gear. When rebuilt as a tender engine the problem ceased. Dean certainly had a preference for tank engines and for many years, following completion of the Armstrong Standard Goods series, all goods engines, even for main line work, had tanks. Construction of Armstrong's '1076' or 'Buffalo' class continued at Swindon until 1881 when an updated version, the '1813' class, was introduced. Side tanks replaced saddle tanks but in general format the design remained much the same as that introduced by Armstrong. Single inside frames were employed although for other classes of the period double frames remained in fashion, emphasizing Dean's open mind on the subject; others might prefer to conclude that it indicated a confused mind. Most of the class, some of which remained in service until 1947, were fitted with saddle tanks and subsequently pannier tanks.

It is probable that running experience with No. 1833 convinced Dean that powerful main line goods engines should be of tender rather than tank form, for in 1883 his famous '2301' class appeared. 'Dean Goods' engines had the same 17 in×24 in cylinders and 5 ft coupled wheels as the earlier Armstrong standard locomotives, but the wheelbase and boilers were slightly shorter. Apart from the initial twenty all later engines had domed boilers. During subsequent years several different boilers were fitted, the large domed Belpaire type giving the latter a more recognizable profile. For reliability and simplicity the class could not be beaten and with the addition of superheating they became very economical. That rugged reliability made them a natural choice for war service overseas during both major conflicts, where ease of maintenance and durability had priority. Fortunately one of the class survives in the Great Western Museum at Swindon, a solid tribute to its designer.

Use of standard components occupied much of Dean's thought and during the 1884-7 period he developed four classes of locomotives, tender and tank for both passenger and goods service, with identical cylinders, motion and undersprung wheels. Passenger engines were of the 2-4-0 type, being the '3201' class with tenders and '3501' class with tanks. An 0-6-0 arrangement found continued favour for goods traffic, these being the '2361' and '1661' classes with tenders and tanks respectively. There was nothing remarkable about any of the engines but as an exercise in standardization it allowed valuable experience to be gained.

Indifferent results with compounding applied to No. 7, and the running of broad gauge Nos. 14 and 16 prompted development of the 'Barnum' class in 1889: these turned out to be the most successful of Dean's 2-4-0 engines. Boiler pressure of 150 psi was 10 lb higher than that normally applied to contemporary engines and boilers had only two rings, taking advantage of the larger boiler plate then available. This class of twenty constructed in 1889 were the last GWR engines to employ sandwich frames.

Other 2-4-0 locomotives followed but they included nothing of major importance compared with earlier stock. The same cannot be said about single wheelers, with the '3001' class of 1891 being, arguably, the final development of the wheel arrangement. Thirty double-framed engines with 20 in × 24 in cylinders, 7 ft 8½ in driving wheels and a boiler pressure of 160 psi started a legend. No other single-wheel British locomotive has had such large cylinders. At 4.625 in valve travel was long for the period, and with generous port openings fast running was assured. Dean obviously knew something about valve travel and steam passageways. The first eight, numbered 3021-3028, were initially constructed as broad gauge engines; they lasted less than six months in that form before the 7 ft gauge disappeared.

During September 1893 No. 3021, *Wigmore Castle*, derailed in Box tunnel when the leading axle broke, and Dean was faced with a similar problem to that of Gooch with *Great Western*. Again the solution lay in the use of four leading wheels but this time employing a bogie. Delivery of an almost identical '3031' class of 4-2-2 express locomotives commenced in 1894 and it is likely that they made use of a leading bogie as a result of the derailment. The new engines had 19 in diameter cylinders but that was the only major difference. Altogether Dean constructed eighty engines of the class and they served West Country expresses until the turn of the century when increasing train loads called for more powerful machines. In their original form with raised firebox and domed boiler, these engines were considered to be amongst the most beautiful and graceful ever designed. Rebuilding with domeless Belpaire boilers tended to destroy the effect.

In 1894 Swindon nominally rebuilt the old compounds Nos. 7 and 8, as well as Nos. 14 and 16, to form the double-framed 4-4-0 'Armstrong' class. Handsome and powerful, these locomotives also made use of the raised top firebox boiler. This gives an insight into Dean's train of thought at that time regarding ample steam space, as domes were also provided.

The hills of Devon and Cornwall required something more sure-footed and powerful than single wheelers and between 1895 and 1899, following gauge conversion, the 'Duke' class duly appeared. These 4-4-0 tender engines had 18 in×26 in cylinders and 5 ft 8 in driving wheels, giving a tractive effort of 16,848 lb at 160 psi boiler pressure. Steam chests were placed below the inclined cylinders allowing valves to be directly driven by the link motion. Valves could also come off the seat when coasting and minimize the risk of exhaust being drawn into the cylinders. Inclined valves below cylinders had originated with Stroudley on the LB&SC Railway but had been adopted by James Holden on the GER and it was Holden's layout which Dean followed. Cylinders larger than 18 in diameter left little room between the frames and so it became convenient to mount valves below the cylinders rather than alongside. That arrangement was introduced in 1886 with No. 10 and applied to most subsequent Dean designs.[27]

The 'Dukes' had extended smokeboxes with a

Top *'3031' class, No. 3021* Wigmore Castle, *in original 2-2-2 form* (courtesy GWR Museum, Swindon).

Above *'3031' class, No. 3027* Worcester, *as subsequently rebuilt to 4-2-2 form* (courtesy GWR Museum, Swindon).

Right *'3031' class, No. 3027* Worcester, *in final form with Belpaire firebox boiler* (courtesy GWR Museum, Swindon).

'Duke' class No. 3261 Mount Edgcumbe, *as built with extended smokebox and flush top boiler. Note Mansell wheels on bogie and tender* (courtesy GWR Museum, Swindon).

diaphragm plate and netting spark arrestors of contemporary American pattern. Obviously Dean had been influenced by American practice and the influence cannot have been due to Churchward who did not move to the Locomotive Works until 1896. A further novel feature, also applied to certain '3001' class engines, lay in feed heating, where a portion of the exhaust was piped back to the tender. Crank driven feed pumps supplied the boiler but hot feed presented problems and adoption of the exhaust steam injector superseded the practice.[28]

A variation on the 'Dukes' were the 'Bulldogs', the main differences being straight frames and improved boilers operating at a higher pressure. The class originated with *Bulldog* of the 'Duke' class when it was provided with Churchward's prototype standard No. 2 boiler. Construction of 'Bulldogs' continued until 1910 and, during the 1930s, both classes had a new lease of life when the 'Earl' class came about through the use of 'Duke' cabs and renewed boilers on 'Bulldog' frames.

1896 saw production of a powerful 4-6-0 freight engine, No. 36, with a massive boiler having a 7 ft long × 5 ft wide raised top firebox. Dean's thoughts were on the large size.

During his latter years in office Dean's mental capabilities declined and Churchward took an increasing role in design. Most commentators consider that Churchward's influence with regard to boilers showed up almost immediately because of the adoption of Belpaire fireboxes. Dean was a keen experimenter and, it would appear, always open to new ideas. When Churchward moved to the Locomotive Works Belpaire fireboxes had already been fitted to a number of British and foreign locomotives with varied success. A trial on the Great Western was natural, especially as Dean

had turned his mind to increased steam space through the raised firebox. It is just as likely that Dean influenced Churchward towards large boilers as the other way round. After all, Churchward had little locomotive experience before his move to the Locomotive Works in 1896.

The 'Badminton' class of 4-4-0 locomotives followed a basic 'Bulldog' pattern of double frames curved above the driving axles. Cylinders 18 in×26 in were the same as on 'Duke' and 'Bulldog' classes but 6 ft 8 in driving wheels allowed for higher speed. Raised round top fireboxes had been intended in 1896 when the design was first conceived, but new drawings were issued early in 1897 stipulating Belpaire fireboxes on traditionally domed boilers. It may have been at Churchward's suggestion that the change came about or it may have been part of Dean's natural progression towards enlarged steam space. There is no conclusive evidence either way and to conclude the former simply from the fact that Churchward later developed his standard boilers with Belpaire fireboxes is rather speculative. Churchward did not become Dean's chief assistant until September 1897 by which time the decision on Belpaire boilers had long since been made.

Sometime in the early summer of 1897 Dean personally provided a conducted tour of Swindon Carriage Works for the correspondent from *The Railway Magazine*. The subsequent article, published in July 1897, indicates that Dean was still in charge, mentally aware and capable of making decisions, during the first part of that year at least.[29]

Waterford, of the 'Badminton' class, came out early in 1899 and had an almost identical boiler to the rest of the class but without the dome. That boiler became standard No. 2. There was considerable discussion at the time as to the advantages or otherwise of boiler domes. In his paper, 'Large Locomotive Boilers', Churchward indicates that he carried out tests with two identical engines and identical boilers, save for the dome, in order to 'settle this much disputed point. The engine without the dome proved to be decidedly freer from priming than the other.'[30] A Dean's assistant, Churchward was obviously in a position to make such tests but the statement may also indicate that he then directed much of what was going on in the Locomotive Department. It would be reasonable, therefore, to consider all developments after 1900 as Churchward's doing, especially with regard to boilers. In many mechanical respects locomotives in the 'Atbara', 'City', 'Aberdare' and other classes

were pure Dean, and his successor continued production to meet demand. The 'engine' part of the locomotives worked well and time could be spent getting the boilers right before a standard group of machines entered production.

Dean left the GWR with a good range of locomotives and there was little immediate need for new types. Churchward had time to develop his boilers and standard designs. The fact that construction of these 'old-fashioned' double-framed machines continued well into the first decade of the twentieth century is an indication of a sound design. Later renewal brought in many other standardized parts with the result that some locomotives remained in service after the Great Western ceased to exist.

Below *'Atbara' class No. 3374,* Baden Powell, *temporarily fitted with* Britannia *nameplates for Royal Train duties in October 1902* (courtesy GWR Museum, Swindon).

Bottom *'Earl' (or 'Dukedog') class No. 9024 in July 1958, a class formed from 'Duke' cab and boiler on 'Bulldog' frames* (D. K. Jones Collection).

7. Twentieth-century locomotives

'The modern locomotive problem is principally a question of boiler.'[1] Thus Churchward began his famous paper, 'Large Locomotive Boilers', presented to the Institution of Mechanical Engineers in 1906. When he became Dean's assistant in 1898 it is highly likely that the ageing, and ailing, Locomotive Superintendent encouraged him to direct his talents towards perfecting the steam generator part of the machine. Churchward, therefore, enjoyed the luxury of time in which to develop his own ideas. Meanwhile the Dean products could meet the railway's needs and also provide valuable test-beds for new boiler designs. Without any change in the 'engine' part it was possible to observe how new boiler arrangements affected performance.

In 1899 an amazingly shaped boiler found its way onto No. 2601, nicknamed *Kruger*. A double-framed 4-6-0, that machine incorporated many new ideas, perhaps too many, including 28 in stroke inside cylinders inclined at 1 in 7, single slide bars and piston valves above the cylinders. It was, however, the visible straight barrel boiler which attracted most attention. The large Belpaire firebox continued forward some 3 ft 6 in into a combustion chamber supplied with supplementary air by a valve positioned below. A large saddle sandbox sat on the boiler barrel just behind the smokebox. Coil and volute springs were employed for driving axles in, aparently, no organized or logical way. Sister locomotive No. 2602, appearing in 1901, was of similar form but with a pony truck instead of the leading bogie. There were so many new ideas that the locomotives appeared to have

been designed by a committee; possibly they were, with Dean and Churchward contributing most ideas. In view of some earlier designs, Dean's experimental urges might have found a final outlet in the 'Krugers'. Eight more of the design were constructed during 1903 but the entire group had ceased work by January 1907.

Construction of the 4-4-0 'Atbara' class began in 1900 and, with their straight frames, they looked very much like the later group of 'Bulldogs' although coupled wheels were 1 ft larger. Some of them had piston valves instead of the usual slide valves, possibly to provide a comparative test of qualities not obtainable from the 'Krugers'. A domeless, parallel No. 2 boiler had been originally supplied but the coned boiler, working at 200 psi pressure, later became standard. Fitting of a larger standard No. 4 boiler to one member of the class, *Mauritius*, produced the famous 'City' class. Ten new engines, the real 'Cities', were constructed during 1903 and nine further rebuilt 'Atbaras' brought the class up to twenty. Churchward's 200 lb pressure large boiler certainly did wonders for performance and the 'Cities' soon became noted for high speed operation which their smaller boilered 'Atbara' sisters could never match. In providing different steam generators for what was basically the same Dean form of 'engine' unit, Churchward proved his point regarding boilers. An engine is only as good as its steam supply and the exploits of *City of Truro* down Wellington Bank, following an arduous climb, provides ample evidence as to the speed and performance capabilities of the class, even if the 100 mph claim is debatable. For high

'City' class, City of Truro, *operating on the Severn Valley Railway following restoration in 1985.*

speed running the Dean bogie and wheel arrangement were ideal.

Coal trains demanded strong, capable engines and a goods version of the proven 'Bulldog' class seemed appropriate at the turn of the century. Of 2-6-0 form with coupled wheels 4 ft 7½ in in diameter, the 23,222 lb tractive effort 'Aberdare' class was introduced during 1900 and continued in production until 1907. Piston valves below the cylinders were fitted to the first groups but more common slide valves appeared on later batches. Parallel No. 2 boilers, fitted to the initial forty engines, were replaced by the standard No. 4 for later construction and the earlier engines rebuilt to that form. Though of basically antiquated design the class performed well, some members not being scrapped until after nationalization.

The classes mentioned above continued in construction because Dean had provided a basic design which was sound and practical. Later provision of standardized cylinder blocks and piston valves added to the capabilities and eased maintenance but, below the frames, they remained very much a late nineteenth-century design. Churchward's boilers with top feed and superheating also added to performance and allowed them to remain in service long after their styling had disappeared from other British lines. To a great extent the 'Bulldogs', 'Atbaras', 'Cities' and 'Aberdares' were constructed as stopgaps whilst development of standard classes continued. That they lasted so long is a credit to both men.

In January 1901 there appeared a drawing which outlined six projected standard engines with common components.[2] Although at the time he was still only Assistant Locomotive Superintendent, there is little doubt that Churchward was the originator of the plan, but Dean must have been aware of it and have given his approval; evidence presented in chapter 2 indicates that Dean was not as demented as some have supposed. All six classes were to have two outside 18 in×30 in cylinders with 8½ in diameter piston valves; only two sizes of boiler, constructed using the same flanging blocks, and three sizes of coupled wheels were required. The plan was masterly and obvious in its simplicity, but it was also the logical extension of the parts standardization policy which had been applied by Gooch, Armstrong and Dean.

Only one of the six proposed classes, a 4-6-0, was not constructed during Churchward's lifetime. Three of the designs appeared in 1903, these being No. 97, a 2-8-0, No. 98, a 4-6-0 and No. 99, a 2-6-2 tank. The 4-4-0 'County' class came out in 1904 and, as already mentioned, was really an exercise in the use of standard parts rather than an attempt to fulfil a real need.[3] The 'County Tank', 4-4-2T, lasted slightly longer than its tender counterpart but was not as versatile as expected. In terms of the standard design concept, neither could be considered a success apart from the fact that use was made of components common to other classes.

In February 1902, some four months before Churchward officially became Locomotive Superintendent, an outside-cylindered 4-6-0, No. 100, emerged from Swindon Works. It was so different from any other existing GWR design that the retrospective conclusion must be drawn that Churchward provided the guiding hand. Again, as evidenced from chapter 2, Dean appears to have been mentally alert during the first part of 1902 and must have been aware of No. 100's existence. It is inconceivable that he can have been duped, as some have suggested, into believing he was

'Aberdare' class No. 2669 entering Stapleton Road Station (G. H. Soole Collection/NRM, York).

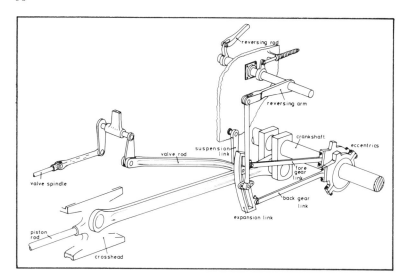

Left *Stephenson link motion as applied to Churchward's two-cylinder standard designs.*

Below *'Saint' class No. 2912,* Saint Ambrose, *with the tender formerly attached to* The Great Bear *(G. H. Soole Collection/NRM, York).*

Bottom *French compound No. 103,* President, *with the boiler from No. 104, at Old Oak Common circa 1913 (courtesy National Railway Museum, York).*

responsible for the design, or had any part in it, if that was not the case. Without doubt Dean was ill for a period towards the end of his reign and Churchward will have had to take over. The exact nature of the illness is unknown but was probably what now classes as a nervous breakdown. Upon his return to work Dean must have been made aware of changes which had taken place and, knowing retirement was due, allowed Churchward to continue his development, probably even making suggestions himself.

Some features from the standard list of 1901 applied to No. 100 but in most respects it was a 'one-off' and did not fit the anticipated pattern. That begs the questions, why was it constructed and who was responsible? Piston valves were smaller and between the frames rather than part of the casting as they ultimately became in all two-cylinder designs. The usual Stephenson valve gear was applied but with motion transmitted to the valves through rocking levers in a different way to the later standard. The domeless boiler had a parallel barrel and Belpaire firebox, but that appeared to be very much an interim arrangement as it gave way to the standard No. 1 type within a year. With so many features not part of the standard list to which Churchward rigidly adhered, was No. 100 merely an aberration or Dean's parting shot? We shall never know as neither man left a diary.

Design of No. 98, the standard pattern 4-6-0, must have continued alongside that for No. 100, but changes will have taken place in the light of operating experience. The later engine, No. 98, copied an American feature, with identical cylinder castings being bolted back-to-back in order to form a complete cylinder block which also incorporated the smokebox saddle. Identical standardized castings could be used but only so long as the cylinders remained horizontal, an arrangement which Churchward favoured anyway. Inside, Stephenson link motion of modified form operated 10 in diameter piston valves through a rocking lever. The system became standard for all two-cylinder designs, producing a 6¼ in travel in full gear.

Churchward preferred the Stephenson arrangement because lead could be varied from −⅛ in when fully notched up for starting to +⅛ in at about 25% cut-off whilst running at speed. At high speed the valve opened early, thereby admitting steam to a cylinder before it had reached the end of its previous stroke. That provided a cushioning effect but also ensured that full steam pressure was available in the cylinder as soon as the piston began its next stroke. A similar situation exists with the need to provide a timing advance mechanism on a car engine so that combustion of the fuel takes place just as the piston is ready to move down on its next power stroke. In full gear, when starting or moving slowly, steam would not be admitted until the piston was ⅛ in down its stroke, but pressure was almost immediately available at the piston due to the slow speed. Long travel valves also found favour as they provided full steam port and exhaust port opening very quickly, thus reducing the steam energy loss due to throttling.

A further 4-6-0, No. 171 *Albion*, came out in December 1903, only nine months after No. 98. They were identical mechanically and had the same coned boiler, but for *Albion* it was rated at 225 psi pressure instead of 200 psi. Behind the increased boiler pressure was a foreign influence. Churchward had been impressed by the performance of de Glehn four-cylinder compounds on the Nord line in France. Determined to give compounds a further trial on GWR metals he sought, and obtained, approval for the purchase of a compound 4-4-2 engine, suitably westernized to suit the different loading gauge.

La France, No. 102, entered service during October 1903, being tested on main lines to the west in competition with the new 4-6-0s. Both 13⅜ in diameter H.P. cylinders were outside the frames driving the trailing coupled axle whilst the 22⅛ in L.P. cylinders were inside the frames and drove the leading coupled axle. Each cylinder had its own Walschaert valve gear and screw reverser, all of which could be operated together or in isolation depending upon circumstances. A driver-controlled intercepting valve, placed between the H.P. exhaust and L.P. steam chests, allowed the locomotive to be worked as a simple if required.[4] *La France* had a boiler pressure of 227 psi; to make comparative trials fair, *Albion's* boiler was pressed to 225 psi. Even then a major difference existed with the wheel arrangement and so, in October 1904, *Albion* was converted to a 4-4-2. For Churchward, reduction in the number of test variables had priority.

A single compound could not be expected to provide fair trial and two larger machines, *President*, No. 103, and *Alliance*, No. 104, were obtained in 1905. Though they had the same boiler pressure, coupled wheels, stroke and valve travel as their younger sister the H.P. cylinder was 14⅜ in diameter and the L.P. 23⅝ in. To run against the compounds, nineteen engines similar to *Albion* also entered service in 1905. All were identical except that six were 4-6-0s and the others 'Atlantics'. Not only was Churchward interested in comparing simples against compounds, he also wanted to identify the better wheel arrangement.

Tests involved running throughout the GWR system but *La France*, and presumably also the other compounds, had not been designed for working heavy gradients.[5] On reasonably level ground the compounds performed well and *La France* easily met Churchward's design requirement of a two ton draw bar pull at 70 mph. The 'old man' was satisfied as 'it took a remarkably good locomotive to do that'.[6]

In the end Churchward decided against compounding on the basis that the extra complication was not warranted and similar fuel saving could be obtained through control of expansion in a simple engine. The exercise with the French engines did not, however, end until they were disposed of in the late 1920s, standard No. 1. boilers having been fitted. The bogie was developed for use on later Great Western locomotives, whilst the advantages of smoother running from four cylinders with reciprocating masses balanced and driving force divided between two axles were noted and used.

'Atlantics' were converted to 4-6-0s during 1912 and 1913 when it became obvious that adhesive power was better with six coupled wheels than with four. Further similar 4-6-0 locomotives were constructed during 1907, 1911, 1912 and 1913, producing the famous 'Saint' class which performed so effectively throughout the system until the arrival of Hawksworth's 'County' class. All had the same characteristics as the original groups

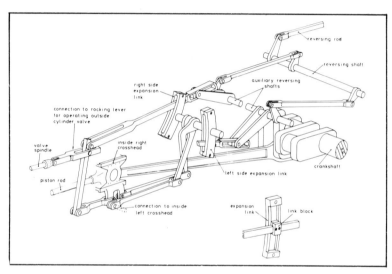

Left *Scissors valve gear as developed at Swindon.*

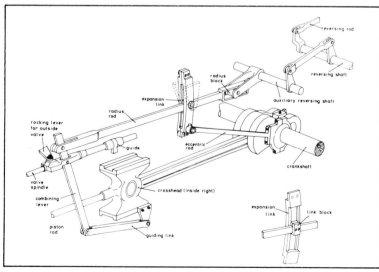

Left *Walschaerts valve gear as fitted by Churchward to all of his four-cylinder engines.*

Above right *'Star' class* Queen Berengaria *as built* (courtesy GWR Museum, Swindon).

except that fully coned standard No. 1 boilers with superheaters were fitted. Some 'Atlantics' received superheaters prior to conversion with the remainder being so treated upon rebuilding.

Not only did the French engines provide food for thought regarding compounds as opposed to simples and 4-4-2 against 4-6-0, they also set Churchward thinking about the benefits of a four-cylinder simple design. No. 40, produced by Swindon in 1906, incorporated many of the desirable features found in the de Glehn compounds but it was a simple 4-4-2 with a 225 psi boiler pressure and allowed for more direct comparisons not available with the two-cylinder designs. Outside cylinders drove the rear coupled wheels whilst the inside cylinders connected with the front pair. The usual Churchward restrictions of horizontal cylinders and no outside valve gear applied, but space prohibited inside Stephenson link motion.

W.H. Pearce came up with a solution to the valve gear problem and produced a form of 'scissors' gear whereby the inside crosshead on one side of the engine operated valves for both cylinders on the opposite side. Compensated rocking levers allowed each outside cylinder valve to be driven by the linkage moving the inside valve spindle. The system was ingenious and avoided the use of operating cranks or eccentrics. However, a problem arose in that R.M. Deely had come up with a similar arrangement whilst assistant to S.W. Johnson on the Midland Railway. Deely revived the idea when he succeeded Johnson and fitted it to a large 4-4-0, but he did not apply for a patent until August 1905 and that was not granted until the following June. Meanwhile No. 40 had appeared. Strongly worded letters flowed between Derby and Swindon with Deely accusing Churchward of making use of his idea without acknowledgment.[7] Pearce's arrangement predated the patent and so Swindon had a right to make use of it.

Scissors gear was not used on later four-cylinder engines for two good reasons unconnected with the argument about its inventor. Valve setting was a very time consuming process which could not be tolerated with a large class and, more importantly, there was a flaw in the design. A defect in the linkage on one side of the engine would result in complete failure of the locomotive as each valve set was dependent upon movement of the opposite inside crosshead. Inside Walschaert gear was applied to later four-cylinder locomotives, with the compensated rocking shaft being retained to drive the outside cylinder valves. Compensation was produced by having the rocking shaft slightly cranked rather than straight and became necessary because inclination of the connecting rod results in piston motion not being symmetrical with crank angular motion; *e.g.* when the crank is at 90° and midway between top and bottom stroke positions, the piston has not yet reached the middle of its stroke. Where one cylinder operates another set of valve gear, compensation for the angularity of the connecting rod is essential. Churchward also insisted that subsequent four-cylinder locomotives incorporate a device allowing any set of valve gear to be easily disconnected and fastened in mid position.[8] It would then be run using the cylinders on one side only; with scissors gear that was impossible.

Having 14¼ in×26 in cylinders, 6 ft 8½ in driving wheels and No. 1 standard boiler working at 225 psi pressure, No. 40 could produce a tractive effort, at 85% boiler pressure, of 25,090 lb. That exceeded *La France* but not the other compounds, but Churchward was well pleased with the results, particularly the freer working when pushed hard. Tractive effort is only one measure of a locomotive's theoretical ability, based upon boiler pressure and dimensions; other criteria such as drawbar pull must be considered when investigating true potential. A few months after construction No. 40 received the name *North Star*. A year earlier Churchward had arranged for the original broad gauge holder of this name to be broken up, so the naming would appear rather insensitive. It may have been a gesture of contrition or he may have considered it appropriate, presuming that his

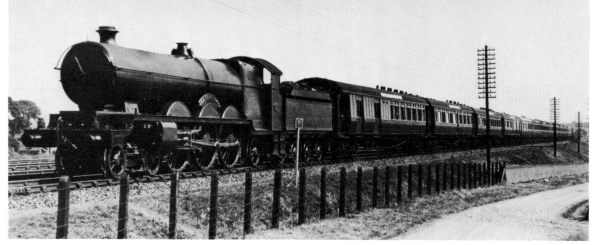

No. 111, The Great Bear, *with a down express in the Thames Valley* (courtesy National Railway Museum, York).

'Stars' would provide a new locomotive beginning just as Stephenson's had done. Whatever the reason, Churchward did not divulge it to anybody.

Conversion to the more acceptable 4-6-0 form followed in 1909 when a short cone superheated boiler was fitted. Sharp angular lines were smoothed out to give a more pleasing appearance. The first true batch of 'Star' class engines followed in 1907 and they continued to be constructed regularly until 1914, Collett building more during 1922-3.

Western Star became test engine for superheating, a Cole type superheater being provided in 1907. Trials with other engines, 'Stars' and 'Saints', followed until the final design of Swindon No. 3 type superheater was developed in 1909. From 1910 all 'Stars' were provided with superheaters and earlier locomotives converted. In that final condition 'Stars' formed the basis for future GWR four-cylinder locomotive design, except in one case.

Over the years there has been much speculation as to Churchward's reason for building the first British 'Pacific', *The Great Bear*. Publicity seeking directors have been blamed but it does not appear to have been part of the incumbent CME's character to follow the engineering dictates of others, particularly when they had little or no engineering training. Policy for locomotive construction developed at Swindon with permission being sought from the Locomotive Building Committee at Paddington. In view of Churchward's success in getting his vast construction programme approved there can be little doubt that he would not have had much difficulty over a single engine, no matter how big. His persuasive nature and commanding personality ensured that he generally got his own way. Cutting-up of the remaining broad gauge engines would indicate how effective his style could be.

O.S. Nock concludes that production of No. 111, *The Great Bear*, was an exercise in large boiler design.[9] F.W. Hawksworth was closely involved in the design work, being responsible for the general arrangement drawings. Nock had many conversations with Hawksworth and gathered from him that building and running of the locomotive gave valuable experience towards the day when a larger machine than the 'Stars' would be required. There was no obvious need for the locomotive and its route availability was severely restricted, but the Publicity Department at Paddington could, and did, take advantage of the size and unique nature of the beast. If construction had been purely for publicity there must have been a less expensive way of getting it.

The Great Bear was over boilered. To make full use of the steam raising capabilities of the boiler's heating surface, some 2,855 sq ft compared with 2,149 sq ft of a 'Star', cylinders larger than 15 in diameter would have been required. However, adherence to standard front end details and horizontal cylinders dictated a maximum cylinder diameter of 15 in. Much more effective use of the boiler's capabilities could have been made with larger cylinders; the locomotive was a 'one-off' and the normal standardization restrictions should not have applied. Although the large boiler concept was good, Churchward did not 'grasp the nettle' and complete the task by developing a front end to suit. A locomotive, after all, consists of boiler and cylinder units and Churchward's preoccupation with boilers wasted a valuable opportunity for real progress.

Without suitably sized cylinders the boiler could not be steamed at its full rate and so the exercise must have been limited in its application, effectively a waste of time and money. Collett was certainly right in rebuilding No. 111 as a 'Castle' when its boiler came up for heavy repair in 1924, but the legend of Britain's first 'Pacific' proved difficult to erase even though it had been of extremely doubtful value. The original eight-wheel bogie tender did not stay with *Viscount Churchill*, as 'The Bear' became, but was attached to several other locomotives before being condemned in 1936.

It is frequently forgotten that Churchward also introduced another wheel arrangement to British railways, the 2-8-0. One of the early trial locomotives, No. 97 of 1903, pointed the way to a heavy freight design which lasted until the end of steam traction on GWR rails. So successful was the prototype that few changes were made when the design went into steady production as the '2800' class two years later. Standard No. 1 boiler, working at 225 psi, was applied throughout with but minor modifications in terms of taper and superheating. Two outside 18 in×30 in cylinders were fitted to all members of the class, piston valve diameter being increased to 10 in from the 8½ in of No. 97. Without doubt Churchward had produced a winning design but its application to freight use kept it from general public gaze, preventing the '2800' from attracting similar affection to that lavished on 'Stars' or 'Saints'

Collett constructed further locomotives to the same pattern but with updated features, the most important of which were outside steam pipes. Some problems with leakage of high pressure live steam at joints between the cylinder block castings had been experienced on two-cylinder locomotives. Introduction of outside steam supply pipes made troublesome joints more accessible and subjected the casting to low pressure exhaust steam only. The casting itself was simpler and less expensive to produce.[10]

The first outside steam pipes appeared on the '4700' class of more powerful 2-8-0 locomotives. A prototype of Churchward's final design, No. 47, appeared in 1919 being very much like the '2800s' but having 19 in diameter cylinders and 5 ft 8 in coupled wheels instead of 18 in and 4 ft 7½ in respectively. Originally a No. 1 boiler with extra long smokebox had been fitted but it could not supply sufficient steam. In May 1921, during Churchward's final year in office, the new standard No. 7 boiler and replacement cylinder blocks with outside steam pipes were provided. To what extent the redesign was pure Churchward is unknown. At the time Collett was Assistant Chief Mechanical Engineer and had spent many years in the Locomotive Works where problems concerning steam leaks must have been obvious. Possibly he had an influence on the new design as Churchward had taken no steps to rectify an obvious defect until then.

Standard 2-8-0 design, '2800' class of freight locomotives. No. 2857 as fitted with outside steam pipes.

The Traffic Department had requested construction of suitable locomotives for working heavy but fast vacuum-braked freight trains which had been hauled successfully by *The Great Bear*. Increased route availability necessitated a relatively light, powerful machine and so the mixed traffic '4700' locomotive came about, the only Churchward design produced to satisfy a definite demand.[11] The class consisted of nine locomotives, all but the prototype being constructed after Collett took charge. In later years the Running Superintendent requested more of the same type but Collett decided to construct additional 'Castles' which, although a little more costly, were better suited to passenger train duplication during peak periods.[12]

The original Churchward standardization proposal of 1901 called for 4-4-0 and 4-4-2 tank locomotives and these were constructed as the 'County' class and 'County tanks' respectively. No prototypes were built, the classes were basically produced using standard parts and, as already mentioned, did not really fit successfully into the standard range. Another tank locomotive in the scheme was to be of 2-6-2 formation, with No. 99 being constructed as a prototype in 1903. Apart from the driving wheels, which were 5 ft 8 in in diameter, cylinders, boiler and most other items were identical to those used two years later on the 'County tanks'. With the prototype successful, a further batch of almost identical machines was ordered for delivery in 1905-6, forming the '3100' (later '5100') class. The only major differences between the prototype and production models lay in the standard No. 2 boiler, later engines having fully tapered boilers, and the side tanks, which were straight topped on No. 99 but sloped to match the boiler taper on production locomotives.

4-4-2 'County' tank standard design, No. 2250 (courtesy National Railway Museum, York).

Collett update of Churchward's '3100' class, the 2-6-2 tank No. 5164 of the '5100' class.

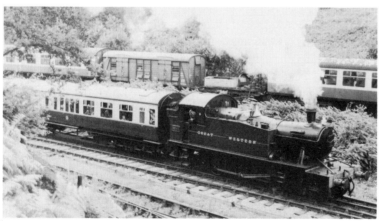

2-6-2 tank, '4500' class No. 5541 at the Dean Forest Railway, 1985.

Heavy freight 2-8-0 tank No. 5239 of the '4200' class at Paignton.

By placing a No. 4 boiler on a '3100' class locomotive, No. 3150, Churchward created a larger and more powerful machine which proved to be ideal for banking duties. The production group of forty locomotives, which formed the '3150' class, had cylinders 18½ in in diameter instead of 18 in, giving a 25,670 lb tractive effort. Buffing strains at the front end resulted in the introduction of struts which later found application on all classes with leading pony trucks.

In 1919 the boiler pressure of the '3100s' was raised to 200 psi, thereby increasing the tractive effort at 85% boiler pressure to 24,300 lb. Superheating had been applied some nine years earlier. Modified cylinder block castings with outside steam pipes, enlarged bunkers, lower cab roofs and curved drop ends were the main alterations applied at the end of the 1920s, thus updating the locomotives to produce the '5100' class. Swindon constructed a further fifty before identical '6100s' were turned out with boiler pressure increased to 225 psi. The success of the design for local passenger, pick-up freight and banking duties guaranteed survival until the end of GWR steam.

Reconstruction of the '3100s' reached the planning stage during the mid-1930s and it was proposed that the extensive work be financed from the capital renewal fund rather than revenue. As far as Collett was concerned, simple replacement of parts on a like-for-like basis would constitute repair, which had to come from revenue. Use of money from the renewal fund for basic repairs he considered as a wangle and that he would not countenance. However, if reconstructed with new larger cylinders, a higher pressure boiler and reduced diameter coupled wheels, the 'new' locomotives would be a greater asset to traffic and the work could be financed as part of the capital renewal programme. According to K.J. Cook, Collett loved to engage in the mental gymnastics such an accounting problem presented.[13]

Churchward digressed from his policy of using standard parts with the introduction of two smaller 2-6-2 tank classes, both miniature versions of prototype No. 99. Cylinders were non-standard at 26 in stroke and 16½ in diameter for the '4400' class, those of the '4500' class being 17 in in diameter. In both cases a No. 5 standard boiler was fitted, but the '4500s' had driving wheels 6 in larger than the '4400s' at 4 ft 7½ in. Both classes operated on branch lines with considerable success, the larger wheeled class having a greater turn of speed for passenger use. Again Collett continued production of the more useful '4500' class during his tenure.

Another Churchward design which found favour with his successor and continued in production relatively unchanged apart from outside steam pipes was the tank version of the 2-8-0 locomotive. Originally, a 2-8-2 tank had been proposed but the wheel base was considered undesirably long. A prototype, No. 4201, entered service during 1910. With a standard No. 4 boiler working at 200 psi and 4 ft 7½ in driving wheels these heavy mineral locomotives performed valuable service in the Welsh valleys right up until the end of steam.

Trade depression in the 1920s-30s brought a decline in mineral traffic and Collett took the opportunity of increasing coal and water capacity in order to equip the design for long-distance work. Some locomotives had frames extended at the rear to accommodate a radial axle which was essential for the extended bunker carrying an additional 2 tons of coal and 700 gal of water. The envisaged 2-8-2T thus came about in the '7200' class, but by Collett's hand not Churchward's. It is a good example of the former's ability to make full use of what was available, adapting good machines to suit changing needs.

Though he had set out a standard range, Churchward was not averse to the introduction of additional designs if they filled a need and if standardized parts could be used. He was also willing to allow others to take decisions relating to design. By 1910 the standard main line types had been built, and attention turned to secondary services with a view to replacing the double-framed 'Atbara', 'Bulldog' and 'Aberdare' classes. It was intended to employ inside cylinders on a 2-6-0, and Holcroft proposed the use of single slide bars as a means of reducing the cylinder inclination required to clear the leading axle. Churchward, remembering problems with similarly fitted 'Krugers', would have none of it.

Holcroft had recently returned from an investigatory trip to Canada which left him impressed by the 'Mogul' type (2-6-0) in service there. Churchward learned of the visit and, after due consideration, approached Holcroft with his proposition. 'We will have a 2-6-0 with 5ft. 8in. wheels, but use 18in. × 30in. outside cylinders, the No. 4 boiler, and work in all the standard parts possible.'[14] Holcroft was left to get on with the work and within a few days had completed the design. Standard parts meant that most drawings were already available and only layout diagrams had to be made. Thus the '4300' class was born, with No. 4301 appearing in 1911. As a general utility locomotive it was ideal, being at home on heavy freight workings or running passenger trains at up to 70 mph. Production continued over many

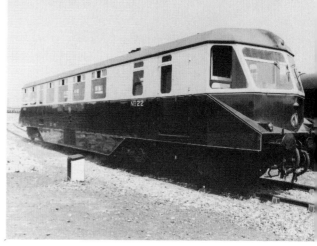

years with only minor modifications such as outside steam pipes and strengthened main frame in way of the pony truck. No fewer than 342 examples were constructed altogether, several seeing service in France during World War 1.

A form of rail car consisting of combined locomotive and carriage unit had been constructed for the Bristol & Exeter Railway during its early years but had not been a success. Dugald Drummond revived the idea when two steam rail motors were constructed for a service between Havant and Fratton. In 1903 one was loaned to the GWR for trials and Churchward found the idea useful enough to design a fleet of such vehicles. Eventually the Great Western became the most extensive user of steam rail motors in the country, many South Wales lines also adopting the idea.

Churchward's vehicles consisted of car with a power unit at one end. A vertical boiler supplied steam to two outside 12 in×16 in cylinders which connected to the trailing pair of 3 ft 8 in coupled wheels. Walschaert valve gear operated balanced slide valves. Gas lamps provided illumination in the passenger compartment though electric lighting was later fitted.[15] Over a five-year period no fewer than ninety-nine coach bodies and 112 engine units were constructed, the additional engine units providing spares. The drive unit could be replaced by a spare allowing for overhaul away from the coach part which would then continue in service.

The increased traffic which the cars generated on branch lines and short-distance main lines often necessitated the connection of an additional carriage which the power unit was not strong enough to take. That limitation resulted in the introduction of locomotive-hauled services and development of the auto trains. Engine units and coaches were withdrawn separately over a period, but the last complete unit remained in service until 1935. A number of coach bodies were converted for use in auto trains. The concept was sound but suffered from a defect in that, as designed, steam rail motors were not flexible enough to cope with changing traffic patterns.

Collett reintroduced the concept in 1933 but with diesel propulsion rather than steam. Diesel mechanical rail cars were constructed by the Associated Equipment Company, with body work supplied by Park Royal Coachworks and the Gloucester Railway Carriage and Wagon Company. In total thirty-eight vehicles were constructed, two for parcels only. Passenger capacity differed between batches and some vehicles were geared down for use on branch lines where they could haul 60-ton tail loads at speeds up to 40 mph. Others were streamlined for high speed main line operation. Auto train fittings allowed additional coaches to be taken if necessary. Twin 121 hp engines gave these machines the flexibility and performance their earlier steam powered sisters lacked. With their introduction Collett obviously had his mind on alternatives to steam traction. A diesel mechanical and seven diesel electric shunters were purchased from outside suppliers during the 1930s, but straight electrical propulsion never found favour at Swindon.

When Collett took over from Churchward the main line locomotive stock was well organized in the standardization scheme, but increasing demands on the Running Department called for higher power than that supplied by the 'Stars'. Axle load restrictions of 20 tons precluded a proportional enlargement of parts, so compromise was necessary. A completely new design was totally unnecessary as the 'Stars' performed effectively and maintenance problems were well understood. Collett has been criticized for not showing more individuality in his designs and merely updating the Churchward locomotives. Had he done otherwise it would have been gross folly both economically and in a practical sense.

Building on a proven design was the best way forward.

Caerphilly Castle stole the show when exhibited alongside *Flying Scotsman* during the British Empire Exhibition at Wembley in April 1924, Britain's most powerful locomotive, at least as far as tractive effort was concerned. To achieve 31,625 lb at 85% boiler pressure, cylinder diameter had been increased to 16 in but length of stroke remained the same as the 'Stars'. A new standard No. 8 boiler was produced, being larger than the No. 1 but smaller than the No. 7 as fitted to the '4700' class. Driving and bogie wheels were identical to those of the 'Stars' but the wheel base was slightly shorter. The 'Castle' may have been an updated version of the earlier four-cylinder design, but it was an improvement and superior. In many respects it was a development which Churchward should have made, but he 'rested on his laurels' following completion of the standardization scheme. Holcroft

certainly thought he did.[16]

As 'Castles' entered service they proved themselves superior to all other British locomotives in fact and not just publicity. The LNER did not take kindly to the downgrading of its 'Pacifics' but, even burning hard Yorkshire coal, *Pendennis Castle* forced the message home when working out of Kings Cross. *Caldicot Castle* provided Collett with valuable data for his paper to the 1924 World Power Conference[17] and, for five weeks during 1926, *Launceston Castle* gave the LMS a lesson in real locomotive performance. Steady output continued, apart from the war years, up to 1950 when No. 7037, *Swindon*, brought 'Castle' production to a close. A number of 'Stars' were rebuilt because maintenance costs had been shown to be one old penny per mile less for 'Castle' class locomotives due to their larger boilers having a lower evaporation rate. Conversion took place when cylinder renewal came due but Collett later

Above far left *'4300' class 2-6-0, No. 4377, on an up freight near Patchway* (G. H. Soole Collection/NRM, York).

Above left *AEC Diesel Railcar No. 22 built at Swindon in 1941.*

Above *Collett's 'Castle' class No. 5051, Drysllwyn Castle, leaving Swindon with a Gloucester excursion during August 1985.*

Right *Cylinder, valve and steam pipe arrangements on a 'Castle'.*

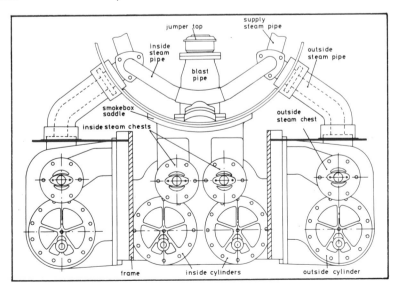

decided to reconstruct relatively new 'Star' locomotives rather than the older ones. That was because frames would be in a better condition and more usable.[18]

If the 'Castles' raised GWR locomotive development to new heights, the 'Kings' pushed it to its pinnacle. 'Castles' were designed to the limit imposed by the Civil Engineer, further advancement in power only being possible if some easing of the restriction took place. Collett knew that he could build a better locomotive if an axle loading of 22½ tons could be permitted and was not slow in telling Felix Pole, the General Manager. Having made enquiries, Pole soon discovered that the axle load limit on the main Bristol line was already 22 tons and could be increased an extra ½ ton by the following year. Lack of communication between Mechanical and Civil Engineering Departments created a problem which did not really exist. Collett got his increased axle loading and Pole a golden opportunity for publicity. The CME was instructed to have his new locomotive ready for the summer traffic of 1927.[19]

Again Churchward's 'Star' formed the basis for the design but Collett took it to the absolute limit. Pole had been promised power, in the form of tractive effort, and that came through a combination of factors. A large No. 12 standard boiler was constructed especially for the 'Kings' and operating pressure increased to 250 psi. Originally, cylinders of 16 in×28 in had been specified, with driving wheel diameter reduced to 6 ft 6 in compared with 6 ft 8½ in for the 'Castles'. Early on, Collett had decided upon reduced driving wheel diameter as a means of increasing tractive

effort, having witnessed the performance of a '4300' locomotive in overtaking a Swindon–Paddington express. New tyres turned down to the intended diameter were fitted to *Ludlow Castle* and tests confirmed Collett's view.[20]

Unfortunately, tractive effort fell just short of 40,000 lb and Pole wanted it just over, publicity value being important. By boring out the cylinders to 16¼ in a tractive effort at 85% boiler pressure of 40,300 lb was achieved. Everybody was satisfied and the Great Western once again had the most powerful passenger locomotive in Britain, at least as far as Pole's tractive effort criterion was concerned. When replacement came due 16 in diameter cylinders were fitted in order to give a longer life, that being more important than the already-gained publicity.

King George V, first of the class, was turned out rather hurriedly in order to represent Britain, and the GWR in particular, at the Baltimore and Ohio Railway Centenary celebrations during late 1927. Thorough road testing was not possible before shipment to the USA in August. Had road trials been carried out a major design defect in the bogie might have shown up. Because of adherence to Churchward's horizontal cylinder concept, without offsetting the cylinder centres insufficient room existed for standard 3 ft 2 in bogie wheels. A plate-framed bogie was considered desirable due to the failure of a number of Churchward bogies through rivet breakage, but plate frames took up more room. One solution lay in having the bogie frame outside the leading wheels and inside the trailing wheels, which were 3 ft in diameter. Axles were individually sprung.

Left King Henry V *at Narroways Junction with the up 'Bristolian' towards the end of 1935. Part of the streamlined casing has already been removed.* (G. H. Soole Collection/NRM, York).

Right *Streamlined arrangement for* Manorbier Castle.

In August the bogie of *King George IV* was partially derailed whilst travelling at speed and suspicion fell on bogie springing. That proved to be the case and tests showed that if the axle dropped 1½ in it was relieved of all load. There was, therefore, little margin for track defects and coil springs were added to the hangers in order to soften the springing.[21] *King George V* had to be similarly modified in order to allow operation on dubious quality American track.

In the 1930s streamlining became a fashion if not an obsession and smoothed lines were applied to all manner of items whether they moved or not. There were, and are, obvious applications for the technique in order to reduce resistance to motion, aircraft being a prime example. Wind tunnel tests at the National Physical Laboratory allowed Sir Malcolm Campbell's *Bluebird* to be designed for very high sped running. Technology provided the means by which the shape of any fast transport vehicle might be optimized and, to some people, an express locomotive fell into that category. Collett came under pressure to apply streamlining on the GWR ahead of the other railways, particularly as the centenary of the Company's incorporation was to be celebrated during 1935. There would, however, be no headlong rush into construction of an unwanted streamlined class. Trials could be carried out on suitably modified existing locomotives.

He appeared to approach the task with little relish and is said to have curtly produced his streamline arrangement by smearing plasticine over a paperweight model of a 'King' which was then sent to the drawing office for working drawings to be made.[22] The tale is probably apocryphal in its attempt to denigrate Collett, but there would have been no better way of starting the process. Collett was no fool and realized that factors other than head-on wind resistance exerted drag on a train; however, the positioning of his streamlined casings indicates a knowledge as to the major wind drag and eddy regions. Even the railway's own journal, *The Great Western Railway Magazine*, had its doubts. Text alongside a photograph of the streamlined *King Henry VII* contained the comment, 'Rigorous application of the principles of scientific streamlining becomes not only difficult but practically inexpedient, as the net reduction in the total resistance may be relatively small.'[23] That text must have been cleared by the CME's department, and probably Collett himself, prior to publication.

Manorbier Castle was similarly treated to streamlined casing, but neither locomotive was subject to any comparative testing in order to determine the fuel saving value of the additional metalwork. Maintenance problems became evident at the front end and, gradually, parts of the casing were removed, the tender cowling and some of the skirting failing to see out the first year. Collett's half-hearted attempt quickly proved the point that streamlining of a steam locomotive increased maintenance difficulties for very doubtful fuel savings. That cautious approach must have saved his employers a small fortune.

Although the '4300' class 'Moguls' performed well, they lacked boiler power for some applications and tended to 'nose' about under certain conditions. In reply to requests from the Running

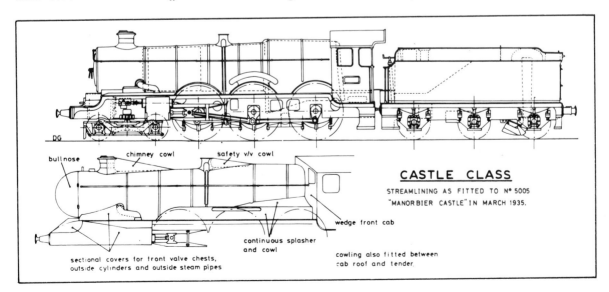

CASTLE CLASS

STREAMLINING AS FITTED TO N° 5005 "MANORBIER CASTLE" IN MARCH 1935.

bullnose

chimney cowl

safety v/v cowl

wedge front cab

continuous splasher and cowl

sectional covers for front valve chests, outside cylinders and outside steam pipes

cowling also fitted between cab roof and tender.

DG

Department for an uprated version, Collett decided that a modified 'Saint' would fit the bill. It had the longer wheel base and large boiler requested but had also proved itself reliable in years of service. Why, in fact, attempt a radically new design when an adequate base, which fitted the standard pattern, already existed? In 1924 *Saint Martin* was rebuilt with 6 ft coupled wheels and became the first 'Hall'. There were other minor changes but nothing of note except cab side windows. The 225 psi boiler pressure and 18½ in diameter bored-out cylinders gave a tractive effort of 27,275 lb compared with 20,530 lb for the original 'Saints'.

The prototype enjoyed considerable success resulting in an order for eighty production locomotives which differed in having a higher pitched boiler, outside steam pipes, modified frame and longer travel valves. So popular was the machine that construction continued until 1946 by which time over 250 had been built. When Hawksworth became CME he introduced new ideas, building seventy-one 'Modified Halls' between 1946 and 1950.

The Hawksworth modifications were radical and moved away from Churchward's standardized pattern. Plate frames applied throughout, extension pieces at the front end no longer being fitted. Separate cylinder blocks were bolted to the outside of each main frame and a fabricated smokebox saddle formed part of a stay between the cylinders. A plate frame bogie replaced the bar frame variety with wheels reduced to 3 ft in diameter and wheel base increased by 2 in. A larger superheater provided increased steam temperature. Hawksworth was obviously applying his own ideas to an already successful design but greater use of fabrication as opposed to casting must have reflected American wartime manufacturing influences.

Though the 'Halls' could not be faulted they did not fully comply with the Running Department's requirement, that of an enlarged '4300'. In 1936 Collett nominally rebuilt some members of that class as 4-6-0s in order to produce the requested design. These 'Granges' were, in effect, new locomotives and were basically smaller-wheeled 'Halls'. By fitting wheels of 5 ft 8 in diameter to the 'Hall' design Collett had produced a standard 4-6-0 as advocated by Churchward in his scheme of 1901. Having a higher axle loading than the '4300' locomotives they replaced, the 'Granges' were more restricted in route availability and so were less useful.

With route availability in mind a second 'rebuild' of the '4300s' produced the 'Manor' class in 1938. A lighter version of the 'Grange', it

Left *No. 4930,* Hagley Hall, *in service on the Severn Valley Railway in 1985.*

Below left *Collett's 'Grange' class No. 6859,* Yiewsley Grange, *at Bristol Bath Road shed on 23 October 1965* (Chris Surridge).

Bottom left *'Manor' class No. 7827,* Lydham Manor, *enters Paignton on the Torbay and Dartmouth Railway, August 1985* (Patrick Griffiths).

Right *'5600' class 0-6-2 tank No. 6697 at Didcot* (Sarah Griffiths).

differed mainly in having a new standard No. 14 boiler which was shorter and of smaller diameter than the standard No. 1 used for 'Halls' and 'Granges'. Superheating surface area was consequently less. To compensate for lower boiler power cylinder diameter had to be reduced to 18 in from the then standard 18½ in. With a tractive effort of 27,340 lb, marginally more than a 'Hall' and slightly less than a 'Grange', the 'Manors' proved extremely popular because of their route availability. Collett had finalized the Great Western plan for a range of 4-6-0 passenger tender locomotives to replace the 4-4-0s on similar duties.

From the above it might be concluded that Collett was preoccupied with 4-6-0 tender engines to the exclusion of all others. In reality he expended considerable energy on locomotive design for secondary and shunting duties as well as reconstruction, to fit a standardized format, of many engines absorbed at the grouping. The load placed upon him matched that of Armstrong and Dean when faced with gauge conversion. Also, he was not averse to participation in co-operative schemes with other railways through the Association of Railway Locomotive Engineers. That open approach differed from the secretive world of Churchward. Harold Holcroft considered that the 'iron curtain' mentality which had previously resulted in Swindon's 'splendid isolation' was greatly relaxed under Collett.[24]

Grouping brought over 800 locomotives of many different classes into the Swindon fold, almost exclusively tank engines. Although certain of the grouped companies had adopted standardization, it was limited to that particular railway and offered very little help to the enlarged Great Western as far as repair and maintenance was concerned. In some instances old locomotives could be scrapped and replaced by new standard machines, but in other cases such a step was not considered economically worthwhile. Collett instructed the drawing office to investigate each class in order to ascertain which, if any, of the existing standard boilers would be most suitable for fitting as a replacement. Three standard boilers were modified to produce an enlarged range, thus allowing more of the grouped engines to be so treated. By changing boilers to a standard type Collett was able to centralize much of the repair work at Swindon, allowing him to downgrade the maintenance facilities at depots on the absorbed railways, thereby cutting costs. Mechanical parts could not be standardized and the grouped locomotives remained very unpopular with Swindon repair gangs as they slowed down the work rate.[25]

Scrapping older stock from the grouped railways necessitated replacement by a class which could operate on lines with tight curves and reduced clearances. In the stock then existing there was nothing of sufficient power and so Collett set about producing a design new to the GWR. Conditions dictated an inside-cylindered tank engine with a pair of trailing wheels to support a large bunker. The '5600' class 0-6-2 tank broke new ground on the Great Western when introduced during 1924, although many of the grouped engines scrapped had a similar wheel arrangement. By fitting 18 in×26 in cylinders with 8 in piston valves operated indirectly by Stephenson link gear, a number of modified standard parts could be incorporated. The boiler was a standard No. 2 but coupled wheels were of a new size at 4 ft 7½ in diameter. Use of standard, or modified standard, parts presented a challenge to the design team as it must have been more convenient in many cases to produce a completely new design.

Churchward appears to have had a dislike for locomotives without guiding wheels, his only 0-6-0 design being the '1361' saddle tank class of which five were constructed for dock shunting duties. Collett suffered no such inhibitions and made use of that wheel arrangement whenever it suited. First of a long line was the '5700' class of pannier tanks, introduced in 1929 for shunting and light goods work. In effect the design followed closely Dean's '2021' class of 1897 but with an improved boiler working at 200 psi pressure and pannier instead of saddle tanks. Wheels were 4 ft 7½ in in diameter and cylinders 17½ in×24 in. Such parts did not fit into the standard range but with some 853 '5700' and derivative tank locomotives being constructed over the years, parts became standard.

A slightly smaller design, '5400', '6400' and '7400' classes of 0-6-0 pannier tanks commenced production in 1930 specifically for small branch and auto train working. Variations between the groups included boilers and cylinder diameter but all followed the same basic pattern. Particular advantage lay in their ability to negotiate curves down to 3½ chains radius. Although the pannier

tanks may have looked dated they were very reliable, covering all parts of the system on light passenger, freight and shunting duties.

Hawksworth updated the '5700' design in 1947 through his '9400' class, making use of the coned and domeless standard No. 10 boiler. In effect the design might be considered as the pannier version of Collett's '2251' class 0-6-0 tender engine which, in turn, developed from the '5700' class. Dean's '2301' goods engine had performed sterling service but by the mid-1930s heavier loads demanded a more powerful machine for secondary routes. Remaining 'Dean Goods' could then be released for working upon the very light absorbed lines. It seemed reasonable to modify the successful '5700' as a tender engine. Framing and motion were almost identical but the cylinder castings had to incorporate a saddle for supporting the drumhead type smokebox of the standard No. 10 boiler. Although intended for main and intermediate pick-up freight services, the '2251' engines also worked passenger trains on branch and country lines.

When Hawksworth developed his '9400' class the wheel had turned full circle, pannier to tender to pannier. That example illustrates the basic

Left *Pannier tank '5700' class No. 7752 as preserved at Tyseley* (Sarah Griffiths).

Below *Collett's 0-6-0 tender locomotive No. 3205, of the '2251' class.*

Above *Modified 'Hall' No. 6998,
Burton Agnes Hall, at Didcot* (Sarah
Griffiths).

Right *'County' class No. 1009,* County
of Carmarthen, *at Shrewsbury on 26
August 1962* (D. K. Jones Collection).

evolutionary nature of many GWR locomotive
designs. Although Collett, and even Hawksworth,
have been criticized for their designs it would have
been excessively wasteful not to make use of
successful patterns already existing. Churchward
set the style of standardization and his successors
attempted to work within it. Not to have done so
would have been the height of foolishness. In many
respects working with standard parts imposed
greater restrictions than defining those standard
items in the first place.

Departures from a standardized component
system were natural, if not essential, in producing
locomotives to meet changing demand. It was not
only demand which influence design but also
outside factors such as fuel, developments in
construction techniques and maintenance patterns.
Hawksworth had the final say in Great Western
locomotive design but, as already mentioned, one
of his schemes, the 'Pacific', failed to materilize
because of wartime restraint. Second best as far as
Hawksworth was concerned turned out to be his
'County' class.

A two-cylinder express passenger design appears
to have been out of keeping with multi-cylinder
trends, especially as the 'Castles' and 'Kings' could
meet all requirements. Features such as the bolt-on
outside cylinders and plate bogies had been
introduced with the 'Modified Halls', but the 280
psi pressure high superheat boiler was a complete
change. The boiler pressure and 6 ft 3 in coupled
wheels gave the 'Counties' a tractive effort nearly
1,000 lb greater than that of the 'Castles', but there
was a price. Being a two-cylinder design, hammer
blow was excessive and that severely limited route
availability. In fairness to the designer it should be
added that his machines cost less than a 'Castle' or
'King' and were easier to maintain. The fact that
later BR standard 'Pacifics utilized a two-cylinder
arrangement for the same reasons indicates that
Hawksworth had foresight.

Austerity and the need for maintenance accessibility could be observed in another of Hawksworth's designs, his '1500' class pannier tanks
needed for carriage shunting duties around Paddington and in freight yards. Outside cylinders

Left *'1500' class with outside Wals-chaerts valve gear, No. 1508 at Padding-ton on 24 March 1961* (D. K. Jones Collection).

Below *Proposed Collett design for a 2-10-2 tank locomotive.*

with outside Walschaert valve gear allowed easy access to the motion without resort to a pit. Absence of an unnecessary platform above the wheels and extensive use of welding provided a glimpse of future design possibilities.

Had nationalization not intervened and had Hawksworth remained in command at Swindon it is probable that GWR locomotive development would have progressed along the lines eventually adopted for the BR standard classes. Hawksworth appears to have been very much in tune with developments. Plans were drawn up not only for a 'Pacific' but also for a lightweight 4-4-0 and 2-6-0 pannier tank, both of which showed slightly inclined cylinders and rather austere lines. There

were also alternative arrangements for the 'Coun-ty' class using outside valve gear and different boilers. Other interesting propositions included the fitting of a 'Hall' with an LMS class '8F' boiler and the use of a Southern Railway 'Merchant Navy' class boiler on a 'King'. It is unlikely that Churchward would have been amused. Even Collett had speculated as to future trends but had rejected many schemes including enlarged 'Saint', 'Star' and '2800' together with the 'Compound Castle'. One plan which almost reached fruition was the 2-10-2 tank in 1937-8. Intended for Ebbw Vale iron ore traffic, at 41,465 lb tractive effort it would have been the heaviest and most powerful tank engine in Britain.

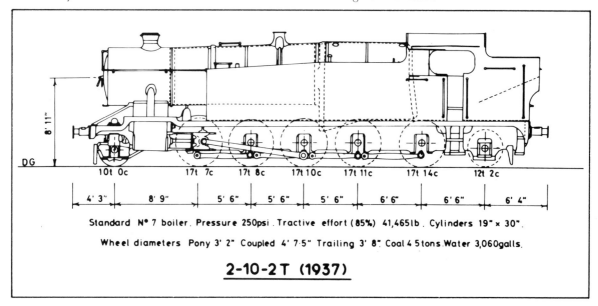

Standard Nº 7 boiler. Pressure 250psi. Tractive effort (85%) 41,465lb. Cylinders 19" x 30".

Wheel diameters Pony 3' 2" Coupled 4' 7·5" Trailing 3' 8". Coal 4·5 tons. Water 3,060 galls.

2-10-2 T (1937)

8. Testing and innovation

Locomotive and train testing was a forte of the Great Western Railway from its early years; in fact, testing was forced upon the Company due to animosity regarding the gauge. Charles Babbage, that eminent man of science, was called upon by the directors to offer his opinion regarding the line but he felt uneasy about speaking without making certain experiments. The directors lent him a second class carriage in which to set up his equipment that, in effect, became the first true dynamometer car. Babbage used the carriage framework as support for a long table which was independent of all carriage motion. Along the table slowly rolled a sheet of paper, about 1,000 ft long, and several pens were used to trace lines upon the paper. These lines represented traction force as well as carriage motion, vertically and horizontally, at the carriage ends and middle. A chronometer also marked the paper every half second.[1] It was possible to regulate the paper speed to suit conditions, particularly where measurement of the effect of rail junctions on carriage movement was required. Under such circumstances the paper would travel at up to 60 ft per mile, whilst for normal running the paper speed would be only inches per mile.[2]

After early problems with the pens and clock the machinery functioned well and many valuable sets of data were obtained. In 1839, following his experiments, Babbage reported his findings regarding the track to the directors and also presumed to offer advice upon the adoption of means for obtaining regular readings of tractive power and carriage movements on all trains. With the growth of rail operations that was not a real possibility as it would have involved a permanently connected dynamometer car. Babbage was sceptical that such a plan would ever be adopted but, later in life, he still fervently believed in regular testing of track and locomotive.

> I have a very strong opinion that the adoption of such mechanical registrations would add greatly to the security of railway travelling. . . .I have, however, little expectation of their adoption unless Directors can be convinced that the knowledge derived from them would, by pointing out incipient defects, and by acting as a check upon the vigilance of all their officers, considerably diminish the repairs and working expenses of both the engine and the rail.[3]

Though these opinions generally fell on deaf ears, one man was listening and prepared to act. Daniel Gooch, himself very tied up in the gauge war, saw merit in the proposals and, at a later date, set about devising a scientific means of train testing. There can be little doubt that Babbage's work influenced Gooch but it was his own determination and ability which got the work done. His dynamometer car also registered results on a single roll of paper which traversed a table within the car. Tractive force was measured by means of a spring 7 ft 6 in long containing five plates kept $\frac{1}{2}$ in apart by rollers. Oil-filled damping cylinders were provided between the spring and pencil in order to smooth out any vibration but Gooch rarely used them for fear that the accuracy of his results might be doubted. A measuring wheel, in contact with the track, caused the paper to be moved and marked every $\frac{1}{16}$ mile, a clock making marks every $\frac{1}{5}$ second. A wind gauge 5 ft above the carriage roof allowed wind speed and direction to be monitored and recorded.[4] In all matters Gooch was meticulous and took great pains to avoid any of his results being brought into question.

The engine itself needed to be monitored and Gooch again designed his own steam indicator. The device consisted of a piston operating within a cylinder which was allowed steam contact with the engine cylinders by means of a valve. That piston was connected to a double elliptical spring and, via a lever, moved a pencil. A system of rollers driven by a pulley from the engine axle caused a roll of paper to be drawn across a table. As the paper moved the indicator pencil scribed a line directly related to the cylinder pressure, other pencils marking the atmospheric pressure and cylinder half strokes. Knowing the strength of the indicator spring, the actual cylinder pressure could be determined. The piston stroke was divided into twenty-four parts in order to allow the production of conventional indicator diagrams from the paper roll.[5]

The indicator was a piece of ingenious design and precision manufacture, producing the most accurate locomotive power measurements which had then been obtained. What makes the results even more amazing is that the operator, Gooch himself, had to sit exposed at the front of a speeding locomotive, nobody having thought of the protection hut used for later GWR road testing. 'The difficulty in taking steam cards at 60 miles per hour will be readily understood when it is considered that it is necessary to sit on the front buffer beam of an engine, and in this windy position take four sets of cards in three quarters of a minute.[6]

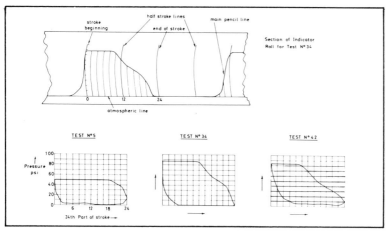

Left *Gooch's indicator.*

Below left *Section of indicator roll and resultant diagrams.*

Above right *Gooch's dynamometer car test results of train resistances at different speeds.*

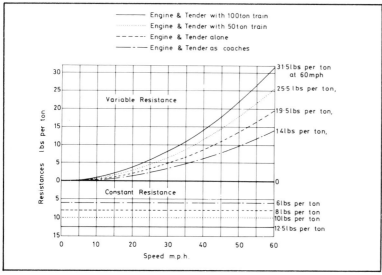

Left *Gooch's final graphs showing the relationship between resistances and speed for locomotive and train.*

Right *The inside of Churchward's dynamometer car during Collett's regime.*

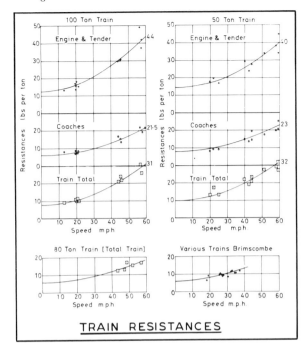

TRAIN RESISTANCES

Following a series of very rigorous tests Gooch presented a paper, entitled 'On the Resistance of Trains at Different Velocities', to the Institution of Civil Engineers. The paper was presented during the evening of 18 April 1848 and such was the interest that the discussion lasted several evenings. Following a description of the dynamometer car and indicator Gooch went on to detail the tests carried out and results obtained. On level track and with loads of 100 tons and 50 tons a number of runs were made at different speeds, the power developed by the locomotive and tractive effort being measured in each case. Further runs were made with an 80-ton train and also on the Brimscombe incline. Graphs of resistance against speed were plotted for the engine and tender, the coaches and the total train.

Gooch reasoned that there would be constant resistances which had to be overcome just to get the train in motion, and variable resistences due to motion. He also considered that the engine and tender resistances could be divided into that of the machinery itself and that due to the wheels and windage, *i.e.* engine and tender as coaches. Nobody to that date had actually considered a train in such detail and Gooch was forced to derive his own equations for determining the resistance in each case.[7] The paper was not, unfortunately, published but a detailed account of the experiments, results and derivation of equations is given in Clark's *Railway Machinery*. It is unnecessary to give further details here save to say that the final graphs allowed Gooch to analyze power requirements for different loads and speeds. They also allowed consideration of the aspects contributing most to train resistance.

Gooch had set the pace in train testing and his approach provided the basis for future developments, but major changes in train testing were a long time coming. Even then thorough analytical testing of the locomotive's thermodynamic performance was not attempted.

In 1901 Churchward decided that a modern dynamometer car was required and had the construction authorized by Dean who was still nominally in control. The new vehicle weighed 27 tons and was carried upon two four-wheeled bogies. As with the Gooch car a special spring was used to measure the draw-bar pull. This consisted of a number of tempered steel plates separated by rollers in order to eliminate friction. The paper roll was moved across its table at a rate of 1 or 2 ft per mile traversed. Again the paper drive was similar to the method employed by Gooch in that a flangeless wheel was allowed to contact the rail and that, via a gear arrangement, turned the rollers.

Train speed and time intervals were recorded and an electric bell connection with the footplate allowed the point of any regulator, cut-off or boiler pressure change to be noted. Mileposts and stations could also be noted by an observer at a car window. A mechanical 'integrator' allowed the work done on the draw-bar to be recorded.[8] Apart from its refinements the car followed closely the format laid down by Gooch.

Churchward made extensive use of the dynamometer car, testing his new designs and laying down performance characteristics for each type. The testing programme aimed to gather information which could be used for the serious purpose of assessing the merits, or otherwise, of particular combinations of parts.

For each class tested a 'Characteristic Curve' would be produced with cut-off graphs being superimposed upon the hp graphs. Using the set of 'Characteristic Curves' for different classes having the same size of cylinders, a 'Traction Chart' could be drawn. From that chart, which was based upon empirical formulae, it was possible to predict the performance of an engine with a particular cylinder size, whatever the boiler pressure or driving wheel diameter. With a chart for each desired cylinder size Churchward had, in effect, obtained a valuable design tool for his standardization programme.

The draw-bar pull could be calculated under a variety of conditions from an empirical formula using the chart, the equation being:

$$\text{Pull (tons)} = \frac{\text{Boiler Press' (psi)} \times \text{Traction Factor}}{\text{Driving wheel diameter (in)}} \times \text{constant}$$

The constant was the traction force coefficient which for cylinders of 14¼ in diameter and 26 in stroke was 0.04714.

Given driving wheels of 5 ft 10 in (70 in), boiler pressure 180 psi, cut-off 15% and speed 50 mph, the chart could be used as follows: The horizontal line opposite 70 in is followed until it intersects the 50 mph curve and that point is followed downwards until it cuts the 15% cut-off line. That intersection is followed horizontally until the table of 'Traction Factors' is reached which, in this example, is at 15. Inserting the values in the equation gives a draw-bar pull requirement of 1.8 tons.[9]

Testing continued over many years until a complete set of charts had been produced. Such a set of charts became invaluable during later years, allowing combinations of standardized parts such as cylinders, boilers and wheels to be checked with 'paper' engines before any serious design work was undertaken. Churchward's legacy was not just in

his machines but also in the information he provided.

He was not, however, interested in publishing the results of such tests as the data obtained were intended for use at Swindon in order to perfect performance and provide information for future machine designs. It was not until Collett presented his paper, 'Testing Locomotives on the Great Western Railway', to the World Power Conference in 1924 that some of the information became readily available. Why Churchward kept the results a virtual secret is difficult to imagine, particularly as they showed his locomotives to be better than most then in service. One reason may have been a suspicion that his dynamometer car was defective. In was in 1914.

At that time few dynamometer cars were available and loans would be arranged. Shortly before World War I Nigel Gresley, CME of the Great Northern Railway, borrowed the GWR car and that belonging to the North Eastern Railway in order to carry out rolling stock tests. He adopted the same procedure some years later for testing his 50-ton bogie brick wagons, one dynamometer car being positioned next to the engine and the other in the middle of the train.[10] The reasons for, and effectiveness of, such an arrangement fall outside this work; what is important is that Gresley found

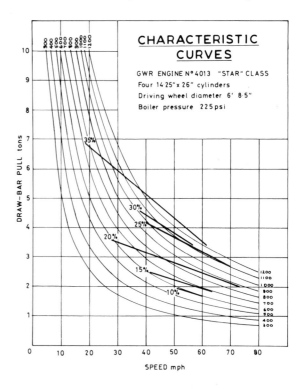

CHARACTERISTIC CURVES

GWR ENGINE Nº 4013 "STAR" CLASS
Four 14 25"x 26" cylinders
Driving wheel diameter 6' 8·5"
Boiler pressure 225 psi

Below left *Characteristic curves for 'Star' class locomotive No. 4013.*

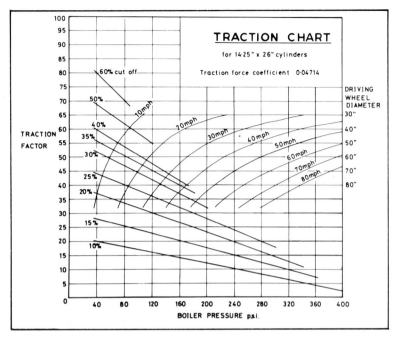

Right *Traction chart for 14¼ in × 26 in cylinders.*

differences in the cars. Vincent Raven of the North Eastern Railway asked Gresley to check both cars and he found that although both showed errors, that belonging to the Great Western had most defects. The distance recorder was 2¾ yd/mile in error, whilst main spring and integrator produced defective results.[11] Churchward's 'Traction Charts' will still have been valid although slightly in error if the dynamometer car was defective during those earlier tests.

Collett improved the dynamometer car by fitting additional apparatus, allowing more information to be gathered during any particular test. This included temperatures in smokebox, superheater and feed water as well as smokebox gas analysis by means of Orsat apparatus. Gas composition was analyzed at the instigation of the operator in the dynamometer car who would signal to the footplate for the gas cock to be opened. An electric bell sufficed for the purpose and two gas sampling points would be tested on each occasion, one near the superheater tubes and the other at the bottom row of flue tubes. Coal composition, including calorific value, together with the composition of ashes in the smokebox and ashpan were determined following the trial. A temporary wooden shelter was constructed around the front of the locomotive in order to afford protection for those engaged in the taking of cylinder indicator diagrams. Clearly things had improved since the days of Daniel Gooch. Indicator diagrams were

obtained from all cylinders at predetermined positions during a run and at the same time temperatures in the smokebox and superheater would be taken.[12]

Though locomotive testing continued throughout the Collett era it is for one set of tests he is particularly well known. *Caldicot Castle* was the subject of the tests and the results were presented by what must have been a rather smug Chief Mechanical Engineer to the delegates at the World Power Conference in 1924. On three occasions during March of that year the 'Castle' hauled its train from Swindon to Plymouth, returning the next day. Eight-wheeled 70 ft coaches were used, the load varying at different points on the journey from a maximum of fourteen plus dynamometer car to a minimum of eight plus the car. In order that the tender might hold sufficient fuel for a run to Plymouth and back the coal space was temporarily increased by adding 1 ft to its height. Comprehensive data sets were takien throughout the runs with emphasis being on fuel, water and lubricating oil consumption as well as on power developed.

During the tests conducted on 19 and 20 March 1924 *Caldicot Castle* consumed coal at the rate of 2.83 lb per draw-bar horse power,[13] a staggeringly low figure compared with the 4 lb or so which was the best that most machines away from the GWR could accomplish. During 1908 Churchward had attained a remarkably low 3½ lb with his 'Star' class *Knight of St. Patrick* but had not published the fact, possibly disbelieving the value.[14] In view of the dynamometer car errors discovered by Gresley the value may have been in error. Though Collett's figure was based upon the average of a number of runs and with a relatively new engine, it was exceptional for the day and became the benchmark for all other locomotives. Other test values indicated a boiler thermal efficiency of 79.8% and overall thermal efficiency of 8.22%,[15] both of which compared more than favourably with the best which could be achieved on other railways. Clearly Collett had designed a very good express locomotive.

A point often raised in an attempt to limit credit for this notable performance is that only selected good quality Welsh steam coal was employed for the test runs. GWR fireboxes were designed to burn Welsh coal and to select other than best grades and correct size of lumps would have been foolish in the extreme. Even accounting for the use of better quality coal the results obtained were superior to anything considered possible with steam traction. The results also indicate the thoroughness with which the tests were carried out and the level of skill and performance achieved by the test team. GWR locomotive testing at that time was certainly ahead of the rest.

The same dynamometer car was employed by Hawksworth and remained in use with but minor modification until the mid-1950s. Road testing progressed over the years but the main precepts laid down by Churchward and Collett remained in force. However, testing on the road did introduce certain problems regarding weather and gradients which could influence results related to locomotive efficiency. Churchward was well aware of the difficulties and sought ways of minimizing the problem. American locomotive practice greatly influenced him during his early years in the CME's chair and the work carried out by Professor Goss at Purdue University provided an answer. The stationary locomotive test plant at that establishment fitted the bill and Churchward decided that the GWR should have one of its own.

Following the Purdue pattern Churchward designed a test plant to suit what he considered to be the GWR's needs. The plant was built in 'A' shop at Swindon Works and came into use during 1904. A bed of cast iron was bolted onto a concrete foundation with timber baulks being interposed to lessen vibration. Upon the bed were five pairs of bearings which could be moved longitudinally in order to suit the wheel centres of any locomotive placed on the plant up to and including a maximum of ten wheels. The bearing axles were provided with wheel sets upon which the wheels of the locomotive would run, tyres on the wheel sets being profiled in a similar way to the GWR rail section. Axles were also provided with brake drums upon which hydraulically operated brake bands could act in order to absorb some of the generated power and so regulate speed. Outside the brake bands on each side of the plant were broad pulley wheels. These allowed all axles to connect by means of a long continuous belt, tension being maintained by jockey wheels. Such an arrangement ensured that all wheels would be turned even when the locomotive had only a single pair of driving wheels.

That facility was considered to be important as Churchward wished to use the machine for running in new or recently overhauled locomotives, thereby avoiding disruption on the main running line should any defect occur. The name 'home trainer' soon attached itself to the machine but little use seems to have been made of it for running in.

The locomotive to be tested would be run onto the test plant table, its wheel flanges bearing in grooves on that table. When the locomotive was positioned the axle bearings would be adjusted so that the running wheel centres matched the locomotive wheel centres and the bearings were then locked. By means of an electrically operated lay shaft the rail jacks lowered the table, thereby bringing the locomotive wheels into contact with the test plant wheels. The rear of the locomotive was connected to the draw-bar mechanism and the headstock stop screws tightened. That prevented fore and after oscillations, due to unbalanced reciprocating masses, whilst the locomotive was running. A movable chimney could be positioned to suit any locomotive and the firing platform could also be adjusted for the same reason.

In order not to waste all the energy developed on the plant an air compressor was driven through a shaft extension and belt arrangement. Air could be supplied to the works system. The hydraulically tightened brake straps were not very effective and the draw-bar gear could only absorb some 500 hp.[16] That gear was, in fact, relatively weak and during the early years of testing it actually broke once, causing the locomotive under test to propel itself through the shed doors. Subsequent testing was usually carried out with a tank engine, brakes fully on, positioned in front of the engine undergoing testing.[17]

Whilst the test plant was sufficient for the locomotives existing at the beginning of Churchward's term of office, it did not suit those locomotives he developed over the succeeding

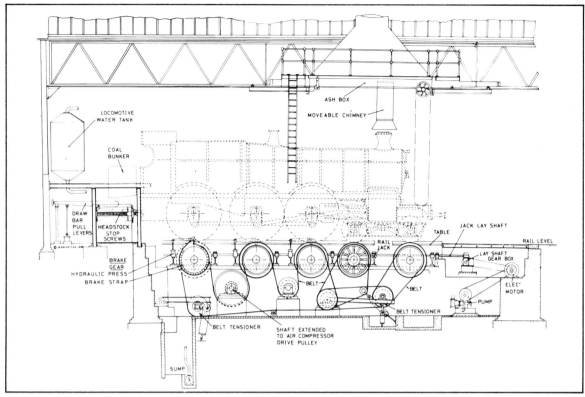

Diagram of the Swindon Test Plant showing the system of pulleys connecting all wheels.

years. Not surprisingly, it quickly fell out of favour for testing and was not much more effective for running in. It is difficult to understand why Churchward did not design the plant for greater power and even more difficult to imagine why he did not upgrade the plant when his own locomotives far outstripped its capabilities. Churchward initially expressed high hopes for the plant.

It is hoped that this plant will enable many questions of the relative economy of different classes of engine, either simple or compound, to be settled definitely. The question of superheating and the efficiency of various forms of smokebox arrangements might be investigated on it. The effect of various percentages of balancing can be investigated, and, in fact, any of the experiments which are at present being made on the road may be made on this plant, with the great advantage that any engine which may be selected can be placed in position ready for testing, and all connections made in a time probably not exceeding an hour.[18]

Maybe the novelty of the 'toy' just wore off after a while, or maybe the high scientific hopes were just

for public consumption as, in December 1905, *The Engineer* felt confident enough to report, 'The principal use of the apparatus is to run engines to get all the bearings right, and at this work it is very fully employed.' Original plans for 'A' shop made in August 1900 show provision for no less than four test plants, probably for the testing of locomotives with different wheel arrangements.[19] With the 'universal' plant later installed there would have been no need for so many but, in 1905, the intention was still to install two further test plants at Swindon, space having been provided for the purpose.[20] The fact that plans were made during 1900 indicates that Dean must have had some say, but the enthusiasm of Churchward for American practice would appear to have been the driving force.

Clearly, Churchward changed his mind as to the benefits of a stationary test plant, but the reasoning will never be known. Later engineers such as Collett, Stanier and Gresley found considerable merit in such plants but the one which Churchward designed does not appear to have been capable of any really useful work. Its inability to deal with the higher powered locomotives was a serious drawback and one which Collett amended admirably. But why didn't Churchward attend to the problem? After all, he was the designer. Road testing with the dynamometer car provided valuable data regarding train running, but thermodynamic performance of the locomotive, engine and boiler could be better assessed on a stationary plant. As a locomotive designer Churchward should have been enthusiastic about thorough testing of his machines both indoors and out.

During the early years of the 1930s Stanier and Gresley developed plans for the construction of a joint high powered stationary testing plant, hoping that the GWR would also take part. However, Collett was already making arrangements of his own. He had a senior draughtsman, C.T. Roberts, investigate the operation of trains on the fastest schedules from Paddington to Exeter and Birmingham. Roberts reached the conclusion that a constant boiler evaporation rate would meet all the requirements for a complete run rather than the desire to maintain point-to-point timings. It was agreed that future locomotive testing would be based upon constant evaporative rate, thus removing one of the variables from any test. Approval was given for the stationary test plant at Swindon to be modernized in order to deal with the recent higher powered locomotives. Removal of the belt-driven compressor and an upgrading of the roller braking system were necessary parts of that modernization, but an essential feature was renewal of the draw-bar lever arrangement to raise the pull capacity above 2,000 hp.

By the time an approach from Stanier and Gresley came, work was well advanced and representatives from the LMS and LNER were invited to Swindon in order to view the test plant. They were, however, given no indication of any changes. Instead of the 500 hp 'home trainer', the visitors saw a thoroughly modern piece of apparatus in operation with *Arlington Court* belting away at a road speed of 70 mph and developing in the region of 1,200 hp.[21] Upon being informed that the plant could absorb at least 2,000 hp, the visitors from the north realized that there was no chance of the GWR participating in their scheme. Collett appears to have taken great delight in dropping bombshells.

It has often been said, usually in a derogatory manner, that Collett was a works man and not a locomotive designer. The statement has a great deal of substance and a works man was desperately required at Swindon. Locomotives not only have to perform well, they must also be capable of running for prolonged periods without much maintenance. Collett provided that facility through good production practice, the introduction of optical alignment being a major weapon in his arsenal.

A locomotive comprises many axles, pins and bushes, each of which must be fitted correctly in relation to its mating parts and the engine framing. The smaller the initial tolerance on mating parts, the less rapidly will wear take place and the greater will be the interval between overhauls. That simple fact was obvious to everybody connected with locomotive construction but the problem lay in obtaining close tolerances. Alignment of cylinder

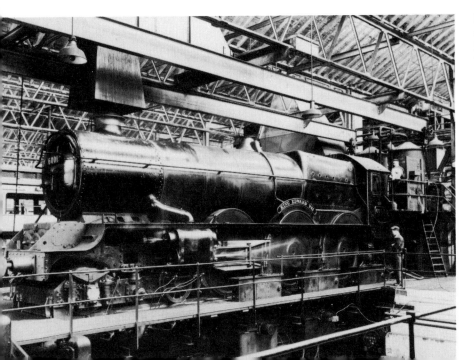

Left King Edward VII *running on the Swindon test plant as modified by Collett* (courtesy National Railway Museum, York).

Right *Diagram of the Zeiss Optical Alignment system.*

centres with the hornblocks, which carry the axle bearings, was critical and traditionally carried out using piano wire, calipers and rule. Subsequent chipping or hand grinding in order to get the hornblocks correctly positioned was time-consuming and open to errors. Overall the system was inaccurate and resulted in considerable differences between locomotives leaving the works. Some were very well set up whilst others could barely last out until the next overhaul.

In 1933 Collett discovered that the German firm Carl Zeiss had developed an optical system for locomotive alignment. Following investigation it was decided to purchase the equipment for use in setting up new locomotives as well as for assessing the condition of locomotives brought in for repair and overhaul. The manufacturers had to be supplied with dimensions of all locomotives in the standard range in order that necessary length bars could be provided.

A telescope held within a tube was set up in one of the cylinders, a self-centring spider being provided on the tube for that purpose. The front of the tube had a zero datum surface for measuring and spirit levels ensured that vertical and horizontal axes were correct. The width across each pair of horns had to be measured using a vernier and a sighting scale would be placed against each driving horn in turn and read through the telescope. That distance plus half the width across the horns gave the distance of the cylinder centre to the theoretical engine centre line. If the distances either side of the engine were not the same then the cylinder axis was not parallel to the centre line of the engine.

Some tolerance would be allowed and the telescope realigned to account for that if it was within acceptable limits.

With the telescope set parallel to the theoretical centre line of the engine the sighting scale would be removed and a collimator clamped to the end of a tube so that it was exactly at right angles to the tube. Using an adjustable stand the tube was then moved until the telescope cross lines cut the illuminated collimator wires, thereby indicating that the collimator and telescope were parallel. As the collimator would be at right angles to the tube, the tube must be at right angles to the cylinder axis. Using a dial gauge between the tube and horn cheeks it was possible to check that the horn sets, and hence the axles, were themselves at right angles to the cylinders. A length gauge between datum surface at the telescope and gauge point on the tube gave the distance from the cylinder face to the centre of the axle. Similar measurements between locating studs allowed all other horns to be checked, with the actual centre line being obtained by means of a straight edge across the frames at a set distance from the locating studs. A dial gauge measured the distance from straight edge to horn cheeks.[22]

Optical alignment was just one stage in the process, accurate machining of the horn blocks being essential for correct assembly. To that end Collett searched for an effective grinding machine which would suit the Swindon design of locomotives. There was in existence a German machine and another produced by the Churchill Machine Tool Company, but neither suited entirely. In the

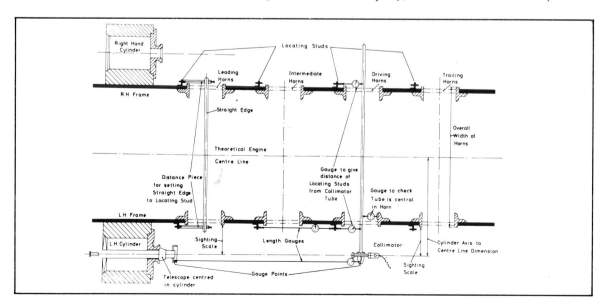

end a special grinding machine was designed by James Say, a freelance consultant. That device, constructed by H. Broadbent of Sowerby Bridge, had a grinding wheel mounted on a long arm, enabling both horn blocks to be ground without moving the machine. The purchase of a second machine with a shorter arm, and the use of a shorter arm on the original machine, allowed both to work simultaneously on opposite frames, thereby reducing machining time.[23]

Collett was delighted with the result and the system became standard practice for all locomotives. Alignment became so good that the motion clanking which characterized locomotives on other railways was eliminated. Although boiler condition generally dictated the interval between major overhauls, attention to the motion would usually be required at intermediate repairs. That might be at 60,000-mile intervals for a locomotive aligned in the traditional manner, but experience with the first batch of 'Castles' built using the optical technique allowed a doubling of the mileage. Even then sideplay at the trailing end was not particularly bad. Some Swindon hands denigrated the engineering prowess of those elsewhere, commenting that the GWR scrapped locomotives which had clearances the others started with. Whilst that may not have been completely true, it was getting close.

Optical alignment and setting up allowed repair time to be reduced and operating intervals to be extended, and it reduced the wear on other engine components due to the initial accuracy of assembly. The Great Western locomotive became 'A Machine of Precision', restoring the supremacy given by Churchward. If Collett did nothing else during his term of office, he turned locomotive manufacture from a craft into a skilled science and in doing so probably prolonged the steam locomotive's operating life on the railways of Britain.

A later development by Hawksworth was also an attempt to extend the operating capabilities of steam traction when events tended to conspire against its use. That was in the introduction of oil firing, the reason for and demise of which have already been mentioned in chapter 3. Initially, oil firing was authorized for ten '2800' class and eight '4200' class freight locomotives, all working in the South Wales area. Conversion basically centred around the firebox and tender, the cylinders being unaffected. Instead of a coal bunker, the tender was provided with a 1,800-gal fuel tank and a filling pipe with connections so that the tank could be filled from either side. Fuel oil was of the 'heavy' or bunker grade which required heating in order to reduce its viscosity so that it flowed from the tank to the engine. Steam heating coils were provided for the purpose, the steam supply valve being on a manifold in the cab.

The firebox grate was replaced by a plate firepan containing air supply openings, air regulation being by means of a firepan damper door. Firebox floor and lower part were lined with high alumina firebricks due to the changed nature of combustion. At the front of the firepan was the single burner designed to project the combustion flame towards the back of the firebox and slightly upwards. Steam atomization was used, and the original design of

Oil firing arrangements for a '2800' class locomotive.

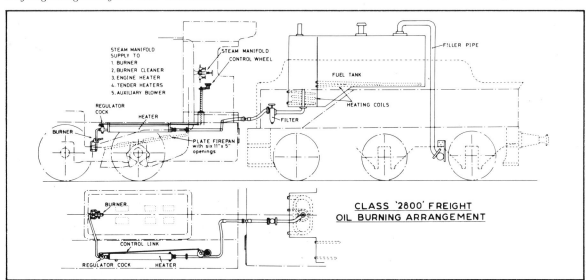

burner had hot oil flowing over a weir into a steam jet which broke the oil into fine particles and formed a spray pattern. Correct regulation of oil and air flow produced effective combustion and maintained steam.

Oil fuelling depots were established at Llanelly and Severn Tunnel Junction, the converted machines being confined to operations west of the Severn Tunnel. The limited experiment, carried out during the winter of 1945-6 in conjunction with the Anglo-Iranian Oil Company, was a complete success with an estimated coal saving for the eighteen engines of about 13,000 tons.[24].

Certain problems, including poor combustion at high evaporation rates, did occur with the burners and these were soon replaced by Laidlaw-Drew type which provided for better atomization and produced a swirling action in the spray. It was also found that daily removal and cleaning of the atomizers was essential in order to maintain their effectiveness. The fireman, however, still had a less arduous task than with a coal-burning locomotive. Apart from minor problems conversion was a success and, later in 1946, plans were made to convert a number of 'Castle' and 'Hall' class locomotives for work in Cornwall. That work was also highly successful and it seemd that Hawksworth had a winning idea, at least as far as the GWR was concerned. Unfortunately, 'Whitehall Wizards' in the Ministry of Fuel and Power came to hear of the scheme and considered it a suitable one for interference. Had it not been for the lack of foreign exchange to purchase oil, extension of oil firing to other railways might have been beneficial. However, had there been sufficient foreign exchange available there would have been no need to export good steam coal.

Hawksworth was requested to supply information to the other railways and that he did, but the obvious dawned on those in power before any real progress had been made and the general conversion plan quickly came to a halt. It is interesting to speculate what the development of steam traction would have been in Britain if the oil experiment had been allowed to continue. Oil firing was easier on the fireman, less labour was required for fuelling and no labour was needed for ash removal as there wasn't any. Depots would certainly have been cleaner, fuel transportation costs lower and, in the days of relatively inexpensive oil which existed until the 1970s, operation more economical. Hawksworth had a good idea but circumstances worked against it.

Some good ideas do, however, come to fruition and play an important part in general railway development; others remain fairly localized but are nonetheless extremely important. In many respects the Great Western went its own way, developing ideas to suit its own needs, not those of other concerns. Train braking was one such field. In the early days locomotive brakes had been notoriously weak and Brunel's comment on the effectiveness of the brakes used on the original GWR locomotives, 'tolerably useless', typifies the early attitude.

Brakes did, fortunately, improve on locomotives but as longer and heavier trains came into use a more effective system was required. The Sanders-Bolitho system for continuous braking found favour with many companies and, in 1876, Joseph Armstrong arranged for a trial. He died before it was completed but his successor, William Dean, though generally satisfied with the system, considered improvements to be possible. In 1880 he instructed 'Young Joe' Armstrong to develop a better arrangement for the GWR. With the assistance of Churchward 'Young Joe' did just that and provided a system which was effective and efficient.

Each carriage was provided with a brake cylinder which had the unusual arrangement of a fixed piston and moving cylinder. Trunnions connected the piston rod to the carriage frame and the cylinder moved the brake shaft arms, thereby operating the brakes. The space below the piston would always be maintained at high vacuum and when the space above the piston was evacuated the

'2800' class No. 4809, formerly No. 2845, operating with oil firing at Ilmer Halt on 25 September 1948 (J. Russell-Smith Collection/NRM, York).

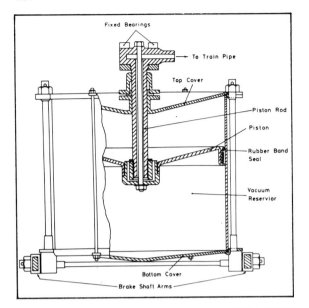

cylinder weight would force it downward, keeping the brakes off. In applying the brakes air would be allowed into the train pipe and hence the space above the piston, thus forcing the cylinder upwards. Any air which leaked into the space below the piston was removed whenever the brake pipe was evacuated as the piston rubber band seal acted like a non-return valve.

The vacuum formation mechanism constitutes an essential part of any brake system and 'Young Joe' again showed his genius by combining, in a single unit, a valve supplying steam to the locomotive brake, the air/vacuum valve to the train pipe and the air ejector. With but minor modifications that arrangement continued to be fitted to many GWR locomotives until the end of steam. A steam-operated air ejector is very effective at raising and maintaining a vacuum but the GWR system called for a relatively high vacuum of 25 in of mercury. The maintenance of a vacuum does not require as much energy as the raising of one and so a smaller air ejector might be used for that purpose. However, such a device consumes a fair quantity of steam and its effectiveness reduces if boiler steam pressure falls. Poor steaming could, therefore, increase the engine workload as brakes might creep on. The Armstrong-Churchward team overcame that problem by the provision of a vacuum pump driven from a cylinder crosshead. The double-acting pump consumed less energy than a small ejector and had no difficulty in maintaining a high vacuum whenever the locomotive moved. It was a triumph of ingenuity and, again with but minor alterations, remained in GWR service until the end of steam.[25] One such later modification was the provision of a relief valve in order to limit the vacuum to 25 in of mercury.

Armstrong cylinder design remained in force until 1903 when a more conventional arrangement was introduced. That had a fixed cylinder and moving piston connected to the brake rod. With a vacuum in the cylinder reservoir above the piston

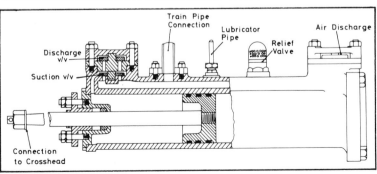

Top left *The Armstrong/Churchward brake cylinder.*

Above left *Vacuum pump drive arrangement on a 'Manor' (Sarah Griffiths).*

Left *Double-acting crosshead-driven vacuum pump.*

Right *Churchward brake cylinder arrangement with direct admission valves.*

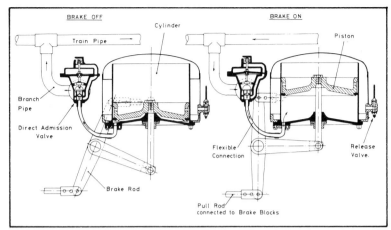

Below right *Diagram of Instanter type coupling showing long and short connections.*

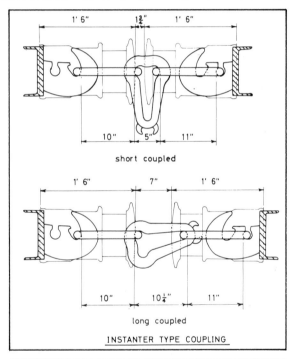

Bottom right *Instanter coupling.*

and the space below evacuated, the weight of the components kept the brake off. In order to provide for rapid release of brakes should the need arise, a release valve was fitted to each cylinder. That valve could be opened remotely, thereby allowing air into the space above the piston and forcing it downward. Other railways employed a vacuum of 23 in of mercury and when GWR coaching stock moved onto lines where it would be pulled by different locomotives, it was frequently the case that all brakes had to be released prior to starting under reduced vacuum conditions.

Fitted freight trains were introduced to the GWR during 1905, vacuum brakes being fitted to all wagons if less than thirty-five were used or to at least that number if the train consisted of more than thirty-five wagons. With such long trains evacuation of the train pipe took considerable effort, whilst brakes would only be applied slowly. There was no particular problem with freight trains but for the safety of passenger trains rapid application of brakes was required. Churchward arranged for a modification to the system through the introduction of a direct admission valve fitted between each brake cylinder and the train pipe. Any reduction in train pipe vacuum, due to the introduction of air as the brake was applied, caused the diaphragm to lift because of increased pressure below. That in turn lifted the atmospheric valve which allowed air to flow directly from the atmosphere into the brake cylinder.[26]

Vacuum-fitted wagons needed to be closely coupled so that pipe connections might be readily made and damage whilst working might be avoided. Screw couplings found favour with coaching stock which remained connected for long periods but it caused problems if applied to wagons which had to be shunted. The GWR developed a three-link instanter coupling which had a triangular centre section. Use in the long position was similar to loose coupling whilst the short connection would be the same as a screw coupling. A major advantage was to be seen when shunting as the shunter could couple up from the wagon side. Skill would be required; the wagons would first be long-coupled with an end link being thrown over a draw hook and then, with the wagons drawn together, the shunter would twist the centre link over to the short position using a pole engaged in the projecting hook. Later connection of vacuum pipes would be required but the whole operation was quicker than for screw coupling. That system remained in use on the GWR and was later adopted by the nationalized British Railways.[27]

Churchward appears to have been particularly interested in braking systems, no doubt influenced by his earlier work alongside 'Young Joe' Armstrong. During 1905 he took out two patents concerned with modifications to the system introduced during 1903. The first was in conjunction with Messrs Dumas, Rayer and Snell, probably all members of the Swindon team, whilst the second, for a local venting valve, was a solo effort. That 1903 arrangement, with its later improvements, eventually became the standard British Railways vacuum braking system.

Upon the introduction of the stationary test plant Churchward expressed the hope that it would enable smokebox design to be perfected. How much testing with that in mind actually went on is difficult to determine but GWR locomotive smokebox proportions certainly became larger than those which persisted elsewhere. The free running and good steaming of the Great Western engines is in part claimed to be due to their generous smokebox space.[28] A standard formula connecting blast pipe tip, chimney height and throat diameter was eventually derived, thus simplifying design calculations.

Experience with some two-cylinder engines engaged in heavy banking work showed that the sharp exhaust blast caused considerable disturbance to the fire when working with a cut-off exceeding 40%. Churchward's design team tried several ideas until the jumper top blast pipe showed itself to be very effective. Surrounding the main blast pipe was a jumper ring which, when the cut-off remained below 40%, stayed in its lower position, allowing the main blast pipe to exhaust the steam. At increased cut-off the steam pressure, acting on the jumper ring due to a number of radial holes just below the main orifice opening, caused it to lift. That lift increased the effective blast area and reduced the severity of the blast. Through a combination of blast pipe tip diameter and weight of jumper ring the whole range of locomotives could be catered for, thus keeping exhaust back pressure at a reasonably low value.[29]

Piston valves have a great advantage over slide valves and Churchward considered no other form suitable for modern locomotives. Effective sealing of piston valves operating at higher pressure was,

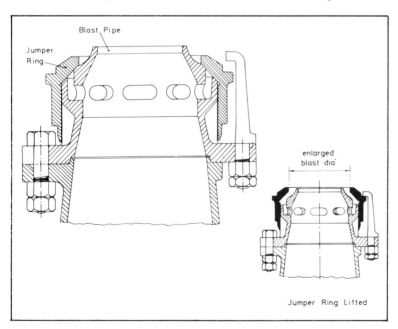

Left *Jumper ring blast pipe.*

Above right *Valve arrangements for long travel and inside steam.*

Right *Semi-plug piston valve.*

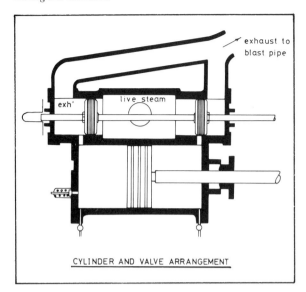

CYLINDER AND VALVE ARRANGEMENT

however, difficult with the technology which existed when he entered office. Wear of the valve chest due to rubbing by the piston valve rings resulted in leakage and a fall-off in efficiency. The broad piston valve rings which then existed were a problem. Ever on the look-out for good ideas, Churchward was attracted to an American-designed semi-plug piston valve. In fact he was so impressed that he purchase the rights of manufacture in Britain and obtained a trial pair of valves from America.

Serrated steam rings for maintaining steam tightness were forced into contact with the walls of the steam chest by steam pressure whenever the regulator was opened. A locking ring, also activated by steam pressure, held them there and the valve functioned with minimal leakage, due to the effectiveness of the rings. Closing the regulator reduced steam pressure in the chest, thus releasing the locking ring and allowing the steam rings to contract slightly and move away from the steam chest wall. Absence of contact during the free-wheeling periods considerably reduced valve chest wear. Initially all valve rings had to be scraped by hand but later precision manufacture removed the need for such hand finishing. The valves functioned perfectly and it was found that even with a steam chest wear of $\frac{1}{40}$ in they were still perfectly tight when the regulator was opened.[30]. Churchward set a wear limit of $\frac{1}{33}$ in at which the steam chest should be rebored. Later research showed that this value was ideal.[31]

It would be easy to form the opinion that nobody else connected with the Great Western Railway

was responsible for any new or reshaped ideas. That is far from the truth, but Churchward was extremely good at selecting schemes which possessed potential and which could be utilized effectively in modernizing the GWR locomotive fleet. It was not only the power and performance fields which were of interest: as might be seen from his involvement in brake development, Churchward had a passion for safety. Signalling played a vital part in train safety but came under the control of the Signals Engineer, not the CME. However, developments in that field were of considerable concern to the Locomotive Department and the Automatic Train Control system fell into that category.

Experiments with audible warning systems began during 1906 and Churchward encouraged development of the apparatus which was first introduced on the Fairford branch. Should a distant signal be clear a bell would ring in the cab, but if it was at danger a steam whistle would sound, thus allowing the driver time to take whatever action was necessary. By 1910 the system was in operation on all four lines between Reading and Paddington. Later developments brought about automatic control of the train braking sytem as well as giving an audible warning.

Ramps 40 ft long were placed between the rails at distant signals and a metal plate on the ramp could be electrified from the signal box. It would be 'live' if the distant was clear and 'dead' if the signal was at danger. Upon reaching the tamp a contact

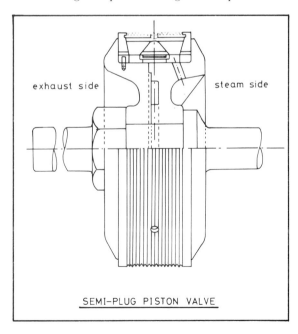

SEMI-PLUG PISTON VALVE

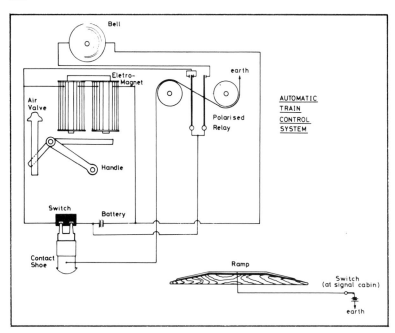

shoe beneath the locomotive was lifted, thereby opening the electrical circuit connected to the electromagnet. That electromagnet would be de-energized and open an air valve which allowed air into the train brake pipe. The driver would release the brakes by lifting the handle in order to bring the armature back into contact with the electro-magnet, which would re-energize once the locomotive had cleared the ramp. With that arrangement the brakes were applied whenever a distant signal was at danger.

If the distant was clear the ramp would be 'live' and the contact shoe would lift as before. However, current would be picked up from the ramp and energize the polarizing relay. (The electrical circuit was completed by the locomotive structure and rails back to the battery at the signal box.) A contact switch would be operated by the relay, forming a different circuit between battery and electromagnet; this ensured that the electromagnet remained energized and that the air valve was not opened.

A later modification introduced a separate bell circuit, also operated by the polarizing relay. If the distant signal was clear a bell would ring in the cab indicating that it was safe to proceed.[32] That arrangement was most useful during pierods of poor visibility.

By 1931 all Great Western main lines, and locomotives, had been provided with the equipment and it proved to be extremely safe and valuable. Following nationalization, however, a different system of automatic warning was adopted elsewhere, though many considered it to be inferior to that of the Great Western.

Broad gauge locomotives as developed by Gooch were generally superior to locomotives developed on other railways, but the 7 ft gauge was unique to the Great Western and the technology was not readily transferable. The broad gauge did, however, limit development during the Armstrong and, to a lesser extent, Dean eras. Joseph Armstrong had to contend with gauge conversion and he developed some magnificent 'convertible' locomotives which were a major challenge to his skill. That work has been described elsewhere in this book but it was a 'dead end' in design terms; apart from Dean, nobody else would make use of it. The fact that the works of Armstrong and Dean have not been given space in this chapter does not imply that they were neither imaginative nor innovative; they were, perhaps more so than many of their contemporary engineers.

The chapters on locomotives and carriages deal with aspects of Armstrong and Dean design work, it being left to the reader to decide what influence the two men had. A point worthy of consideration is that involving the limitations imposed on the men by the broad gauge. What indeed would their influence have been had not the creeping abolition of the 7 ft gauge absorbed much of their energy and time? Churchward had no such encumbrance, and look what he achieved.

9. Carriages and wagons

Just as with locomotives, Brunel had certain ideas appertaining to the coaching stock of the GWR, although manufacture lay in the hands of outside concerns. He considered that large diameter wheels would result in a slower rotational speed and thus minimize frictional losses. Present-day lubrication technology does not agree with the premise but, at that time, lack of effective lubricant control dictated matters. Large diameter wheels necessitated that the coach body be placed between them, and two types of four-wheeled vehicles were actually constructed to that form. One of these, a Posting Carriage, was the ultimate in comfort for railway travellers of the period. A detailed description is given in Whishaw's *The Railways of Great Britain and Ireland*, with the comment that only Royal Carriages exceeded the elegance of its furnishing. Eight india-rubber air bags were placed between carriage and steel frame in order to cushion any shocks from the extremely rigid 'baulk road'. Although the very height of luxury, these vehicles did not appear to be popular and were only used on specific occasions.[1]

The other form of vehicle in which the body rested between the wheels was the carriage truck, designed to convey an empty, or occupied, road carriage. Other vehicles had bodies which overhung the wheels and all were of the four-wheeled type. It quickly became obvious that four-wheeled carriages were incapable of operating safely at sustained high speeds and plans had to be laid for the production of six-wheeled versions. In fact, as early as August 1837 Brunel had submitted schemes for three-axled vehicles and later obtained approval for the alteration of some previously ordered four-wheeled carriages to six wheels.[2]

From the start Brunel appears to have been convinced that passenger carriages would be safer with a six-wheeled arrangement than four, even informing the Gauge Commissioners of his beliefs.

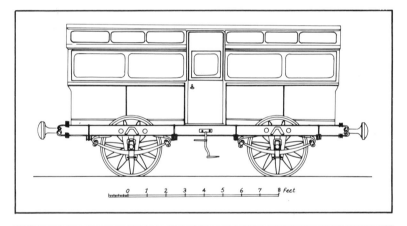

Posting carriage of 1838.

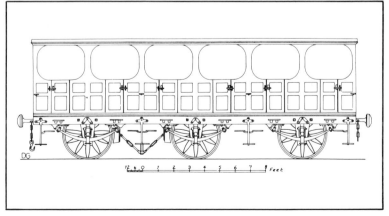

Open second class carriage of 1840.

Early second class carriages were open at the sides but at least had a roof to protect their occupants from some effects of the elements. No such luxury was afforded to 'the very lowest order of passenger' whom the Company deigned to convey by goods train in open trucks with wooden seats.[3] As a result of pressure in Parliament the Cheap Trains Act was passed in 1844, consequently 'the lowest orders' were offered covered accommodation. The vehicles were little better than enclosed cattle trucks but they complied with the law and that, it would appear, satisfied the Great Western. Luxury abounded in first class carriages but then passengers paid more and expected greater comfort. Apart from better springing there was little difference in an engineering sense below the body on all three classes of vehicle.

Gooch was faced with the task of keeping early locomotives in running order, but no such brief existed regarding carriages and wagons. Craftsmen trained in the manufacture of road coaches were employed for that purpose and Brunel soon realized that it was a mistake. Many coaches had revealed an alarming propensity for sideways motion and that, he discovered, was due to excessive bearing wear coupled with the habit of using short bearings. In addition, the thumping of wheels when running fast turned out to be because of unequal thickness of tyres. Both defects, Brunel considered, would never have been allowed by a reasonable mechanic and, in 1842, he wrote to Saunders, the Company Secretary and General Superintendent of the line, expressing his view that railway carriages required engineering superintendence just as much as locomotives.[4] Rolt, in his biography of Brunel, concludes that carriage maintenance originally lay with the Traffic Department but, as a result of the letter, responsibility was transferred to the Locomotive Engineering Department, probably at the new Swindon Works.

Most carriage construction remained with outside contractors although maintenance and repair would have been undertaken by the Company's own personnel. Daniel Gooch operated from a base at Paddington and it is likely that the Locomotive Works Manager at Swindon had responsibility for mechanical maintenance of the carriages. During 1844 a number of four-wheeled, iron-bodied luggage vans were constructed by the Great Western, but the designer is unknown.[5]

The use of iron extended to third class carriage construction in 1845, ten such six-wheeled vehicles being built at the Company's works whilst others came from contractors. Wood still remained in favour for the frames of first class carriages, bodies generally being supplied by specialist coach builders although, in 1851, some bodies were constructed at Paddington for iron frames supplied by an outside contractor.[6] It would appear that engineering construction and repair were undertaken at Swindon whilst wooden bodywork and interiors fell to a squad at Paddington.

Construction of a Royal Saloon in the early 1840s presented a challenge and every effort was

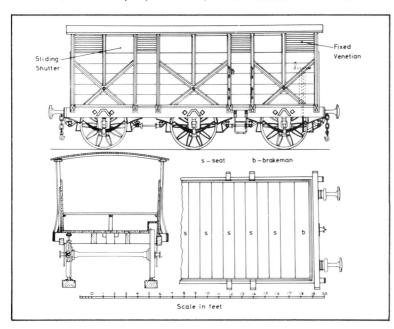

Closed Parliamentary third class carriage.

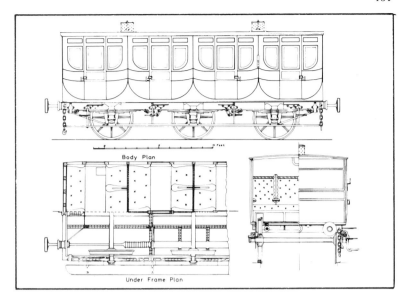

Body Plan

Under Frame Plan

made to ensure Queen Victoria's satisfaction. Coach work went to David Davies of London and the intention was to mount the coach on a four-wheeled frame until Brunel insisted, on the grounds of safety and comfort, that an eight-wheeled frame be used.[7] A second Royal Saloon was constructed in 1848 and that also had eight wheels. Axles were grouped in pairs at the frame ends, axle-boxes being connected by compensating beams. Carriage weight was carried by single long springs connected to the middle of each compensating beam. The arrangement did not constitute a swivel bogie but the axles must have had some lateral freedom to allow the coach to negotiate curves.[8] That arrangement provided valuable experience towards the design of eight-wheeled vehicles and bogies.

In 1846 Mr James Gibson was appointed Superintendent of the Carriage and Wagon Department. Whether that came about as a belated result of Brunel's letter or due to pressure from the locomotive section is unknown. Gooch's 'Diary and Memoirs' offer no information and the lack of comment upon carriage matters would indicate that he had little interest or involvement. It would appear that Gibson worked independently of Gooch and so carriage matters of that era do not really fall within the scope of this book. However, it is important to mention some developments of the period, if only to ensure a degree of continuity.

Carriage bodies were constructed from wood, or in a few cases from iron, but 1850 saw the introduction of papier-mâché body panels on a first class carriage. Such was the success of the

experiment in terms of durability and passenger reaction, as well as cost, that most first and second class carriages built between 1851 and 1858 utilized the material for bodywork. Outside contractors continued to supply most carriage stock but in 1853 a board decision was made to construct, whenever possible, all iron frames at Swindon.[9]

1852 saw the introduction of the first eight-wheeled, normal service carriages to run in Britain. Known as 'Long Charleys', these 38 ft long first and second class composites had four axles arranged in pairs in a manner similar to that of the Royal Saloon. It was not a bogie system but shows the awareness of a need for axle pivotal freedom in order for long carriages to negotiate curves. This stock was for the broad gauge but absorption of the Shrewsbury lines in 1854 introduced narrow gauge items into Gibson's domain. Outside contractors supplied most coaching stock and continued to do so for many years, whenever the powers at Paddington allowed. Repair shops of the former Shrewsbury & Chester Railway, at Saltney, had to attend to narrow gauge vehicle maintenance. Gibson's retirement in 1864 allowed Joseph Armstrong to take control of all rolling stock matters throughout the system.

A major preoccupation during Armstrong's short reign at Swindon was construction of the new Carriage Works which opened early in 1869. Throughout that period there was a reduction in the need for broad gauge stock and an accompanying requirement for narrow gauge vehicles. Gauge conversion brought about the change in emphasis and there seems to have been a concerted effort to run down the 7 ft stock, retaining only the best items. Absorption of the lines in Devon and Cornwall brought other carriage and wagon stock into the fold, thus minimizing the need for new construction. That situation allowed the recently built Carriage Works to concentrate on narrow or standard gauge stock.

It was not until 1876 that any quantity production of broad gauge carriages resumed, and even then the vehicles were designed for future conversion to standard gauge. James Holden was manager at the Carriage Works from 1873 until 1885 when he moved to the Great Eastern Railway as Locomotive Superintendent. In view of his subsequent design work it would be reasonable to assume that many of the carriage designs originated with him. Joseph Armstrong was, however, in overall command with responsibility for approving, rejecting or modifying plans. Just as with locomotives, convertible coaching stock found favour with Armstrong. The arrangement favoured was basically a standard gauge coach with a removable centre section inserted to bring the width to 10 ft for broad gauge running. Different frames were needed for operations on broad and standard gauges and considerable effort was required in conversion.[10] How many were actually converted is unknown as a later system proved to be much simpler.

Eight-wheeled stock constructed during the Armstrong era utilized the earlier axle grouping system, the bogie concept not yet being developed. Wheels were, however, an improvement, being of the wooden-centred Mansell type which gave a smoother ride. All stock built after 1868 was so fitted and that remained a standard wheel type long after the turn of the century.

Another improvement in general passenger well-being, the application of continuous brakes, came about at the instigation of Parliament. Armstrong tried the Sanders automatic brake on a carriage in 1876 and its success heralded general adoption, in the modified Sanders-Bolitho form, shortly afterwards. The untimely death of Armstrong brought William Dean to Swindon in 1877, and he soon became rather disenchanted with the braking arrangement, considering that improvements were possible. Those improvements, at the hands of 'Young Joe' Armstrong and Churchward, are detailed elsewhere in the book and need not be further described. Suffice it to add that the system became standard and lasted until the end of the GWR itself with but minor changes. Dean knew a good idea when he saw one.

The introduction of sleeping cars to the Great Western also came during the Armstrong/Dean transition period. Two six-wheeled, 29 ft vehicles commenced operation on the London–Penzance service during December 1877 but it is difficult to determine exactly who was responsible, Armstrong having only recently died. Dean is given credit as he then occupied the seat of power but delay between conception and delivery indicates some probable involvement on the part of his predecessor. Then again, Holden may have had a hand in the matter. There were two sleeping compartments, one for men with seven beds and the other for women with four beds. Separate lavatories were provided, as befitted the social climate at the time. In the event, passengers did not like the dormitory-style sleeping arrangements and both carriages were rebuilt as ordinary saloons a few years later.[11]

Dean seems to have taken a certain amount of interest in coaching stock and many innovative ideas were introduced during his period in office. In 1881 two new sleeping cars were produced, these being such an improvement as to make the earlier pair positively antiquated. In many respects they were the forerunners of modern sleeping stock, being very much in advance of anything in service on British lines. The clerestory-roofed vehicles had six two-berthed compartments and three lavatories, all having direct access from the side corridors. An attendant's pantry, positionined at the centre of the carriage, provided service whenever required. Built with conversion in mind, the bodies were to standard gauge dimensions but on broad gauge frames and with broad gauge bogies. Conversion was to be simply by replacement of the frames and bogies. Both broad and standard gauge bogies at the time were of the Dean suspension type.[12]

Carriage suspension bogies followed much the same pattern as that applied to locomotives although slight variations did occur. Four brackets, two on the outside of each soleplate, supported four links on hemispherical bearings. These in turn carried a pair of transverse beams on volute springs, stanchions on the beams being attached to the underframe. A certain amount of swing was allowed by the hemispherical bearings but it was limited by a central bogie pin which took none of the weight. For earlier bogies the support links were at the ends but on the longer bogies which appeared later, suspension points were placed between the axles. Two support links were then provided at each location, one on the inside of the frame and the other on the outside. Dean's suspension bogie provided the Great Western with an advantage over other railways. It gave a comfortable ride, allowed for high speeds and was relatively simple to maintain.

Dean insisted upon high quality materials and the setting up of his chemical laboratory was one way in which he could keep a check on standards. Steel axles and tyres for all standard coaches had to be case-hardened in order to improve operating life and Dean considered that the superior operational performance of his vehicles was attributable to that process.[13]

Apart from a group of six-wheeled carriages for the Torbay branch, to which bogie arrangements were not applicable, all broad gauge coaching stock built after 1882 was of similar format to that used for the sleeping cars, namely standard gauge bodies on broad gauge frames and bogies.[14] The adoption of independent bogies in 1888 further simplified the arrangements for conversion. From that date all coaching stock was constructed to standard gauge dimensions on standard gauge frames, only the bogies requiring replacement when conversion became due. Although conversion from broad to standard gauge was that intended, the possibility existed to convert the other way if stock requirements so dictated. Many earlier convertibles had their frames altered to standard gauge form, thus allowing for rapid final conversion when the broad gauge ceased to exist.

To facilitate conversion a special hydraulically operated arrangement was constructed in the Carriage Works. Carriages, in batches of about six, would be run into the changing shed on their broad gauge bogies. The frames and bodies were then supported on trestles, the bogies detached and the platforms upon which the bogies stood lowered below floor level. The bogies were run underground until clear of the carriage body units and then raised to floor level before being moved out of the building. Narrow gauge bogies found their way under the body units by the same underground route. Connection of new bogies to the carriage frame completed conversion. A. H. Malan, a well-known railway enthusiast and commentator of the time, witnessed such a conversion and considered the process took less than half an hour.[15]

The ingenuity of the conversion machinery leads to the conclusion that Dean's must have been the guiding hand. It is the sort of scheme his agile mind would have relished designing. Publicity was also close to his heart, journalistic tours of locomotive and carriage plants being encouraged. At times he personally conducted such tours, especially when an item of major interest was available for inspection. One notable occasion was the visit of Herbert Russell, from *Railway Magazine*, to report upon the newly constructed Royal Jubilee Train. During the discussion another facet of Dean's character came to light; a willingness to

Dean suspension bogie (Patrick Griffiths).

offer public praise to members of his staff. In the Royal Saloon he enthused about the sliding doors which ran upon bicycle ball bearings, 'a notion introduced by my ingenious assistant Mr. L.R. Thomas'.[16] Presumably the idea, for which a patent was granted, found application with all sliding doors.

Thomas was then manager of the Carriage and Wagon Works and he is also credited by Churchward with the design of the first class sleeping carriages which appeared in 1897. The carriages accommodated eight passengers, each having his/her own compartment, with one lavatory shared by two compartments. Provision of a special lever bolt arrangement prevented one passenger from gaining access to the lavatory whilst the other was using it.[17] It was another ingenious device of which Dean must have approved.

Carriages throughout most of the nineteenth century were independent units with no connecting passageway. Although corridors were provided within many coaches it was not possible to pass along the length of a train. The change came in 1892 with complete corridor trains introduced by James Holden on the Great Eastern and William Dean on the Great Western. It is worth remembering that Holden had moved to the Great Eastern from Swindon in 1885 and may have developed or learned the idea there. Whoever was responsible for the concept, the honour of introduction goes to Dean as his four-coach train commenced operation on the Paddington–Birkenhead service in March 1892. The idea of the corridor was to give access to

separate ladies' and gentlemen's lavatories, most interconnecting coach doors normally being locked so that 'inferior' second and third class passengers could not enter the first class world.

Success of the prototype corridor train led to rapid introduction of similar trains on West Country and South Wales services. Abolition of the compulsory refreshment stop at Swindon in 1895 brought a need for on-train catering, particularly with long-distance services. Passengers had to wait until the following year before the Great Western's first dining car was incorporated in the 'Cornishman' corridor set, the 10.15 a.m. from Paddington to Penzance.

Corridor stock, indeed most coaches during the later years of Dean's term in office, was of the clerestory type. It was a style he preferred even though it had fallen out of fashion on other railways. Churchward, Carriage Works Manager between 1885 and 1895, had no regard for that pattern of roof and quickly abandoned it in favour of the semi-elliptical when he became 'Chief' at Swindon. His arguments were that it harboured dust and caused condensation, with the result that dust-laden moisture dripped upon ladies' expensive dresses.[18] That particular problem could have been solved by a better form of decklight, so the real reason is likely to have been the higher initial and maintenance costs. In addition, Churchward held the view that a clerestory was a source of structural weakness. Why Dean persisted with its use is unknown but the clerestory roof looks more stylish than any other form, and Dean's vehicles certainly had style. The elegance of clerestory-roofed stock behind a Dean single-wheeler is difficult to surpass. The fact that clerestories remained under construction until Churchward

actually took over as Locomotive, Carriage and Wagon Superintendent is a strong indicator that Dean still controlled matters at Swindon.

An operating feature which Churchward did perpetuate was that of the 'slip coach'. Although the idea of slipping coaches from a normal service train did not originate on the Great Western, it was perfected there. The first appearance came during December 1858 but it was not until May 1861 that the term 'slip coach' actually appeared in the timetable. Early methods of slipping entailed the guard pulling on a rope attached to the coupling, no attention being required to brakes as the continuous vacuum arrangement had not then been applied.[19]

During Dean's period in office the system was developed so that train and slip vacuum systems were maintained following a slip. The carriage was detached by moving the slip lever in the slip guard's compartment. That pulled away a slip bolt which released the upper part of the hinged slip hook, freeing the slip coach from its train. Flexible vacuum pipes would be pulled apart as separation took place, the guard having previously leaned through his window to close the slip cock, thus sealing the train vacuum. In the slip guard's compartment was a cock which sealed the slip coach vacuum. A linkage prevented the slip lever from being moved until that cock had been closed. The guard had to exercise skill and judgement in applying his brakes, for once he had lost vacuum, brakes could not be released and assistance had to be summoned.[20]

A Churchward modification of 1909 allowed the guard to regulate his braking as and when required. Large vacuum reservoirs enabled a vacuum to be restored in the brake lines following

Top left *No. 3813,* County of Carmarthen, *with mixed rake of Dean clerestory vehicles. The leading coach is 56 ft first class sleeper No. 9037 of 1897 (courtesy of the National Railway Museum, York).*
Above left *'Bulldog' class No. 3357,* Exeter, *temporarily renamed* Royal Sovereign, *with the 1897 Royal Train on 7 March 1902 (courtesy GWR Museum, Swindon).*
Left *'Bulldog' class No. 3363* Alfred Baldwin *with two Dean clerestory coaches. Leading coach, diagram F10, slip combo of 1903 with vacuum reservoirs on roof. Rear coach third class, diagram C23 (G. H. Soole Collection/NRM, York).*
Right *Slip mechanism.*

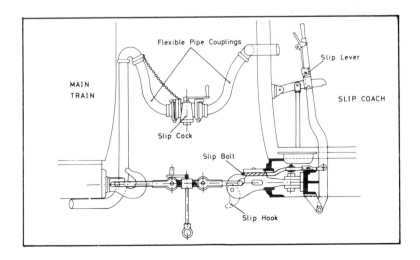

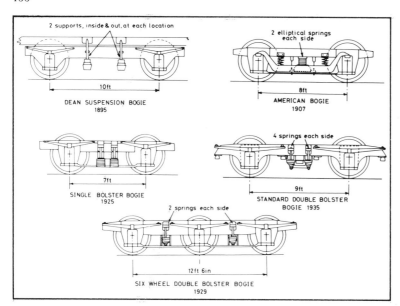

Left *Diagram showing different types of carriage bogie.*

Right *'Star' class No. 4012,* Knight of the Thistle, *hauling a rake of 'Dreadnought' stock on the Cornish Riviera Express* (courtesy GWR Museum, Swindon).

Below right *Churchward 'Toplight' special purpose vehicle No. 9055, a 1912 'one-off' replacement for a Dean clerestory* (Patrick Griffiths).

Bottom right *Churchward steel-panelled 'nondescript' saloon without toplights, designed for private party travel. Shown at Bridgnorth following restoration on the Severn Valley Railway.*

limited brake application and thus the slip coach speed could be more accurately controlled. Clerestory slip coaches were provided with long vacuum reservoirs on the roof either side of the clerestory section. The ends of the brake pipe connections were fitted with self-sealing valves which automatically closed when the slip was made and the pipes pulled apart.[21] A similar automatic adaptor enabled steam heating of slip carriages to be provided for the first time.[22]

With the appointment of Churchward as Locomotive, Carriage and Wagon Superintendent it was not only locomotive design which changed. An early casualty, along with the clerestory roof, was the suspension bogie. A number of different bogie arrangements were tried during his early years in office, including some based upon American practice. There was even a six-wheeled American-style bogie for use with the 70 ft long sleeping cars of 1907 and a few restaurant cars of the period.[23] The majority of 70 ft stock actually ran on four-wheeled bolster bogies introduced in 1910. Collett seemed to pay special attention to bogie design, carrying out many tests before he settled upon a particular type. His tests with the whitewash coach have already been mentioned in chapter 3.

Churchward's new broom certainly appears to have made a clean sweep of the carriage department. Passenger/weight ratio in American coaching stock was higher than that on the GWR, where wasteful features such as separate ladies' and gentlemen's lavatories remained in fashion. Long steel-panelled coaches could improve the

ratio and Churchward set about designing his 'Dreadnought' stock. That assortment of coaches, introduced between 1904 and 1907, varied in length from 68 ft to 70 ft whilst the body sides bulged out to a 9 ft 6 in width, thereby making full use of the loading gauge. Many criticized the length, including the Civil Engineering Department which considered there to be potential problems at point locking-bars. Churchward got his way, characteristically suggesting that savings from the new stock would far outweigh any costs involved in modifications to the locking-bars.

The 'Dreadnoughts', nicknamed after the massive Royal Navy battleships of the same name, did not prove popular with most passengers as outside doors were not provided at each compartment, access only being possible from the corridor via doors at the carriage centre and ends. Passengers had no liking for the crush when entering or leaving a train. Further 70 ft stock was introduced in 1906, called 'Concertina' on account of the way in which all body doors were recessed to keep within a 9 ft wide load gauge. All were corridor coaches but with outside doors to compartments. That appears to have been one of the few occasions upon which Churchward bowed to the views of others, but then carriages were intended for the passengers.

'Toplight' stock provided the mainstay of coach production during the final ten years of the Churchward era, a wide variety of arrangements being covered by the classification, including some 70 ft long coaches of corridor and non-corridor form. One of the original intentions regarding long coaches had been a high passenger/weight ratio, but that did not really come about. On the basis of passengers per ton weight for third class corridor coaches, a 54 ft Dean clerestory had a ratio of 2.67 whilst for the 70 ft 'Toplight' of 1909 it was 2.38. The steel-panelled 70 ft 'Toplight' of 1914 could only manage 2.25. Modern stock comes off even worse.[23]

In designing passenger carriages Churchward also gave thought to maintenance and cleaning, semi-elliptical roofs and fairly flush side panels being easier to deal with. He also advised a 'float' of 400 new coaches which would allow each coach to be systematically removed from service for regular cleaning and maintenance. At an average of £1,000 for each coach it would have been a high investment, but his mind was on the availability of good quality stock at all times. He also considered that provision of shelter and modern cleaning methods would increase stock availability and reduce maintenance costs. Such an idea contradicted the opinion held by Dean, who felt that the cost of covered storage for coaches was not justified.[24]

The 'traditional' chocolate and cream livery of Great Western coaching stock essentialy came about by accident. In 1864 it was decided that the top portions of coaches, up until then painted brown all over, should be painted white. When varnished that white became the familiar shade of cream.[25] Churchward did not consider the colour scheme suitable and, in 1903, painted some coaches deep brown with gold lining. Over the ensuing years several other schemes were tried, including dark lake. By 1908 his mind was made up and the two-tone livery was discontinued, to be replaced by a colour varyingly described as Tuscan red and chocolate-lake. Churchward had his way in changing even the colour scheme and nobody appeared to question his decision, apart from sections of the railway press with whom it did not find favour. The 'old man' was not a person to be overly concerned about what outsiders thought, or even his directors for that matter.

A change of command in 1922 brought Collett into office and one of his first decisions was to reintroduce the old livery. During the First World War overhaul and repainting of the coaches had fallen well into arrears and a coat of paint was sorely needed on most stock. The reappearance of chocolate and cream was a welcome sight to many.

Although steel-panelled stock had been introduced in 1912 it was not until 1921 that the first all-steel coach commenced operations on the Great Western. Over the years a few other experimental types were produced but there was no overwhelm-

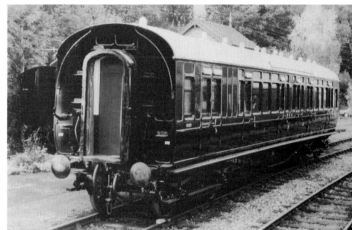

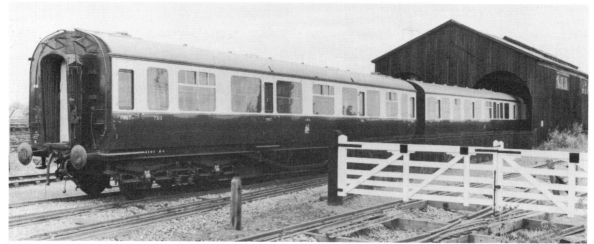

ing desire to discard the composite metal panel on wooden frame form of construction. One factor said to be in favour of all-steel coaches was that of safety in the event of collison, but Swindon took another view. Automatic train control provided better safeguard against an accident in the first place. There was also the weight factor to be considered, heavier coaches required more powerful locomotives. In addition, steel coaches were considered to need 30% more heating surface, they were noisier and liable to corrode. Such were the arguments offered by J.W. Innes in a 1939 Swindon Junior Engineering Society paper.[26] During Hawksworth's time in office experiments were conducted into the use of light alloy but they came too late in the life of the GWR to have any influence.

Collett ended production of 70 ft coaches, as mentioned in an earlier chapter, but not before two sets had been constructed for South Wales services. In view of his contention that such long coaches were unsafe it is likely that they were an interim measure following wartime losses. A number of novel features were applied, the main one being that of Laycock 'Buckeye' couplers. Collett was almost certainly responsible for that introduction as Churchward retired some eighteen months before the trains entered service. In addition to the couplers, special drop-down buffers and gangway adapters were provided to allow for connection with other coaches having normal screw couplers and GWR gangways. When running with 'Buckeye' coupling the hinged buffers dropped down with their heads facing the track.[27]

Articulated sets came into fashion, a number being constructed in 1925 for main line and suburban use. As on the LNER, they were not a great success and the experiment was not repeated. Gradually Collett imposed his own style on coaching stock, producing some very elegant flush-panelled sets, the internal fittings being arranged to match the service. In 1931 the very special 'Super Saloons' commenced operation as part of the Paddington–Plymouth boat train. They were the Great Western's own Pullman cars but with very British internal styling. Bodies were bow-ended with recessed entrance doors set at an angle of 30° to the sides. Furnishing and fitting went to the firm of Trollope & Sons although Carriage Shop craftsmen undertook the ornate internal panel work.

Further sets of special coaches, appropriately called 'Centenary' stock, appeared in 1935 to mark the GWR's centenary. Body design closely followed that of the 'Super Saloons' but the interiors were not so ornate. They were, however, modern compared with most of the first class stock then running and very much appreciated by passengers. As with the 'Super Saloons', 'Centenary' stock had limited route availability. Collett was well aware of the disadvantages and pressed for a change in policy. In 1937 it was agreed that all future stock for general service would have a maximum width of 8 ft 11 in, thus allowing it to run over most other lines in Britain. Yellow discs were displayed at the ends of coaches to designate such vehicles.

Hawksworth took over at a difficult time and, as with his locomotives, was constrained by outside influences. He introduced the concept of body construction directly onto frames to the GWR, thereby saving on weight and construction time. Steel brackets fitted to the underframes held the base of each body pillar whilst the tops were connected with similar brackets welded to longitu-

Top left *Collett Super Saloon kitchen car, 'Queen Mary'.*

Above left *Collett standard 59 ft 10 in composite coaches Nos. 7313 and 7371, constructed to diagram E158 in 1940 and 1941 respectively* (Patrick Griffiths).

Left *'4500' class No. 5572 at Didcot with Collett Excursion third coach No. 1289, diagram C74, built in 1937. At the rear is Hawksworth Auto-trailer No. 231, built in 1951* (Sarah Griffiths).

Right *Hawksworth slab-sided brake 3rd, No. 2202, diagram D133. Built in 1950 as part of the last lot ordered by the GWR* (Patrick Griffiths).

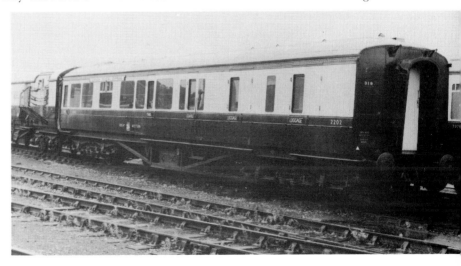

Left *Typical five-plank open wagon with oil lubricated axle-boxes.*

Below right *Dean Goods, No. 2532, hauling mixed fitted freight near Moreton Sidings, Didcot, on 29 September 1951* (J. Russell-Smith Collection/NRM York).

Bottom right *'Crocodile F' bogie well wagon of 1909.*

dinal roof girders. Many long timber sections were eliminated by this method of construction, whilst the floor became part of the frame unit and not the body. There was no general turning away from wooden-framed structures due to the scarcity of light alloys. Flat-sided bodies, just as with locomotive tenders, made for simpler construction, particularly as curved body pillars were avoided. That also made for better use of available timber.

Goods wagons were designed to meet specific requirements and, as with carriages, the original stock came from outside manufacturers. Iron replaced wood for body construction at an early stage and by 1845 Swindon was producing many of the items. No special attention appears to have been given to wagons during the broad gauge era, developments following on from carriage practice. Many items of 7 ft gauge stock were very antiquated and barely lasted until the end. It was for the growing standard gauge that most developments took place, but not in isolation from other companies. Through-working of goods trains, or at least some trucks, required a degree of common practice but many specialist trucks and wagons did appear.

Grease-lubricated axle-boxes were in universal use for freight vehicles but overheating problems frequently occurred at speeds in excess of 30 mph. Churchward's response to the claim of inspectors that dirt was responsible has been outlined in a previous chapter. Production of the O.K. axle-box was a considerable advance and dramatically reduced bearing problems on freight vehicles. With a lubricant film to separate bearing and journal, Churchward concluded that overheating would cease to be a problem.

His simple solution was to provide a lubricating pad which would dip into an oil reservoir and continuously feed lubricant to the journal whenever it rotated. The pad was a mixture of horsehair, wool and worsted, braided in such a way that it would not clog. With the top part of the pad kept in contact with the journal by means of a spring, a supply of oil to that journal was guaranteed provided the axle-box was filled to the correct level.[28]

Another Churchward patent, this time in conjunction with Dean, was the either-side hand brake for wagons. Towards the end of the last century it became a Board of Trade requirement that all modern freight stock be fitted with hand brakes capable of application or release from either side of the wagon. Such brakes were needed when parking vehicles, regulating speed whilst shunting and for assistance in the safe descent of steep inclines.

A number of patents were granted including one to L.R. Thomas but it was the Dean/Churchward either-side brake which found more general favour on the GWR. The link arrangement for application of brake shoes was fairly standard to all brake types, but the method of application differed and was the subject of various patents. Dean and Churchward, patent No. 202 of 4 December 1902, employed a toothed rack and lever arrangement for operating the brake levers. Several modifications were made over the years to suit the system for long vehicles and for vacuum braking, but by the 1930s Morton's type of either-side brake replaced all versions of the Dean/Churchward type. Development of the vacuum brake and its application to fitted freight trains has been related in an earlier chapter and need not be repeated again.

Many wagons were used for cross-country freight but had to be returned to the parent company as soon as the goods were delivered, otherwise fines would be imposed. During World War I a number of companies, including the GWR, decided to form a 'common user' pool of unfitted open wagons and closed vans. Such an arrangement introduced a degree of standardization within the railways but it did not preclude development of specialist vehicles. As far as the Great Western was concerned these were designed and constructed at Swindon to the specific requirements of the Railway.

Bogie trucks were introduced during 1873 but it was not until 1892 that the specialized 'Crocodile' entered service. Designed to carry boilers and other large items, it remained very much the same through its years of construction which lasted until

the late 1930s. The original vehicles had 4 ft bogies but these soon became 5 ft 6 in, and one variation even employed six-wheeled trolleys. 'Loriots' were introduced at the same time, the basic design being perpetuated until 1943. These well designed wagons were employed in the transportation of machinery.

Bogies were employed for a number of goods vehicles, the 'Siphon G' being, perhaps, the most famous. It was basically an item of carriage stock but with a ventilated van body used for the transportation of milk churns. Another carriage-like vehicle for similar non-passenger duties was the travelling post office van. First introduced to the GWR in 1891, they were designed to allow for

Top *'Loriot' well wagon of 1934.*

Above *Collett Travelling Post Office No. 814 of 1940.*

the sorting of mail en route as well as for its pick-up and set-down without the train stopping. Basic styling structure followed the passenger stock of the period and so there is little special to consider about them from an engineering point of view. Mail exchange apparatus had to be designed for efficient operation but there is no reason to believe that it came in for special attention from any of the CMEs.

In general terms the same can be said for all freight stock as little information exists showing that any of them had more than a passing interest. That is reasonable in the overall context of the mechanical engineering department as vehicles, in general, were similar below the frames. Wagon sizes and types were dictated by traffic demands and specialist vehicle requirements did not drain design resources to the same extent that locomotive design could. With brake and bearing conditions satisfied there was little necessity for any of the CMEs to interfere. None of them appears to have done so.

10. Standardization

The word 'standard' may be applied to a group of locomotive classes intended to cover traffic requirements for a particular railway, but in its true technical sense standardization applies to the parts from which the locomotives are constructed. A number of different classes of locomotive could, therefore, be built using a limited range of identical parts. The basic purpose was economic and according to E.S. Cox, Executive Officer responsible for design of British Railways' standard steam locomotives, there were five advantages:

1. Reduction in first cost due to quantity production.
2. Reduction in the cost of repairs
3. Reduction in repair time as items, particularly boilers, could be replaced by previously overhauled units.
4. Reduction in the size of a spares stock.
5. Better trained personnel, constructional, repair, servicing and operational, due to greater familiarity with the product.[1]

Benefits to be gained from the use of standard parts are now obvious, but that was not always the case. Not until the Industrial Revolution was firmly entrenched did such procedures become possible. Railways, and the Great Western in particular, led the way although the situation was not so refined as it was later to become.

Brunel actually applied the concept during construction of his lines in using spans of 66 ft or 50 ft for timber viaducts in Cornwall. That allowed standard-sized units of timber to be used throughout and his design enabled any unit to be replaced without interrupting traffic.[2]

Locomotive construction during the early years of the railway age was basic, each machine being very much an individual. Design to a particular class was often the aim with similar castings being employed, but final fitting suited that machine only. Interchangeability played no part. A few engineers realized that, as the railway system expanded, some form of standardization would be essential. Fortunately for the Great Western Railway, Daniel Gooch was one of them.

His baptism of fire when faced with the almost impossible task of keeping Brunel's 'freak' locomotives in working condition must have hammered home the essential need for consistency in quality, performance and parts. The locomotive debacle following commencement of services soon prompted a rethink on traction policy. Gooch was instructed to prepare drawings for two locomotive classes, later known as 'Firefly' and 'Sun'. Harrowing nights spent at Westbourne Park in the early days when he was forced to 'rebuild one half of the stock'[3] in order to maintain a service provided an invaluable lesson for the future. Parts had to be interchangeable.

Gooch decided that certain components would be common to both classes, the 'Sun' being but a smaller version of the 'Firefly'. Two later classes, 'Leo' and 'Hercules', also fell within the scheme, with the four 'Hercules' engines making use of 'Firefly' boilers. The important feature, however, was the way in which he ensured that all members of each class would, as far as possible, be identical. Several manufacturers had to be involved in order to guarantee rapid delivery of sufficient locomotives. Drawings were lithographed, thus avoiding the possibility of errors during tracing or copying, and iron templates provided for parts which had to be interchangeable. Finally, but of equal importance, regular visits were made to the contractors' workshops in order to check on progress.[4]

Having set the pattern, future designs could be produced with relative ease, manufacturers knowing exactly what was required of them. In demanding perfection for GWR locomotives Gooch must have raised the standard of construction for all locomotives. It is unthinkable that any of the approved manufacturers would have produced lower quality machines for other contracts.

A centralized construction and repair facility at Swindon offered economic advantages compared with the use of outside contractors. It was, however, only of real benefit if an effective parts standardization policy existed. Gooch had already instituted such a scheme for dealing with other manufacturers and its extension to Swindon presented no real difficulty. Maintenance problems could be eased if repair squads dealt with well-known classes of locomotive, thus allowing for swifter return to service. Once the manufacturing side became operational, standard parts for spares could also be made 'in house', thereby saving time on procurement.

Control over the construction side allowed Gooch to advance his scheme for a fleet of standard locomotives. Not only were machines to be identical with a class but many common parts would be used across a range of classes. Table 1 illustrates how that came about with identical boilers, cylinder units and wheels being employed for several groups. Valve gear, crankshafts, pistons

Table 1

Gooch's later standard locomotives

Class	No built	Boiler barrel length	diameter	No tubes	Firebox casing		Wheel diameter drive	other	Cylinder diameter stroke (in)
Prince	6	10ft	4ft	178	4ft 5in	× 4ft 10in	7ft	4ft	16 × 24
Iron Duke	29	11ft	4ft 9½in	303	5ft 0in	× 6ft 0in	8ft	4ft	18 × 24
Premier	12	10ft	4ft	178	4ft 5in	× 4ft 10in	5ft		16 × 24
Pyracmon	6	10ft 6in	4ft 3in	219	4ft 11in	× 5ft 3½in	5ft		16 × 24
Bogie (Corsair)	15	10ft 6in	4ft 3in	219	4ft 4in	× 4ft 8¾in	6ft	3ft 6in	17 × 24
Waverley	10	11ft	4ft 6in	249	5ft 0in	× 5ft 4in	7ft	4ft 3in	17 × 24
Victoria	18	11ft	4ft	193	4ft 6in	× 4ft 10in	6ft 6in	4ft	16 × 24
Caesar	8	10ft 6in	4ft 3in	219	4ft 11in	× 5ft 3½in	5ft		16 × 24
								later	17 × 24
Std Goods	102	11ft	4ft 6in	249	5ft 0in	× 5ft 4in	5ft		17 × 24

All boiler tubes 2in diameter.

and other items also became standard. Large wheels were constructed from several pieces forge-welded together, thus each was, in effect, a 'one-off' as opposed to the identical cast wheels made years later. Even so there were advantages to be gained from standardization, not least due to the fact that teams became very experienced and could construct a wheel of the desired size virtually from scrap iron.[5]

Gooch left a legacy which placed the Great Western in the forefront of locomotive manufacture. Without that standardization policy development of Swindon is unlikely to have progressed at the rate it did. The works grew up on the policy and was designed for its implementation, so that from the start the Great Western had an advantage over its rivals. Standard parts eventually resulted in better quality products, only tried and tested components remaining in service and production.

With the absorption of narrow gauge lines it was natural that Gooch should extend the standardization scheme which was not, after all, limited to any particular gauge. Difficulties arose due to the fact that the existing narrow gauge fleet had to be serviced and kept running. However, if that task was centred on Wolverhampton, Swindon and outside manufacturers could supply new machines. Two initial designs, the '57' class 0-6-0 and '69' class 2-2-2, had many parts interchangeable with each other including cylinders and motion.[6] More than that, a number of items were the same as for broad gauge machines.

A boiler may be thought of as a single item but it actually consists of distinct parts, namely barrel, smokebox and firebox. Although wheel positioning prohibited the use of complete broad gauge boilers on narrow gauge frames, individual parts could be and were used. '57', '69' and other narrow gauge classes employed the same sized boiler barrel, and probably smokebox, as used for the broad gauge 'Victoria' class. Complete interchangeability was not possible but certain manufacturing advantages must have been evident.

When Joseph Armstrong moved to Swindon he continued along identical lines for broad gauge construction, employing the same basic parts as set out by Gooch. There was no point in doing otherwise, the 7 ft gauge being firmly entrenched in the regime of standardization. Without such a system it is doubtful if broad gauge stock could have been kept running so effectively for the length of time it was. When replacement did become essential Armstrong produced the ultimate in interchangeability, that of the entire locomotive. Convertibles could run on both broad and narrow gauges as required, the only difference being in axle length. Even there, for final conversion they were simply shortened.

Cylinders of 17 in diameter and 24 in or 26 in stroke became normal for most large-scale construction during the Armstrong era. By building large numbers of a particular class it was possible to achieve a considerable degree of interchangeability without any difficulty. Construction of some 300 'Standard Goods' class locomotives during the ten years between 1866 and 1876 introduced uniformity to the GWR goods engine. The manufacturing advantages of a large class are evident but there was also benefit to be derived from familiarity at maintenance depots throughout the system. Drivers also became more accustomed to the type and, it is assumed, more skilled at operating them.

Concurrent with production of his 'Standard Goods', Armstrong designed the 'Sir Daniel' class of single-wheeled 2-2-2 tender engines with 7 ft drivers and 17 in×24 in cylinders. Of significance was the fact that motion and boilers were interchangeable with engines in the goods class. A group of six 0-6-0 side tanks, built in 1870, also used the same motion parts and boilers.[7] These formed the initial locomotives of what was to become an extensive '1076' or 'Buffalo' saddle tank class, although later engines differed slightly from the earlier types. The entire class cannot, therefore, be considered as a standard group in its own right.

Extensive use was made of standard type boilers, which although differing in minor detail over the period of building, remained of basically the same external dimensions and form. That allowed for upgrading at a later date and also provided for some degree of interchangeability. Both Joseph Armstrong and brother George at Wolverhampton made use of the facility whenever they could. As with earlier manufacture, the same barrel, smokebox or firebox parts were employed for different boiler groups, thus making use of common flanging blocks and jigs.

The task facing George Armstrong on the Northern Division was somewhat different from that at Swindon, for a great many absorbed narrow gauge locomotives already existed. Stock for those smaller absorbed lines had originally been supplied by outside manufacturers, some of whom had subsequently gone out of business. Acquisition of spares, therefore, presented a problem. The only sensible policy was one of extensive rebuilding when major parts required renewal. Standard parts from other classes, including cylinders and boilers, would be used whenever possible, the wheelbase being modified as necessary.[8] Although it was not a complete standardization policy it does show the thinking of both Armstrongs on the matter.

Over the years, George Armstrong concentrated upon construction of tank locomotives which produced a form of standardization in its own right. Some classes, particularly the '1501' 0-6-0, were numerous and long lived, thus establishing a pattern for standard parts and continuity of production. Both Armstrongs obviously saw merit in the idea of standardization and applied it to suit particular circumstances. They did not, however, in any real sense extend it, nor does the concept of a fully integrated system appear to have been considered by them. In many respects outside influences dictated their actions and, to be fair, effective standardization only comes about when large-scale production is undertaken. Gauge conversion together with the need to keep up a service on broad gauge lines hampered the work of Joseph, whilst George was faced with the task of keeping a multitude of assorted absorbed locomotives in operation. Financial restraint due to the depressed economic climate was, perhaps, the major obstacle in the way of any wholesale rebuilding.

Until the latter part of his period in office the same constraints were placed upon William Dean. Absorption of railways in Devon and Cornwall increased locomotive problems and financial restrictions did not ease until after completion of the Severn Tunnel. Only during his final ten years, when dogged by illness, was he free from the burden of Brunel's broad gauge. One facet of Dean's character, his enthusiasm for experimentation, restricted any idea of a complete standardization policy. It is doubtful if Dean would ever have been satisfied with a set group of designs. With a mental agility bordering on the genius he would flit from one experimental solution to another and to rest content, as Churchward did, when a design scheme was completed would have been totally out of character.

Despite that, Dean did continue the work of Gooch and Armstrong along the same lines. More convertibles of Armstrong's 0-6-0 saddle tank class were introduced from new whilst many more were converted for broad gauge use. Others of the 'Standard Goods' class, and Dean's own 2-4-0, 0-4-2T and 2-2-2, followed suit from new, most of them subsequently being converted for narrow gauge work. During the 1884-7 period, as mentioned in chapter 6, a group of four classes was constructed to make use of standard components. Tender and tank versions of 2-4-0 and 0-6-0 wheel arrangements, the '3201', '3501', '2361' and '1661' classes, made use of identical cylinders, motion and other parts. Boilers were very similar but not identical, although some degree of interchangeability might have been possible.[9]

That was Dean's only definite attempt at standardization across a range of locomotives and it apears to have been successful, many lasting until well after grouping with only the boilers being changed. Why the policy was not extended to a logical complete scheme is difficult to imagine,

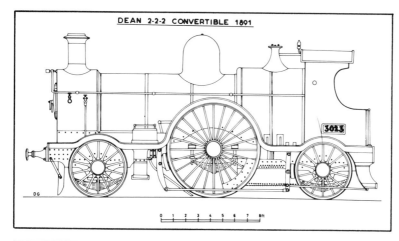

Dean convertible 2-2-2 as arranged for broad gauge running.

DEAN 2-2-2 CONVERTIBLE 1891

'Metro Tank' No. 1499 of 1892 without condensing apparatus, a long-lasting class with a number of variations using many standard parts (courtesy GWR Museum, Swindon).

apart from the outside and self-imposed restrictions mentioned above. The extensive '2301', Dean Goods, class formed a standardized group in its own right, with many parts being similar to previous and subsequent classes. That would have been more for convenience than any fundamental design intention.

Later groups of large tender engines made use of components having the same dimensions, 18 in×26 in cylinders being particularly favoured, but there is no evidence of a plan to organize that in a definite way. As was the case with his immediate predecessor, Dean made use of common components, but it appears to have been for convenience of manufacture in certain restricted cases rather than from a basic desire to arrange a policy.

Towards the end of Dean's period in office it became obvious that locomotive design had to be thoroughly reviewed, due to the increasing demand of the Traffic Department for greater hauling power without the need for 'double heading'.[10] In 1901 Churchward published his famous list of six locomotive classes making use of standardized

parts (see table 3). It is possible that he was influenced by Dean's earlier scheme or even that Dean, still nominally Locomotive Superintendent, requested that the list be compiled. At this distance from the event and without further definite evidence, any conclusion must be speculative. What it important is that Churchward outlined a plan which was to have major implications for future GWR locomotive policy. The time was right for large-scale restocking and sound engineering practice dictated a policy of standardization.

Six classes could not meet all traction requirements but it was a start and illustrated how a range of locomotives could be developed from a limited number of standard components. It can be suggested that Churchward developed his locomotives having already decided upon the parts. That was certainly the case with the 4-4-0 if Stanier is to be believed. Although too powerful for its wheelbase, the 'County' class was built 'tongue in cheek' as Churchward was not going to be 'told what he could do by Webb'.[11] Webb retired as CME of the London & North Western Railway in 1903 and the

'Counties' did not appear until a year later. If Churchward constructed the 4-4-0s knowing full well they would be unsatisfactory then it does seem a strange way for a responsible engineer to behave.

In the light of experience with the French engines and other factors, a more extensive list of standard classes developed over several years.

Naturally, an increased number of standardized parts was required but it was kept to a minimum as far as possible. Only three different-sized driving wheels would be needed. Outside cylinders, cast with part of the smokebox saddle, were interchangeable left- and right-hand sides and all were nominally of the same diameter and stroke. Motion

Table 2

Standard boilers 1903-1949

No	Year	Barrel Outside diameter		Length	Firebox length	Pressure (psi)
		front	back			
1	1903	4ft 11in	5ft 6in	14ft 10in	9ft	200-225
2	1903	4ft 5in	5ft	11ft	7ft	195-200
3	1903	4ft 5in	5ft	10ft 3in	7ft	195-200
4	1902	4ft 11in	5ft 6in	11ft	7ft	195-200
5	1904	4ft 2in	4ft 9in	10ft 6in	5ft 10in	165-200
6	1908	5ft 6in	6ft	23ft	8ft	225
7	1921	5ft 6in	6ft	14ft 10in	10ft	225
8	1923	5ft 2in	5ft 9in	14ft 10in	10ft	225
9	1924	4ft 4in	4ft 5in	10ft 3in	6ft 6in	150-165
10	1924	4ft 5in	5ft 4in	10ft 3in	6ft	150-200
11	1924	4ft 2in	4ft 3in	10ft 6in	5ft 6in	150-165
12	1927	5ft 6in	6ft	16ft	11ft 6in	250
14	1938	4ft 8in	5ft 3in	12ft 6in	8ft 8in	225
15	1945	5ft	5ft 8in	12ft 7in	9ft 9in	280
16	1949	3ft 9in	3ft 10in	10ft 1in	5ft	165
21	1931	4ft 2in	4ft 3in	10ft 6in	5ft 6in	165-180

The No. 6 boiler was fitted to *The Great Bear* only.
No. 8 applied to the 'Castle' class, No. 12 to the 'Kings', No. 14 to the 'Manors' and No. 15 to Hawksworth's 'Counties'. No. 9 and No. 11 boilers were designed as standards to fit on locomotives from absorbed lines.

Table 3

Churchward's outlined classes of 1910

Type	Loco no	Date	Boiler barrel length	dia.	firebox length	Connecting rod length	Wheel diameter Coupled	Other
2-8-0	97	1903	15ft	5ft	9ft	10ft 8½in	4ft 7½in	3ft 3in
4-6-0	–	–	15ft	5ft	9ft	10ft 8½in	5ft 8in	3ft 3in
4-6-0	100	1902	15ft	5ft	9ft	10ft 8½in	6ft 8½in	3ft 3in
2-6-2T	99	1903	11ft 2in	5ft	8ft	6ft 10½in	5ft 8in	3ft 3in
4-4-2T	2221	1905	11ft 2in	5ft	8ft	6ft 10½in	6ft 8½in	3ft 3in
4-4-0	3473	1904	11ft 2in	5ft	8ft	6ft 10½in	6ft 8½in	3ft 3in

Except for No. 100, all cylinders to the same pattern.
Cylinders 18in diameter × 30in stroke with piston valves 8½in diameter.

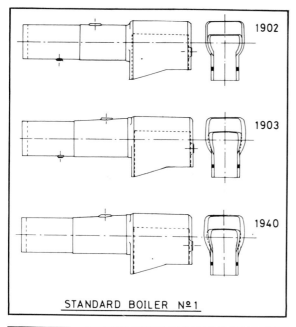

STANDARD BOILER Nº 1

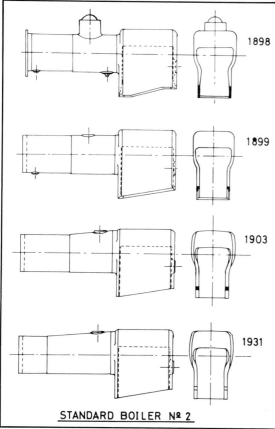

STANDARD BOILER Nº 2

parts and coupling rods fell in with the earlier plan, only two sizes of eccentric and coupling rods being required. Bogies and pony trucks were also to a standard interchangeable design.[12]

Churchward's interest in boilers dictated that standard units would also have to be developed. Evolution was swift as experience grew. Flanged plates and mountings were standardized whilst Churchward was still at the Locomotives Works as manager[13] and the Belpaire firebox appeared in 1898. In May 1899 a domeless raised Belpaire firebox boiler was introduced, working at 180 psi pressure. Although domeless, it had a steam space of 71 cu ft, the casing crown being raised 9 in above the barrel. That dimension remained the same for all standard boilers.

The prototype standard No. 1 boiler with parallel barrel was developed for the 4-6-0 No. 100, but that was quickly superseded by a similarly dimensioned boiler for locomotive No. 98. Although the lower portion of the rear barrel plate remained horizontal, the upper portion was coned. Another difference showed up in a distinct curvature to the firebox side plates and crown, giving increased steam space towards the top of the firebox. Churchward wanted free circulation of water in his boilers and provision of adequate water space around the firebox allowed for that. Whilst developing his designs he carried out experiments in order to determine the direction of water flow in different parts of a boiler. A number of vanes, with spindles passing through lightly packed glands, were placed in the water space where circulation of the water could rotate them.[14] These experiments also led him to the conclusion that top feed would be advantageous in terms of circulation.

A lighter and smaller standard No. 2 boiler appeared in 1903, to be fitted to 2-6-2 tank locomotives of the '3100' class then being developed. With two stages of evolution, the standard No. 4 boiler reached its final form when fitted to the 'Counties'. The No. 4 boiler could use identical smokebox units to the No. 1 boiler and would, therefore, fit onto the same saddle. Only two different saddle units were needed for the three standard boilers and so only two cylinder casting patterns were required, left and right halves being identical for a complete block.

The boilers themselves not only covered locomotives for standard classes but were also suitable for existing classes. A No. 2 boiler could be fitted to the 'Bulldog' and 'Atbara' classes whilst a No. 4 was suitable for the 'Cities' and 'Aberdares'. Standardization of boilers had greater merit and application than any other part. The boilers were also very

good steamers. Design did not stagnate, however, and full taper eventually arrived, but it did not affect the standardization policy as the items which mattered, dimensions and connections, remained very much the same. For smaller tank locomotives a standard No. 5 boiler came about in 1904. The No. 3 boiler was developed not for a standard class under consideration but for fitting to existing 2-4-2 suburban tank engines. Churchward obviously had his mind on an overall boiler policy, not one which applied only to his specific newly designed locomotives.

Although the No. 6 boiler, developed for *The Great Bear*, has been included as a standard in table 2, there is no evidence that it was anything other than a 'one-off', an experiment in large boiler design. The locomotive itself might not have been a success but Churchward was too canny not to see potential in the boiler. At some future time a high

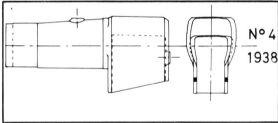

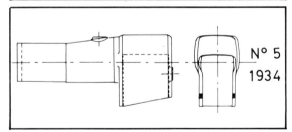

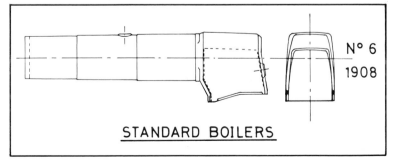

STANDARD BOILERS

Above left *Evolution of the standard No. 1 boiler.*

Left *Evolution of the standard No. 2 boiler.*

Above *'Bulldog' class No. 3357, Exeter, renamed* Smeaton *in October 1903, with original parallel standard No. 2 boiler (courtesy GWR Museum, Swindon).*

Right *Diagrams of standard boilers 4, 5 and 6.*

Left *'City' class* City of Truro, *basically an 'Atbara' with standard No. 4 boiler.*

Below *Diagrams of standard boilers 7, 8 and 12.*

output steam generator would be required and the knowledge gained might be put to good effect. That time did not come until the end of his period in office with development of the powerful 2-8-0 '4700' class. Barrel section diameters of the new standard No. 7 boiler were identical to those of the No. 6 although the length was much shorter. Collett was also able to make use of a similar barrel diameter on his No. 12 boiler for the 'Kings'. Even though all dimensions might not have matched, facilities for plate rolling and flanging were the same, thus allowing for a degree of standardization in production.

A 'one-off' design like *The Great Bear* might be supposed to have been a complete individual, and it really should have been if the potential capabilities of the boiler were to be fully explored. However, Churchward appears to have compromised and made use of as many standard 'engine' parts as possible. Cylinders, valve gear, wheels, axles and bogie were all similar to those fitted to the 'Star' class.[15] It may have been opportune to make use of parts already available in terms of wheels, valve gear and bogie, but small diameter 'Star' cylinders severely restricted the locomotive's capabilities. Having spent a considerable sum of money on the boiler it is possible that Churchward hesitated in spending more than was necessary on other parts if use could be made of standardized items. In fact he insisted upon the 'Star' class general layout for cylinders and motion, being content to leave the cylinder diameter at 15 in.[16]

Standardization of parts has many advantages but, in the opinion of E.S. Cox, there are evils associated with strict adherence to a particular philosophy if it is carried on too long or extended

beyond reasonable limits.[17] Churchward embraced the latter in not making his 'Pacific' a true 'one-off', whilst his successor, Collett, in some instances remained tightly fixed to outdated ways.

Without doubt Churchward put Great Western locomotive production ahead of other British railways but, once the standard range had been designed, he appeared content and failed to lay plans for future continuation of the policy. Apart from the '4700' class nothing new came about during his final ten years in office. A degree of complacency seems to have set in even though

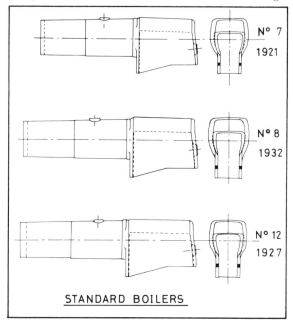

STANDARD BOILERS

much could have been done to standardize the extensive fleet of 0-6-0 tanks required for shunting and branch line work. In fairness it has to be accepted that the war limited scope for production and his main line designs did meet all current traffic requirements. However, in view of Churchward's foresight at the turn of the century, that stagnation is surprising.

At the end of World War I railways remained under Government control and finance was limited. The Railways Act of 1921 proposed a 'grouping' of companies and in January 1923 a

number of minor railways, mainly in Wales, became part of an enlarged Great Western. Collett, who had assumed command at Swindon a year earlier, was faced with the task of 'Westernizing' an extensive array of non-standard locomotives.

Collett wasted no time in having the drawing office investigate each of the absorbed locomotive classes to ascertain which, if any, of the then standard boilers would be most suitable. Subsidiary work was necessary in the form of saddle plates and brackets, but a number of classes could be so treated. In other cases where locomotives were of

Table 4

Churchward standard classes

| Type | Class | Cylinders | | Valve diameter | Coupled wheel diameter | Std No | Boiler Pressure (psi) | 85% tractive effort (lb) |
		No	Size (in.)					
4-6-0	Star	4	15×26	8	6ft 8½in	1	225	27,800
4-6-0	Saint	2	18½×30	10	6ft 8½in	1	225	24,395
4-4-0	County	2	18×30	10	6ft 8½in	4	200	20,530
4-4-0T	2221	2	18×30	10	6ft 8½in	2	195	20,010
2-8-0	47xx	2	19×30	10	5ft 8in	7	225	30,460
2-6-0	43xx	2	18½×30	10	5ft 8in	4	200	25,670
2-6-2T	3100	2	18×30	10	5ft 8in	2	200	24,300
2-6-2T	3150	2	18½×30	10	5ft 8in	4	200	25,670
2-8-0	28xx	2	18½×30	10	4ft 7½in	1	225	35,380
2-8-0T	42xx	2	18½×30	10	4ft 7½in	4	200	31,450
2-6-2T	45xx	2	17×24	8	4ft 7½in	5	200	21,250

Table 5

Collett and Hawksworth outside cylinder standard classes

| Type | Class | Year | Cylinders | | Coupled wheel diameter | Std No | Boiler Pressure (psi) | 85% tractive effort (lb) |
			No	Size (in)				
4-6-0	Castle	1923	4	14×26	6ft 8½in	8	225	31,625
4-6-0	King	1927	4	16¼×28	6ft 6in	12	250	40,300
4-6-0	County	1945	2	18½×30	6ft 3in	15	280	32,580
4-6-0	Hall	1924	2	18½×30	6ft 0in	1	225	27,275
4-6-0	Hall (Modified)	1944	2	18½×30	6ft 0in	1	225	27,275
2-6-2T	51xx	1928	2	18×30	5ft 8in	2	200	24,300
2-6-2T	61xx	1931	2	18×30	5ft 8in	2	225	27,340
4-6-0	Grange	1936	2	18½×30	5ft 8in	1	225	28,875
4-6-0	Manor	1938	2	18×30	5ft 8in	14	225	27,340
2-6-2T	81xx	1938	2	18×30	5ft 6in	2	225	28,165
2-6-2T	3100 (rebuild)	1938	2	18½×30	5ft 3in	4	225	31,170
2-8-2T	7200	1934	2	19×30	4ft 7½in	4	200	33,170

recent construction, modified standard boilers could be used, thus extending the standard range. Because of the work-load, contracts for the boilers were placed with outside manufacturers, tools and plate flanging blocks being loaned as required.[18] By adopting that approach Collett was able to keep much of the absorbed stock running until major replacement of mechanical parts such as cylinders became essential. It was a stop-gap form of standardization allowing newer standard classes to be introduced gradually.

A series of inside-cylindered pannier tank locomotives began to appear in 1929 with the introduction of the '56xx' class. Eventually the class numbered in excess of 800 locomotives, Hawksworth adding to the number with his '94xx' class which differed only in boiler type. At 4 ft 7½ in diameter, the wheel size was fairly standard throughout the pannier tank range, but Collett varied the cylinder diameter in order to obtain the desired power and tractive effort. By making small dimensional changes to cylinders and other components a much wider range of locomotive classes could be produced to meet specific requirements. The range of standard parts was, naturally, increased and Collett has been criticized for that, but such criticism is unjustified. Production of a fleet capable of meeting all the Traffic Department's demands was much more important than strict adherence to a set number of standardized fittings. It has to be remembered that the post-grouping Great Western was larger and more varied than that of the Churchward era. If sufficient numbers were constructed the item became standard anyway.

In some respects Collett did stick rigidly to the Churchward doctrine even though no logical engineering reason existed for doing so. Retention of horizontal outside cylinders remained very much a fetish. In the case of two-cylinder classes it was true that the cylinder castings for left- and right-hand sides were identical and could be interchanged, but producing different castings for opposite sides would have presented no problem. With so many classes making use of identical casting, economy of mass production should still have existed. Certainly by the use of inclined cylinders clearance problems could have been reduced and frame extensions avoided. Only when Hawksworth modified the 'Halls' were the frame extensions avoided, but even there horizontal cylinders remained.

For his 'Castle' class Collett made use of as many standard items as he could and has, again, been criticized for merely enlarging the 'Star'. Tried and tested, the 'Stars' performed well; only upgrading and minor improvements were required. Larger diameter cylinders and a new, bigger standard boiler were the only essentials and possibilities, a fully proportional enlargement of the 'Star' not being available within the weight restrictions imposed by the Civil Engineer. 'Castle' class numbers and commonality of many parts with the 'Stars' enhanced the standardization policy, particularly as a number of 'Stars' were rebuilt as 'Castles'.

Table 6

Collett and Hawksworth inside cylinder standard classes

Type	Class	Year	No	Cylinders Size (in)	Coupled wheel diameter	Std No	Boiler Pressure (psi)	85% tractive effort (lb)
0-6-0	2251	1930	2	17½×24	5ft 2in	10	200	20,155
0-6-0PT	54xx	1931	2	16½×24	5ft 2in	21	165	14,780
0-6-2T	56xx	1924	2	18×26	4ft 7½in	2	200	25,800
0-6-0PT	64xx	1932	2	16½×24	4ft 7½in	21	180	18,010
0-6-0PT	74xx	1936	2	16½×24	4ft 7½in	21	180	18,010
0-6-0PT	57xx	1929	2	17½×24	4ft 7½in	*	200	22,515
0-6-0PT	16xx	1949	2	16½×24	4ft 1½in	16	165	18,515
0-6-0PT	94xx	1948	2	17½×24	4ft 7½in	10	200	22,515
Outside cylinders								
0-6-0PT	15xx	1949	2	17½×24	4ft 7½in	10	200	22,515

* 2301 class boiler, barrel 10ft 3in long×4ft 5in dia., firebox length 5ft 4in. Although not a standard boiler the large numbers constructed effectively made it one.

Former 'Star' class No. 4053, Princess Alexandra, *as converted to a 'Castle'. On a goods train at Twyford, 30 December 1950* (J. Russell-Smith Collection/NRM, York).

Working within slightly less restrictive weight limits it was possible to produce the 'King' class with some pressure from Paddington. In view of the time limit imposed by Pole and the obvious success of the 'Castles', it made good sense to use that locomotive as a basis for the new design. Route availability would be restricted and the class would not be very large, thus allowing scope to divert from the four-cylinder standard without greatly influencing the overall standardization plan. Many of the smaller items could still remain standard. Capital cost of new patterns for cylinders and wheels would be high but those in power were willing to meet it for the prestige of having Britain's 'most powerful locomotive' once again. No standardization policy should be so rigid that it prevents change, otherwise progress is not possible. Collett produced his 'King' design to the limit allowed whilst still keeping within the basic Churchward concept. It was evolution not revolution and it worked. Some parts may not have been standard but the locomotive itself was. 'Kings' fell within the usual pattern which the construction, repair, servicing and footplate gangs knew, thus complying with item 5 on Cox's list (see p. 143).

An obvious evolutionary stage in the standardization scheme is illustrated by the production of the two other 4-6-0 designs. Simply by reducing the wheel diameter of a 'Hall', the higher tractive effort 'Grange' was produced. The 'Manor' was identical to the 'Grange' save for its reduced diameter, though still standard, cylinders and smaller boiler, giving it a lower axle load and greater route availability. Two simple changes in standard items and the usefulness of an already numerous 'Hall' class was extended.

Hawksworth appeared to turn the policy on its head, but his were difficult times and factors such as ease of maintenance predominated. Different manufacturing techniques became available and new ideas in locomotive design, not just steam, developed. The Churchward-inspired Great Western standardization scheme had reached the end of its natural life, although some locomotives similar to those earlier designs continued in production. Faced with many problems, Hawksworth did his best. Certainly his 'Modified Halls' and 'County' class locomotives made use of better constructional techniques and improved accessibility for maintenance. The little '15xx' shunting tank with outside cylinders and valve gear fought a rearguard action against encroaching diesels. Many standard components were used but change was coming.

Nationalization introduced standard classes but the parts standardization as envisaged by Gooch and Churchward did not find complete favour. The requirements of a British Railway system were different from those of a relatively localized Great Western.

Only locomotive standardization has been considered in this section although the technique, obviously, applied to carriages and wagons. Large-scale construction of carriages and wagons introduced a degree of standardization with frames, bogies and wheels being common across whole ranges. Compared with locomotives, carriages and wagons generally required less frequent attention and replacement of parts, their operating lives usually being much longer. In terms of carriage construction the body and interior may have differed, but frames often remained unchanged over many years. Dean, Churchward and Collett, as described in chapter 9, spent time in developing carriage bogies which, in general terms, became standard.

11. Influence abroad

It is possible, without too much imagination, to see a link between many aspects of Great Western engineering practice and that of other railways. For the 'Western' die-hard that link exists because others were influenced by Swindon practice and, in some respects, that is certainly correct. Influence is difficult to quantify or even to define absolutely. By digging deep enough some tenuous connection can usually be made between the practices of one regime and those of another, but such links are often illusory and the evidence is selectively gathered to justify the claim. This chapter intends to look, as impartially as possible, at a number of the ways in which the Great Western influenced engineering practice elsewhere. It is left to the reader to decide how justified the claims are.

Brunel shocked the railway world with his 7 ft gauge, and possibly caused many to ponder the reasoning behind Stephenson's choice of his 'coal cart' gauge. In the end economics dictated that he would lose the battle because it was less expensive to unify the system with rails placed 4 ft 8½ in apart. George Stephenson got in first and laid a great mileage of track before Brunel even set out. There was never any real investigation designed to arrive at an ideal gauge: it was simply a case of majority rule. The fact the Brunel dared to be different certainly cost his employers a great deal of money but it did produce more rapid advances in locomotive and railway development than would otherwise have been the case.

In those early days there was no definite competition between the railways, each having a virtual monopoly in its own region. The real competition developed between the gauges, with parties becoming fervently attached to one or the other. If nothing else, Brunel's individuality united the narrow gauge camp in a way which otherwise might not have occurred. Railways may have had their differences but they united in opposition to the Great Western, not for any particular dislike of that concern but because of its gauge. It was evident that a unified railway system would eventually come about and if it was to be of 7 ft gauge they would lose a lot of money in conversion. In the 'Gauge War' both parties set out to prove that its system was the better and in doing so developed locomotives and track which would provide suitable evidence. It can, therefore, be argued that the difference in gauges promoted a competitive spirit which is unlikely to have existed otherwise, at least to the same extent. More powerful locomotives with better efficiency resulted and trackwork standards were improved.

Locomotive trials before the Gauge Commissioners pitted Gooch's 'Firefly' class *Ixion* against Robert Stephenson's newly constructed 'A' class engine. It has been suggested that the Stephenson locomotive was specially constructed for the trials but that machine was, in fact, approved for construction in April 1845, some months before the Commission was appointed.[1] Differences in operating conditions made true comparisons extremely difficult and both parties made selective use of the

Gooch standard 'Firefly' design locomotive.

results in order to prove particular points. It is reasonable to assume that both locomotives were 'tuned' so as to produce maximum performance but no definite and quantifiable superiority of either type was ever indicated.

The trials did, however, provide a stimulus. Gooch made haste in the design and construction of his superior *Great Western*, whilst other narrow gauge railways became aware of locomotive improvements embodied in the 'A' class engine. Demand for locomotives of that type increased substantially following the trials.[2] Had it not been for Brunel, Gooch and the broad gauge it is doubtful if such orders would have come about so rapidly. It is also highly unlikely that improvements in the 'A' class, as suggested by G.P. Bidder, operating protagonist for the narrow gauge party, would have been made so readily.

Years before those trials took place the meticulous mind of Gooch was exerting its influence over locomotive construction and mechanical engineering in general. Naysmyth, Gaskell & Co. were invited to tender for construction of twenty 'Firefly' class locomotives, being encouraged to do so by a clause in the contract. A premium of £100 was added to the price of each engine after it had satisfactorily performed on trial for a month. Such a clause must have applied to all manufacturers who undertook construction of Gooch locomotives and will have provided an incentive for first class work. Not only was a premium payed but the board of directors, almost certainly at the suggestion of Brunel and Gooch, provided each qualifying building with an unsolicited testimonial as to the quality of workmanship. James Nasmyth was delighted with the testimonial which 'proved extremely valuable in other quarters'.

Nasmyth, Gaskell & Co. later produced the 'Hercules' class, but it was the first order in which James Nasmyth found greatest satisfaction and benefit for other, non-railway, projects:

> . . .in order to effect the prompt and perfect execution of this order, I contrived several special machine tools, which assisted us most materially. These machine tools for the most part rendered us more independent of mere manual strength and dexterity, while at the same time they increased the accuracy and perfection of the work. They afterwards assisted us in the means of perfecting the production of other classes of work. At the same time they had the important effect of diminishing the cost of production, as was made sufficiently apparent by the balance sheet prepared at the end of each year.[3]

If the premium encouraged high quality work and the development of improved machine tools by one manufacturer, it must have had a similar effect elsewhere. The testimonial, a 'Great Western Seal of Approval', is likely to have been of considerable use in obtaining contracts from other concerns. Brunel had certainly learned a lesson from his earlier locomotive ordering. He and Gooch made a formidable team which encouraged development in manufacturing engineering.

James Nasmyth was a very good mechanical engineer in his own right, as his many inventions will testify. One of these, the steam hammer, also came about through another company with which Brunel had connections. The Great Western Steam Ship Company encountered difficulties in finding a manufacturer willing to forge the large 30 in diameter intermediate paddle shaft for its steamer, *Great Britain*. Nasmyth solved the problem with his design for a steam-powered hammer but, ultimately, the shaft was not required as paddle propulsion gave way to screw.[4] Many of the machine tools developed as a result of the 'Firefly' locomotive contract are likely to have been developed at a later date for other work, such was the ingenuity of Nasmyth. The fact remains, however, that Gooch's stringent requirements and his incentives provided ample stimulus.

Necessity may be the 'mother of invention' but the Great Western can claim to have been a midwife. Apart from Nasmyth, Gaskell & Co., other manufacturers also received contracts for locomotives of the 'Firefly' class and many received further work for subsequent classes. High standards must have been set for Gooch to return to the builders again. Considering the state of the locomotive art at the time Brunel ordered his 'freaks', and the quality of the Gooch designs, it is reasonable to assume that the Locomotive Superintendent of the Great Western Railway was instrumental in advancing that art. All railways were to benefit from Gooch's foresight.

An ability to appreciate talent was another forte of the 'young Geordie', for he also gathered around himself other skilful engineers. Whilst Gooch was at the East Foundry, Dundee, he struck up a friendship with Archibald Sturrock, an apprentice barely a month younger than himself. Gooch taught the young Scot mechanical drawing and must have been impressed with his abilities as, in 1840, Sturrock became his principal assistant at Paddington. When the building of the Locomotive Works at Swindon was authorized, the task of supervising construction and managing the plant fell to Sturrock. It was Sturrock who had responsibility for construction of the 8 ft single wheelers as well as other classes. Management of what were probably the best locomotive works in

Britain provided valuable training.

Those years spent with Gooch at Paddington trying to keep Brunel's locomotives in service and subsequent years at Swindon must have left their mark on the talented Scot. Throughout his life he retained a great admiration for Gooch and the work he produced. He was impressed by the superior hauling ability of broad gauge locomotives and attributed it to their high heating surface and pressure. Sturrock took his knowledge and experience to the Great Northern Railway where he became Locomotive Superintendent in 1850.[5] Without doubt Gooch and Brunel would have been sorry to see such a able individual depart. However, it appears to have been a characteristic of both men to take pleasure in seeing a close associate advance to higher office.

At the Great Northern Sturrock found a different type of regime which severely limited his actions. Gooch had considerable freedom in his expenditure but Sturrock had to obtain permission from the GNR board to spend anything. Being aware of the advantages that the repair and construction works at Swindon had given to the GWR, he soon proposed that a permanent repair facility be constructed at Peterborough. Like Swindon, Peterborough was positioned at almost the mid-point on the line (from Kings Cross to Doncaster) and its location was favoured by Sturrock for the same reasons Brunel and Gooch had chosen Swindon. However, other influences prevailed and Doncaster was chosen.[6]

Sturrock got his repair works and equipped them to the highest standard his employers' financial constraints would allow. Unlike the situation which existed on the Great Western, all locomotives were constructed by outside contractors following competitive tendering. Designs were provided by the Locomotive Superintendent. It is inappropriate to consider the Sturrock designs in detail but Great Western practice was evident in many cases. Sandwich frames and large domeless boilers found application to most designs. All of Sturrock's boilers employed round top fireboxes raised above the barrel, a feature common to Gooch's later locomotives. On his famous single wheeler, No. 215 of 1853, he even incorporated a Swindon type 'iron coffin' on the tender.

When, in 1863, the Great Western suddenly withdrew its motive power from the Metropolitan Railways it was Sturrock who quickly stepped in with an offer to provide condensing locomotives. Having been responsible for maintenance of the GWR condensing machines, he knew how to go about adapting GNR locomotives. In the seven days allowed he was able to utilize the whole efforts

of the Doncaster works to make suitable modifications to the necessary locomotives.[7] In view of his experiences in the early days with Gooch at Paddington and in the hurried construction of *Great Western* at Swindon, Sturrock had ideal credentials for tackling the job.

A remarkable introduction by Sturrock was that of the steam tender. Basically an engine-powered tender attached to the locomotive, it was the precursor of the power booster introduced years later. The idea did not originate with him but was dreamed up by M. Verpilleux, a French engineer, in 1843. Sturrock, however, developed the scheme and took out a patent. The Great Northern's mean directors did not appear to take kindly to the idea of paying royalties to one of their own employees. Following protracted negotiations they agreed to pay half the amount which was payed by other railways, subject to a maximum of £50 per engine.[8]

Archibald Sturrock retired from railway service in 1865 and spent the remainder of his long life in country pursuits. He died on 1 January 1909 at the age of ninety-two. Why he put railway engineering behind him whilst still having so much to offer is unknown, but his employers did not appear to offer any encouragement. The Great Northern's loss was also railway engineering's loss.

Contemporary with Sturrock at the GWR was Thomas Crampton, a 'clever fellow', according to Gooch. He held the post of Chief Draughtsman and had, obviously, impressed his superior. It is almost certain that Sturrock and Crampton knew each other even though the former was based at Swindon and the latter at Paddington. Crampton was inventive by nature and work on the broad gauge appears to have suited him. The twin values of a high capacity boiler and low locomotive centre of gravity could be achieved with a 7 ft gauge, but a narrower gauge presented problems. Crampton's solution was to place the locomotive driving axle to the rear of firebox and boiler. The same idea had been tried in America some years before Crampton patented the concept, but no publicity seems to have been given this side of the Atlantic.

After leaving Swindon in 1844 Crampton took on other work but still attempted to interest people in his plan. A year later the Leige & Namur Railway took an option on two locomotives constructed to Crampton's patent. Although the locomotives never did reach Belgium, several others of a similar type were constructed for lines in Britain. Archibald Sturrock found the idea interesting and, in 1850, convinced the GNR directors that the railway should have a number of 'Cramptons'. To what extent Sturrock's decision was influenced by his previous acquaintance is unknown but he appears to have been impressed by the design's merits, at least initially.

Many Crampton-designed locomotives were successfully running on the Nord Railway and Sturrock made a trip to France in order to assess performance. Doubts were expressed as to the adhesive capabilities of the GNR 'Cramptons', which differed slightly from the French engines. The 1849 modification involved an intermediate crankshaft which provided the drive to the main axle by means of outside connecting rods. Concern about adhesion was justified and the GNR locomotives were subsequently modified to a more conventional form.[9]

Despite lack of success in Britain, Crampton's locomotive proved to be popular with European railways. In France and Germany the name of this fine and imaginative engineer is held in high esteem. Like Gooch and Brunel he had many strings to his engineering bow, including that of civil railway engineering. Gooch is famous for his exploits in laying the Atlantic telegraph cable but to Crampton goes the credit of laying the first international submarine telegraph cable. In 1851 Crampton laid a cable across the Straits of Dover using equipment he had designed himself. It may be fanciful to assume that, in those demanding days at Paddington, Gooch and Crampton discussed the intricacies of laying submarine cables whilst they wrestled with a locomotive design problem, but then why not?

Another product of the 'Swindon school of railway engineering' to find fame elsewhere was James Holden. His first senior appointment at Swindon was that of Carriage and Wagon Works Manager in 1873. Five years later, following the sudden death of Joseph Armstrong, he also became assistant to the new Locomotive Superintendent, William Dean. For the next seven years he held both posts and was in a unique position to monitor, and possibly influence, locomotive and carriage design. It is evident that Holden was of considerable importance to Dean in that period which preceded final abolition of the broad gauge. Plans were laid for more convertible locomotives and the convertible coach was introduced.

In 1885 Holden secured the position of Locomotive Superintendent on the Great Eastern Railway and moved to Stratford, in East London. A definite concept he took with him was that of coach conversion, but then it may have been his idea in the first instance. An early scheme for carriage conversion involved the removal of a central portion of body and frame in order to reduce the width. Bodies and frames were not constructed as complete units but were formed from separate longitudinal sections subsequently pegged together. Conversion involved separation of the sections and then reassembly without the central portion. Later conversion techniques simply involved changing the bogies on what were already narrow gauge frames and bodies. That proved more effective. The orignal idea still had merit, however, and Holden put it to good use but in reverse. The Great Eastern wished to improve seating capacity and comfort on some of its trains but did not want to commit itself to new stock. Holden decided that carriages could be modified by simply inserting longitudinal sections after first splitting the bodies.[10] It was a stroke of inspiration based upon previous experience.

Throughout his twenty-three years with the Great Eastern Holden devoted considerable effort towards a policy of standardization.[11] He may have been influenced by similar work on the Great Western, particularly that of Gooch, but the policy was born out of necessity. Prior to Holden's arrival the GER had been 'blessed' with a succession of Locomotive Superintendents. The rapid turnover did little for design continuity even though some of them, including S.W. Johnson, William Adams and T.W. Worsdell, were particularly gifted and went on to show their skills elsewhere. Holden's term in office introduced stability but his training at Swindon must have been useful in formulating a standardization policy. He was assisted in the process by the fact that, like his previous employers, the Great Eastern built its own locomotives and rolling stock.

It would be unfair to attempt any comparison between Holden and those who occupied a similar position at Swindon as their situations were somewhat different. In any case that is not the purpose of this chapter, which aims to illustrate what influence the Great Western had on other railways. Holden produced some very effective designs but will be mainly remembered, it would seem, for his 'Decapod'. With ten coupled wheels and a large boiler working at 200 psi pressure, the machine had an 85% tractive effort of no less than 43,000 lb. Basic design criteria had been for a tank engine which could reach 30 mph in thirty seconds, thus equalling the acceleration claimed for electric traction with a 300 ton train. The big engine met the specification but its life was restricted due to the track damage it caused.[12] It did, however, kill off the notion that electric traction should replace steam on the London suburban services.

Despite all Holden did on the Great Eastern and the service Sturrock rendered to the Great Northern, the most notable of Swindon's expatriate locomotive engineers was William Arthur Stanier.

For most people he *was* Swindon abroad, but many of his practices differed radically from those of Churchward and Collett. Stanier was a product of Swindon and Great Western to the core. There is little doubt that he would not have moved to the LMS if prospects of taking over from Collett had been brighter. However, it was made clear by Viscount Churchill, then GWR chairman, that Stanier had no chance of succeeding Collett.[13] Somewhat reluctantly it would seem, Stanier became Chief Mechanical Engineer of the London, Midland & Scottish Railway in January 1932.

The locomotive situation on the LMS was chronic and urgent action was required. He approached his task in a direct way but first ensured that his senior officers were on his side. Conflict between former LNWR and Midland men had done much to precipitate the crisis and that situation could not be allowed to continue. Stanier made his mark and it is an indication of the strength of his personality that they all pulled together for the new LMS.

It might be supposed that locomotive designs would follow the strict Great Western pattern but that was not the case. Stanier may have been Swindon through and through but he was also a very good engineer with strong views of his own. Pure GWR designs would not suit LMS operations. Churchwardian attitudes to outside valve gear and inclined cylinders found no favour. Stanier's locomotives were for the LMS not the GWR. He did not, however, ignore all former practices but selected those with which he was fully in agreement and which suited the locomotive needs of his new employers. Following his move to the LMS, Stanier seems to have had little contact with Collett but would frequently visit Churchward in order to discuss design details and engineering in general.[14]

In a very visual way some Great Western influence was evident in Stanier's designs; he used a taper boiler with GWR pattern chimney. When the first locomotive, a 2-6-0, emerged from Crewe Works it was even fitted with the GWR style safety valve cover. That touch was without Stanier's approval and he quickly ordered it removed.[15]

Top left *Stanier 4-6-0 'Black five' showing the Swindon influence.*

Middle left *The influence of Churchward's taper boiler is evident in Stanier's 'Jubilee', Leander, as preserved on the Severn Valley Railway.*

Left *Stanier's 'Pacific' design No. 6201, Princess Elizabeth, as preserved. Hawksworth's 'Pacific' designs had a similar external appearance.*

Whilst at Swindon he had attempted to interest Collett in a compound 'Castle' but his first large locomotive for the LMS was a 'Pacific'. Two were constructed initially to allow for testing, with a larger and modified batch appearing later. The 'Princess' class locomotives were imposing and attractive. Initially, in keeping with Swindon tradition, a low degree of superheat was applied and the boilers had a very long barrel but short firebox. Early running showed them to be short of steam and modifications were required. Superheat area was doubled whilst the barrel was shortened and firebox lengthened. They became first class steamers. A further divergence from the Swindon pattern came with the introduction of conventional domed regulators and separate top feed.[16] Stanier had found the secret of a good large boiler to give plenty of steam for hill climbing in Cumbria and across the Scottish border.

Other designs followed quickly, including his famous 'Black fives' for mixed-traffic work, the 'Jubilees' and class 'eight' freight locomotives. After early 'Jubilee' steaming difficulties were sorted out, all classes performed exceptionally well. The fact that no less than 842 'Black fives' were eventually constructed is ample proof of their ability and performance. In the same league were the '8F' engines, both classes serving to the end of steam on British Railways. Stanier had got his boiler design right and had, obviously, heeded the words of Churchward that the modern locomotive problem was principally a question of boiler.[17]

One of the 'Princess' class was constructed with a turbine drive, illustrating Stanier's open views on traction. For high speed services he produced the streamlined 'Coronation' class which were capable of sustaining higher power outputs than any other British design.[18] Again it was all down to the boiler. Rebuilding of 'Royal Scot' and 'Patriot' classes gave them new boilers and some degree of standardization with other Stanier three-cylinder designs.

William Stanier put the LMS at the forefront of British locomotive practice just as his mentor, Churchward, had done for the Great Western. He stabilized the railway's traction regime because he was a good engineer and manager, being given the opportunity to do so because he was an outsider and had no allegiance to any of the railways which combined to form the LMS. Post-grouping LMS squabbles afforded little chance for locomotive progress. It took a strong personality with management talent as well as obvious engineering ability to unify all factions. On the Great Western, Collett had wanted little involvement in public affairs and left Stanier to attend to the social and public

functions of a CME. That experience, and his own thorough training on the Great Western, made Stanier an ideal choice for the London, Midland & Scottish Railway.

Great Western locomotive design talent was appreciated throughout the railways of Britain especially following the advances of the Churchward era. Once the Churchward standard range had been produced there was less need for a large staff and many sought employment elsewhere. R.E.L. Maunsell, Chief Mechanical Engineer of the South Eastern & Chatham Railway, seized upon the opportunity and attracted a small band to Ashford. Harold Holcroft was one of the group which formed a 'little Great Western' in the South East, G.H. Pearson leading the migration when he became Assistant Chief Mechanical Engineer of the SE&CR in 1914. As far as Holcroft was concerned they were 'like a band of missionaries setting out to enlighten the heathen'.[19]

The result of that imported talent was increased adoption of Churchward ideas, including coned Belpaire boilers, top feed, 10 in diameter piston valves with large lap and long travel, steel firebox side stays and bush end connecting rods.[20] Many of the ideas might have percolated through to Ashford anyway but the presence of so many Swindon-trained men certainly speeded the process. Holcroft was a very good engineer in his own right but he has not been afforded the recognition to which he is entitled. Some of his work at Swindon has already been mentioned but his efforts away from Swindon really fall outside the scope of this book. The final form of Gresley-conjugated valve gear for three-cylinder engines has its origins in a modification suggested by Holcroft. Gresley was so impressed with Holcroft that he was invited to join the staff at the GNR but the SE&CR knew a good thing and would not release him.[21]

Final ambassador to leave the 'Great Western School of Locomotive Engineering' was Kenneth Cook, and that did not take place until after nationalization. Reluctantly Cook gave up his post as Chief Mechanical and Electrical Engineer for the Western Region to take up a similar position at Doncaster, on the Eastern and North Eastern Region. Gresley's 'Pacifics' were getting on in years and changed operating conditions meant that they were in need of thorough rebuilding. Many problems resulted from misalignment caused by wear and faulty setting. The only solution was an optical alignment system as installed at Swindon. Contacts with a British manufacturer led to production of an apparatus which was simpler than that originally obtained from Germany.

Optical alignment together with other modifications such as Swindon-type bearings and improved draughting turned these 'old' locomotives into precision machines.[22] Though many LNER enthusiasts might not care to agree, it appears to be the case that Cook gave the 'Pacifics' a new lease of life and actually improved their performance and running.[23]

It was not only its engineers that the Great Western sent to other reailways; locomotives also carried the flag from time to time. Churchward always considered his locomotives to be superior to those of any other railway, and perhaps he was correct. They were, however, more expensive than similar types elsewhere. In 1910 some Great Western directors asked their Locomotive Superintendent to explain why the LNWR could build three of its 4-6-0 locomotives for the same cost as two of his. Typically, Churchward replied with strong words to the effect that one of his could pull two LNWR locomotives backwards.[24]

To prove his point an interchange of unsuperheated 4-6-0s was arranged with C.J. Bowen-Cooke, Locomotive Superintendent of the LNWR. Bowen-Cooke was keen on such interchange trials but it appears that he was more interested in the performance of *Polar Star* than his own 'Experiment' class engine on GWR metals. No special care was given by Camden shed in preparing *Worcestershire* and it showed in the poor performance. Churchward had something to prove and ensured

that his 'Star' was in peak conditon for its foray north. That preparation, and the basic superiority of *Polar Star*, were plain to see. The GWR machine easily managed any task, with a coal consumption far below that of competing 'Experiments'. The trials vindicated Churchward and gave Bowen-Cooke some food for thought.[25]

The next test 'abroad' for a GWR locomotive came about as a result of the 1924 British Empire Exhibition at Wembley. Careful arrangement of exhibits placed the LNER *Flying Scotsman* alongside the GWR's pride and joy, *Caerphilly Castle*. Like schoolboys with imagined pugnacious fathers, directors of both companies argued about technical matters of which they knew little. There was only one possible outcome, a duel. Neither Collett nor Gresley had much interest in such a combat and their approval had not been sought anyway. In 1925 *Pendennis Castle* went to the LNER to work out of Kings Cross whilst *Wild Victor* worked west from Paddington.

Operating with Welsh coal, the 'Castle' had a consumption some 12% lower than the 'Pacific', whilst on Yorkshire coal it was 6% lower. *Wild Victor* did put in some good performances on Great Western metals but the 'A1' design was not then fully developed, hence Gresley's reluctance. Whilst the LNER management appears to have taken the view that test results were private between the two companies, Felix Pole, or someone of similar importance, had other ideas. Publicity was of value

Left Pendennis Castle, *the locomotive which performed so well on LNER metals in 1925. At Exeter St David's on 2 October 1965* (Chris Surridge).

Right *Southern Railway 'Lord Nelson' class No. 850,* Lord Nelson, *as preserved in Bulleid reconstructed form. Through the Swindon expatriates some GWR influence found its way into the design.*

and could not be wasted. Publication of the results with an account of the trials brought complaints from the LNER, especially as they indicated a GWR superiority. To make matters worse for the LNER, *Pendennis Castle* was sent to stand alongside *Flying Scotsman* at Wembley as soon as the trials were over.[26] Gresley subsequently modified his 'Pacific' design, making use of higher boiler pressure and increased valve travel, both of which the 'Castle' had.

Felix Pole could not resist an opportunity for publicity and, in 1926, saw one in the loan of a 'Castle' to the LMS. To give the impression of a locomotive exchange for testing purposes, the Kentish Town depot sent a three-cylinder compound 4-4-0 to Paddington for a short period but it did not hide the fact that the LMS was in desperate locomotive trouble. *Launceston Castle* went to Camden and had no difficulty in maintaining service schedules between Euston and Crewe. Subsequent tests between Crewe and Carlisle illustrated certain shortcomings in the 'Castle' design as far as sanding gear was concerned. The GWR gravity system did not perform satisfactorily in bad November weather when driving side winds blew sand from the rails. In all other respects the results were impressive and Sir Henry Fowler, Chief Mechanical Engineer, was instructed to obtain fifty locomotives of similar capabilities for working services the following year.[27]

The LMS Operating Department had consider-able influence with top management and its indication that a 'Castle' type locomotive would satisfy requirements met with that immediate instruction to Fowler. He was then placed in an unenviable position and anybody with a modicum of engineering knowledge would have realized the problem. To design a new express locomotive in less than a year presented difficulties but it might be achieved. Actually to construct fifty for service within the same time limit was practically impossible. Pole may have asked a lot of Collett but he never demanded the absurd. The lack of understanding between departments was symptomatic of the malaise which afflicted the LMS at that time.

Fowler approached the Great Western to build fifty 'Castles' for him but legal restrictions prevented Swindon from acting as a general manufacturer. The subsequent request for a complete set of 'Castle' drawings was refused by Collett. Why that was so is difficult to understand as there would have been considerable kudos in having another railway reliant upon a Great Western design. It is surprising that Pole allowed the opportunity to escape. Fowler then turned to Maunsell on the Southern Railway and he agreed to furnish a set of drawings for his 'Lord Nelson' class 4-6-0. At the time there was much 'discussion' between GWR and SR parties as to which class, 'Castle' or 'Lord Nelson', was the most powerful. Again the thorny subject of tractive effort tended to obscure the real merits of each class.

Above *LMS 'Royal Scot' class*, The Manchester Regiment (courtesy of the National Railway Museum, York).

Left *The ultimate British 'Pacific'? Stanier's* Duchess of Hamilton. *Few of Churchward's ideas are evident.*

Eventually the North British Locomotive Company was given the task of modifying Maunsell's 'Lord Nelson' design to suit certain requirements of the LMS Operating Department. The Chief Mechanical Engineer appears to have had little to say in the matter. Although 'Castle' drawings were refused, the resultant 'Royal Scot' class owed its existence to Swindon. If it had not been for *Launceston Castle's* performance the LMS might have continued about its confused way. Through the contingent who left Swindon for Ashford there was some Great Western influence on Southern locomotive designs. By a roundabout route that might have reached the 'Royal Scot' class, but only

with Stanier's subsequent rebuilding could any real Swindon influence be seen.

Launceston Castle was the final GWR locomotive to make a foray onto another railway for trial purposes, at least while the independent railways still existed. As locomotive engineering on other railways progressed, any advantage held by the Great Western narrowed and little reason existed for such exchanges. By the mid-1930s Gresley on the LNER, Stanier on the LMS and Maunsell on the Southern had developed machines to suit their needs and operations, so there was no point in comparing designs. Each railway, including the GWR, was satisfied with its own locomotives.

12. Western heritage

The Great Western Railway was not an organization overly interested in preserving its past except where those articles from the past still served a useful purpose. That philosophy extended to many of its servants including some from the engineering side. George Jackson Churchward fell into the category of those who cared little for history or tradition. His actions in calling for the destruction of the two remaining broad gauge locomotives has already been detailed, that single act of folly, or insensitive stupidity, robbing the railway world of its remaining links with Brunel's imaginative dream. There is little doubt that, properly cared for, the original *North Star* and the 'Iron Duke' class

Lord of the Isles would have encouraged many broad gauge projects within the ranks of the preservation movement. That, however, was not to be, but a broad gauge line at Didcot and the replica broad gauge locomotives do allow a tantalizing glimpse of the early years.

Lack of feeling for the past also appears to have extended to Churchward's successor, C.B. Collett, though he did not prove to be so destructive. Imminent withdrawal of the famous *City of Truro* was viewed by some people with a degree of concern, justified in the light of Churchward's actions. The GWR did not want the locomotive when it was withdrawn from traffic but parties at

Right *Replica broad gauge* North Star *at the Great Western Museum.*

Below City of Truro *at work on the Severn Valley Railway following restoration there* (Patrick Griffiths).

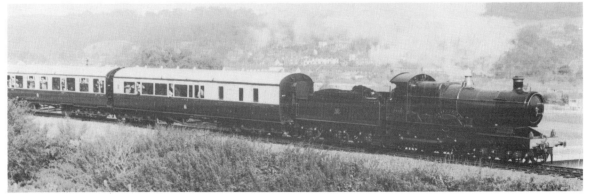

the LNER and York Railway Museum felt differently. Collett was approached and encouraged the group from Yorkshire to contact Paddington. The management of the GWR agreed to the move, with General Manager J. Milne even claiming that he 'did not consider the engine to be of outstanding importance'. Such a claim would appear to have been in keeping with GWR sentiments. Hedging his bets he did, however, indicate that the locomotive should remain at the disposal of the GWR if it was required in the future. Following its sojourn at York and a recall to duty during the latter years of British steam, the 4-4-0 eventually found a Swindon home at the Great Western Museum in 1962. Fortunately, through the skills of those on the Severn Valley Railway and the donations of many, this classic locomotive has returned to steam.

Despite the apparent lack of interest in its own history the Great Western Railway is well represented in the present preservation movement. Credit must go to the many individuals who have given freely of their time and money over the years. It is not only locomotives and rolling stock which survive but also the many artifacts representative of that company. Although a number of locomotives were bought directly from British Railways service it has been from the ranks of decaying giants at Woodham's scrapyard that the majority of GWR-designed steamers in preservation have been drawn. Without that depressing yet rewarding store in South Wales the Great Western would now have the representation its generals seemingly wanted.

In locomotive terms the preserved works of Churchward and Collett are plentiful but that has only been brought about through the dedication of small teams of individuals who turn rusting metal into steaming works of art. Unfortunately there are many classes which have not survived and the last Chief Mechanical Engineer is not as well represented as his work merits. No example of the final GWR-designed tender engine, Hawksworth's 'County' class, exists and many of the earlier classes of the Churchward era failed to escape the cutter's torch upon withdrawal. Understandably, considering the policy of those in command at Paddington, little can be seen of the brilliant efforts of the Armstrongs, Dean or Gooch.

However, it would be churlish to dwell upon what might have been, and all enthusiasts should be grateful for the magnificent display of engineering craftsmanship which is available to public gaze. Throughout the year GWR locomotives may be observed in steam at preserved railways and on British Rail's main lines, 'living' examples of their

designers' skill.

The National Collection includes an example of the ultimate passenger class, namely *King George V*. In the custody of Bulmers, this locomotive is much in demand and performs regularly on main line excursions. Powerful and attractive, 'The King' is limited to certain routes because of weight restriction, even on former Great Western lines. GWR-designed locomotives are mainly confined to territory in Wales and the West because of the ample loading gauge allowed by the company in constructing its lines. Naturally, some designs made full use of this. Two other 'Kings' have survived, both coming via the scrapyard at Barry. *King Edward I* has been restored at the Buckingham Railway Centre whilst, despite driving wheels having been cut through, *King Edward II* is a long-term restoration project at Bristol. From a total class of thirty a survival rate of 10% must be considered exceptional.

Collett's other major passenger class, the 'Castles', are also well represented, though not all of those recovered from the Woodham's scrapyard are intended for full restoration. A number are, quite correctly, intended as a source of spares for members of the class already in steam or shortly to be so. That prudent step will allow some 'Castles' to continue in service long after their present parts become life expired. Apart from *Caerphilly Castle*, now interred at the Science Museum, two other 'Castles' entered preservation directly from British Railways service. One, *Pendennis Castle*, has since emigrated to Australia but *Clun Castle* now resides at the former GWR base at Tyseley. In fact *Clun Castle* was not built until after nationalization and cannot, strictly, be considered a GWR locomotive. However, it is of 'Castle' design with double chimney, revised draughting arrangements and four-row superheater, which shows what the class was capable of becoming. Three other 'Castles' are in the care of the Birmingham Railway Museum at Tyseley, one of which, *Defiant*, has been restored to former Great Western glory.

Amongst its extensive stock the Great Western Society at Didcot also has an allocation of 'Castles', both coming from the scrapyard at Barry. The fourth locomotive actually to leave that place for preservation was No. 5051, *Drysllwyn Castle*. Two names were carried by the locomotive during GWR service, the other being *Earl Bathurst*. It is, therefore, considered reasonable to allow the 'Castle' to operate at the centre or on the main line with either set of name plates in place.

Didcot Railway Centre offers the enthusiast the chance to see a unique collection of former Great Western locomotives, rolling stock and much more.

Right *A candidate for restoration, No. 6023,* King Edward II, *at Bristol Temple Meads Station in 1985.*

Right Clun Castle, *a BR-built example with double chimney, during a visit to the Severn Valley Railway in 1985.*

Below *Three 'Castles' at the Birmingham Railway Museum, Tyseley: residents No. 7029,* Clun Castle, *and No. 5080,* Defiant, *in scrapyard livery, alongside Didcot's No. 5051,* Drysllwyn Castle.

The site itself is, naturally, of GWR origin, its centrepiece, the four-road engine shed, having been constructed during the depression of the early 1930s. Not content with such a prize, the society also boasts a coaling stage surmounted by a 74,000 gal water tank. In typical Great Western fashion coaling of locomotives is carried out using small trolleys. Maintenance of locomotives and other rolling stock comes high on the list of priorities and a lifting shop allows major tasks such as boiler lifts to be undertaken. No voluntary society can hope to match the equipment or space available to a railway company but what is lacking in facilities is made up for in enthusiasm. Locomotives such as *Drysllwyn Castle* bear witness to that fact.

The desire of a small group of schoolboys to see the preservation of an 0-4-2 tank locomotive and auto-trailer began it all back in 1964. Their enthusiasm was infectious and the Great Western Society soon came into being. Large oaks from small acorns certainly do grow. Amongst the locomotive collection is another 'Castle', *Nunney Castle*, though it is not yet restored. No less than three 'Halls' have been preserved, *Hinderton Hall* and *Maindy Hall* being original Collett designs and *Burton Agnes Hall* a modified Hawksworth type. Two are fully operational but the fate of *Maindy Hall* has yet to be decided. It is still possible that it may be rebuilt as a 'Saint', from which the 'Halls' were developed. Though such a rebuilding would be costly, it does show the dedication within the preservation movement and would be a worthwhile endeavour.

The 'Manor' class is represented by *Cookham Manor* which was purchased in 1966 upon with-

drawal from service. Two other tender engines in the fleet are Churchward 2-6-0 No. 5322, '4300' class, built in 1917, and heavy freight 2-8-0 No. 3822, built in 1940 to an original Churchward design of 1903. As with the GWR itself, tank engines abound. The pannier tank '57xx' class, which at one time totalled 863 locomotives, is represented by Nos. 3650 and 3738. Large and small prairie tanks mix with side tanks of other wheel configurations. The oldest locomotive at Didcot is No. 1363, of 1910, the only remaining saddle tank built in Swindon.

To match its locomotive fleet the Great Western Society also boasts an exceptional collection of coaches, amongst which are three Ocean Saloons introduced in 1932. These were designed for use in the transatlantic boat trains from Plymouth. Lunch or tea taken in one of these saloons enables the visitor to capture a little of the luxury enjoyed by the rich 1930s traveller. The remaining coach collection consists of examples from the Dean, Churchward, Collett and Hawksworth eras. A number of Dean four- and six-wheeled vehicles add to the variety. Most of the older coaches survived because they were not conveniently available when scrapping time came around. Some were used for storage, others as accommodation, and one in particular was used as a chicken shed. That vehicle, No. 6824, dates from 1887 and was originally designed for use on the broad gauge. Following conversion to the standard gauge and its agricultural use, long-term restoration is now in hand to renew the broad gauge splendour.

Straddling the divide between locomotive and coach is Railcar No. 22. Built by AEC for the

Left *A trio of Great Western 4-6-0s, No. 5051, Drysllwyn Castle, No. 7808, Cookham Manor and No. 5900, Hinderton Hall, on display at the Great Western Society's Didcot base.*

Right *Hawksworth's '9400' class No. 9466 on display at Didcot. This locomotive is normally based at the Buckingham Railway Centre.*

Below *Visitors at Didcot: '5600' class No. 6619, from the North Yorkshire Moors Railway, and '4200' class No. 5224, now preserved on the Great Central Railway.*

Bottom *Didcot residents No. 1363, of Churchward's '1361' 0-6-0ST class for dock shunting, '4300' class No. 5322 and '5600' class No. 6697.*

Left *Collett's standard pannier tank '5700' class, No. 3738.*

Below left *A visitor at Didcot from the Bluebell Railway, 'Earl' or 'Dukedog' class No. 3217,* Earl of Berkeley.

Right *Modified 'Hall' No. 6960,* Raveningham Hall, *at Bewdley.*

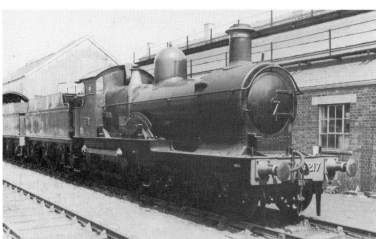

Below right *The Severn Valley Railway's almost mandatory '5700' class locomotive, No. 5764, at Bewdley.*

pioneering GWR diesel services it is not to the taste of many steam enthusiasts but it is, at least, Great Western. Travelling Post Offices found frequent GWR service on trains between the West Country and London, and needless to say one of these vehicles is preserved at Didcot. At regular intervals mail exchange demonstrations are offered to visitors. A wide selection of wagons completes the rolling stock collection. Many have been restored to authentic livery and may also be seen on regular demonstration trains.

As with other railway centres, Didcot offers steam train rides but unlike other centres actually has two demonstration lines. Didcot also has its broad gauge line, or to be more specific its mixed gauge line. This is the only line of its kind in Britain and the only permanent line upon which the replica broad gauge locomotives and stock may operate. A large wooden transfer shed, which

originally stood near the main London–Bristol line at Didcot, allows any visitor to consider the problems which really did exist with a break of gauge. The mixed gauge complex is unique and well worth a visit alone. In all, Didcot offers a complete Great Western experience.

If the Great Western Society is able to provide a condensed view of the GWR on shed, then the Severn Valley Railway offers an operating railway experience. The visitor only has to stand on the platform at Highley or Arley stations in order to be transported back to the age of steam, Great Western steam. The SVR is not solely a GWR-preserved railway but it does have an extensive fleet of Great Western designed locomotives and rolling stock. Through that stock comparisons, if only in a visual sense, may be made, allowing any prejudices to be confirmed; the railway enthusiast rarely changes his spots, or livery.

Based upon a former Great Western branch line, the SVR offers a sixteen-mile journey between Kidderminster and Bridgnorth through some magnificent scenery and period locations. It is a working railway with all stock being maintained to first class standards. Many of the locomotives are on the British Rail list of approved main line runners, a testament to the quality of work produced by the full-time and volunteer engineering staff. Former GWR locomotives include two 'Halls' and three 'Manors'. *Hagley Hall* dates from 1929, being of the original Collett design, whilst modified version *Raveningham Hall* allows Hawksworth design changes to be appreciated if not readily seen. Both restored 'Manors', *Hinton* and *Erlestoke*, come from Lot No. 316 built at Swindon in 1939. They are identical in all respects save that *Hinton Manor* has recently been displaying the early British Railways lined black livery. *Bradley Manor* is currently undergoing restoration.

The only Collett 0-6-0 to survive, No. 3205 of the '2251' class, had the honour of hauling the first train from Bridgnorth when the SVR entered the era of preservation. That machine has seen regular service on passenger trains as well as the occasional demonstration freight train. During Gala Weekends these freights are operated with a magnificent collection of restored stock. As at Didcot it is the authenticity which is important because freight trains carry no passengers and as such earn no revenue. They are, however, popular and certainly provide an attraction, with enthusiasts' cameras consuming film at an alarming rate. Most railway preservation societies now appreciate that they are in the entertainment business and the Severn Valley Railway cannot be faulted on the enjoyment it provides during Gala Weekends and on normal service days.

Heavy freight locomotive No. 2857 of the '2800' class is certainly a popular choice for hauling the demonstration goods trains but it also has a unique claim. To date it is the only steam locomotive to haul a scheduled freight train on BR track since the nationalized railway eliminated steam traction. That took place at Newport as part of the Great Western 150th anniversary celebrations. As might be expected, the goods wagons also came from the Severn Valley Railway, ample proof, if any were needed, of the quality workmanship the 'amateurs' of Bridgnorth and Bewdley consistently produce.

Naturally, tank engines abound, with many classes represented. Pannier and side tanks provide variety but one pannier tank is also unique in preservation just as its class was unique in GWR service. From early days inside valve gear was the norm and only Hawksworth dared vary the

No. 5164 of Collett's '5101' class, developed from Churchward's '3100' class, departs from Bridgnorth on the SVR.

routine. Only one of his '1500' class heavy shunting engines remains, that being No. 1501. It does provide contrast and an indication as to the way its designer must have been thinking. If nothing else, the motion is relatively accessible for lubrication and repair. The only saddle tank in GWR colours is not, in fact, a GWR design but came to that railway from the Port Talbot Railway. It does not fall into the category for discussion in this book but at least shows something of the variety of motive power the GWR absorbed on grouping.

Former GWR coaching stock on the Severn Valley is not as varied as that at Didicot but there is a greater need to provide rakes for daily service. Internal and external restoration is impeccable but coaches in regular service can be subject to abuse and considerable effort is required to ensure standards are maintained. Coaches are of Churchward, Collett and Hawksworth design, including kitchen/restaurant sets, special purpose vehicles, passenger brakes and even sleeping cars. Not all are in regular service but a rake of chocolate and cream coaches hauled by a lined green 'Manor' or 'Hall' must be as close as one can now get to authentic Great Western Railway.

In order to appreciate locomotive design and its problems one must actually see a machine stripped down. Though work is always in progress there are few restrictions placed on the visitor to the locomotive depot at Bridgnorth and a walk around 'the shops' is a must for anybody remotely interested in the workings of a steam engine. It is only close up that an appreciation of scale is obtained. The physical problems of dismantling or assembling the constituent parts are only realized when those parts are seen in isolation, apparently scattered about the shed floor. Swindon and other repair depots had extensive facilities but Bridgnorth, as with other preserved railways, has to

make do with limited equipment. That fact alone highlights the real problems faced by many organizations in preserving our railway heritage. Locomotives were designed for maintenance and overhaul in well equipped workshops; that, after all, is what the designers expected to be available because they also designed and stocked those workshops. It is, perhaps, worth considering what locomotives would have been like if overhaul facilities had been limited to those currently available to preserved railways.

Apart from the track at Didcot there is no broad gauge line in preservation, though there are two railways running on trackbed which formerly located broad gauge rails. Both lines are in Devon and operate under the management of the Dart Valley Light Railway. Naturally, they are Great Western orientated. The Buckfastleigh–Totnes section is on the former Ashburton line, a traditional GWR branch line the character of which the new operators have endeavoured to maintain. On the other hand the Paignton–Kingswear line, although a branch, was very much part of the main line system with through express trains, such as the 'Torbay Express' from London and the 'Devonian' from Leeds, terminating at Kingswear.

The largest locomotives operate on the coast line from Paignton, with *Lydham Manor* preserving the main line image. An example of the most powerful tank engine class preserved in Britain may also be seen in operation. This is the '5205' class locomotive No. 5239, now named *Goliath*. Developed from the '42xx' clas of 1910, the '5205' class locomotives were designed for the heavy South Wales coal trains. Side tanks of the '45xx' class also help maintain services during the peak summer season. For the future, two other tender engines are undergoing restoration at the Buckfastleigh depot. A member of the ubiquitous 'Hall' class, *Dumbleton Hall*, is now nearing completion whilst heavy freight engine No. 3803, of the '28xx' class, is a longer-term proposition.

Along the banks of the River Dart between Totnes and Buckfastleigh the little auto-train locomotives of the '14xx' class are very much at home. Two members of the class, together with members of the pannier tank classes '64xx' and '16xx', maintain a service with typical auto-coaches and other former GWR stock. Two Ocean Saloons, from the same class as those at Didcot, are available for special events whilst other stock of interest includes an Inspection Saloon of 1910 and the former Churchward Dynamometer Car of 1902. The Dynamometer Car is now fitted out as a luxury saloon and so it has lost much of its historical significance.

Throughout Britain there are many other preserved railways, all sporting a selection of former Great Western locomotives and rolling stock. Some projects are still in the embryo stage but many are in full operation. In the beautiful Forest of Dean are to be found prairie tanks large and small, a '57xx' pannier tank of BR vintage and another 'Hall', namely *Pitchford Hall*. Hawksworth designed the inspection saloon and two auto-trailers complement the former GWR coaches. These include four which were converted by the Ministry of Defence to act as emergency telephone exchanges should the need ever arise. It didn't, and now the Dean Forest Railway volunteers intend to reconvert them for use as originally intended.

The Great Central Railway at Loughborough plays host to the powerful tank locomotive No. 5224, of the '5205' class, and also to modified 'Hall', *Witherslack Hall*. The latter engine is now back on former Great Central metals where she performed during the 1948 interchange trials. A member of the side tank '56xx' class has even ventured north into former North Eastern Railway territory on the North Yorkshire Moors Railway. Deep in the heart of former Southern Railway territory, the sole survivor of a hybrid GWR class has found track upon which to rest its wheels. No. 3217 of the 'Earl' or 'Dukedog' class, *Earl of Berkeley* certainly looks like a machine from the last century and belies the fact that she was constructed in 1938. The locomotive was, in fact, a rebuild combining the chassis of 'Bulldog' No. 3425, built in 1906, with the cab and boiler of 'Duke' No. 3282, built in 1899. *Earl of Berkeley* has had a chequered career and deserves her retirement on the Bluebell Railway.

For any Great Western enthusiast the work Swindon evokes a host of deep-seated feelings, for that town is at the heart of the railway. Its Great Western Railway Museum houses a number of fine locomotives in a former Methodist Church which was originally built by the railway as a lodging house for some of the workforce. Externally the building retains its Wesleyan style but inside it is pure Great Western; the ghosts of Brunel, Gooch, Dean and the others seem to pervade the rooms. The place is alive with memories though the exhibits are cold. *City of Truro* spent many years on exhibition before restoration to main line condition, but an assured place awaits her when retirement time returns. For the present her space is occupied by a diesel railcar, GWR of course.

Although only a replica, constructed for the GWR centenary in 1935, Stephenson's *North Star* is impressive in the confined space allowed. The 7 ft gauge is in complete contrast to experience and provides immediate impact. Brunel must have been correct. A number of parts from the original are incorporated into the replica but that does not forgive Churchward for his folly so many years ago. Unfortunately the locomotive cannot steam but it is to scale and openly demonstrates the basic arrangement of the early designs and their complete lack of protection for the crew. To drive such a machine at any speed during the winter months must have been pure hell.

Oldest of the locomotives in the hall is '2301' class, 0-6-0 Dean Goods No. 2516, the only

Dean Goods No. 2516 on display at Swindon's Great Western Museum.

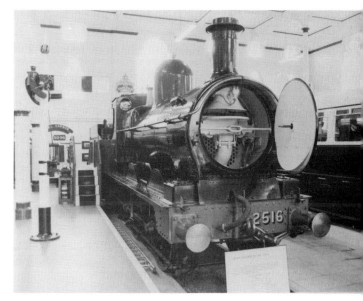

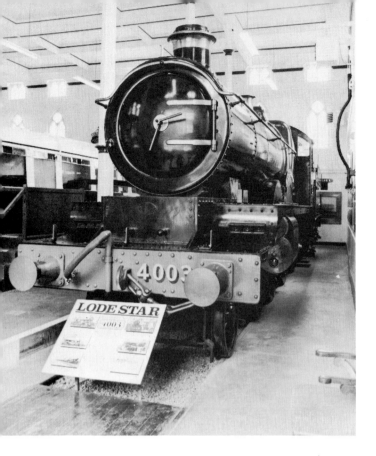

ing design the silver-plated coffee urn modelled in the form of a 'Firefly' class engine has links going back to Brunel. Offended by the unpleasant concoction which the urn produced, the engineer was forced to make a complaint. The refreshment room proprietor took unkindly to the criticism, causing Brunel to respond with his now famous scathing remarks.

> I assure you Mr Player was wrong in supposing that I thought you purchased inferior coffee. I thought I said to him I was surprised you should buy such bad roasted corn. I did not believe you had such a thing as coffee in the place; I am certain I never tasted any. I have long ceased to make complaints at Swindon. I avoid taking anything there when I can help it.

Brunel was never a man to mince his words.

Swindon alas is not the place it was. With the engineering works closed one more link with the old regime has perished. But then of recent years the works had been called upon to deal with modern stock and much of the machinery known to Churchward, Collett and Hawksworth had gone the way of their locomotives. But memories die hard and the spirit lives on. Some of the buildings will survive as monuments to those who toiled for years in the most arduous of conditions: railway factory employment was not as glamorous as the machines that the labour produced. As part of an enlarged, and hopefully working, GWR museum there is an assured future for sections of that Swindon 'shrine'.

As regards the line which Brunel laid out, it is still basically the same today except that the gauge has changed. Model-like trains hurtle through the magnificent Sonning Cutting much as they did so many years ago, although they now sport rainbow liveries and belch foul smelling grey smoke. Though it presents no problem to the sleek Inter-City 125s, Box Tunnel remains a work of engineering genius and the beauty of the portals is still a delight to behold. Standing on the A4 overlooking the western portal, the mind can readily visualize a short man in stove pipe hat busily urging the navvies into renewed effort. At Bristol, the Temple Meads train shed has been restored from its ignominious use as a car park and the creative skill of Brunel may once more be enjoyed there.

In Devon, the Royal Albert Bridge at Saltash defies description. Still in daily use after so many years, it remains a working monument to its dying designer. The legend on the landward sides of both supports says all that is required: *I.K. BRUNEL, ENGINEER. 1859*

Devon also boasts another piece of Brunel's work

survivor from this famous class which saw war service in Europe and the Middle East, being 'drafted' during both world conflicts. Churchward is represented amongst the collection by 'Star' class 4-6-0 No. 4003, *Lode Star*. Magnificent in its domination of the floor area, the locomotive cannot be viewed to advantage as it is impossible to get far enough away to see the lines. That does not, however, detract from the efforts of the museum staff in their display techniques: it merely illustrates the need for a larger museum area. The remaining locomotive on display represents the final era of Great Western locomotive design, being a Hawksworth product. Pannier tanks were the workhorses of the GWR and No. 9400, first engine of the taper boiler '9400' class, has the honour of displaying the charms of that valuable breed.

There is more to the museum than locomotives, but space does not permit a catalogue of stock. The model valve gear is most enlightening and the pair of 8 ft driving wheels from a long gone broad gauge single serve as a stimulant to the imagination. If only people from the past had been more willing to preserve their heritage. Fortunately somebody had the sense to retain an item which is part of Great Western folklore. Though not an item of engineer-

but one much less successful. Following the debacle of the atmospheric system many directors of the South Devon Railway were anxious to expunge memory of the ill-founded experiment. Components were quickly disposed of and in most cases all trace disappeared. Sections of the pipe found a more lasting use in drainage systems and several sections have survived. Of the trains and air pumps there is nothing. However, at Starcross one of the old pumping houses still stands although the chimney is somewhat truncated, the top 50 ft having been destroyed by a furious West Country storm in 1866. Inside the building is an exhibition and a demonstration section of atmospheric railway, operated by vacuum cleaners. Though the lumbering machinery has long gone the building is well worth a visit, if only to reflect on the audacity of the man in attempting such an outlandish scheme on a long stretch of railway.

They may not be original and so have no actual historical significance, but replicas provide a useful means of reliving the past. Reliving is the operative word, for to be of real benefit a replica locomotive must be operational. Much as *North Star* at Swindon provides a valuable insight into the original locomotive designs, it is still just a statue, a stuffed machine lacking soul. Fortunately, despite the problems and shortage of suitable broad gauge track, the Great Western 150th anniversary celebrations in 1985 prompted the construction of a working replica, *Iron Duke*.

Constructed by Resco Industries for the Science Museum, the locomotive is not absolutely authen-

tic as manufacture of a true broad gauge boiler would have been prohibitively expensive. However, *Iron Duke* looks very much an 'original'. With replica coaches coupled behind, the magnificent proportions of the Gooch design may be fully appreciated. Not for some ninety years has the sight of a steaming 7 ft gauge train been observed and a view of that action is certainly worth the construction cost. When seen alongside narrow gauge stock of a similar period the sheer scale of the broad gauge may be fully appreciated. The replica *Rocket* and its coaches are diminutive in comparison. Construction of a full-size replica *Firefly* is also in progress. Two broad gauge locomotives in operation together should be a sight to thrill any railway enthusiast. The major problem with a broad gauge replica is the absence of suitable track on which to operate. At present only Didcot possesses a length of permanent 7 ft gauge track.

Brunel's works are in evidence throughout the West Country and along the former GWR line, whilst the work of Gooch may now be seen through the replicas of his locomotives. Churchward's design skills are very much evident in *Lode Star* and other beautifully restored locomotives including representatives of the '2800' and '4500' classes. In terms of the GWR it is Collett who has most examples of his work preserved. The 'Kings', 'Castles', 'Halls' and 'Manors' still exist in abundance whilst numerous tank engines may be seen scattered throughout the length and breadth of Britain. The absence of a preserved 'County' class locomotive is to be regretted, but Hawk-

Above left *Churchward's* Lode Star *dry inside the GWR Museum, Swindon.*

Right *Replica broad gauge* Iron Duke *at Didcot with the transfer shed in the background.*

sworth's classes in preservation do include 'Modified Halls' and '9400' tanks.

The work of William Dean may be observed in No. 2516, the 0-6-0 goods locomotive at Swindon, whilst his influence is evident in *City of Truro* and *Earl of Berkeley*. A full-size, non-working model of '3031' class locomotive, *Queen*, exists at Madame Tussauds', Windsor, but it is not real, merely a latter-day decoration which does little justice to the engineering skills of its designer. However, the style and beauty which characterized Dean's

period are evident in locomotive and replica Royal coaches. Unfortunately, all of Joseph and George Armstrong's fine works disappeared with elimination of the broad gauge and the restocking projects of Churchward and Collett. Without their skills, and particularly those of Joseph, the GWR would not have progressed as it did. Failure to preserve examples of their work leaves a gap in the living history of the GWR, but that is in the past and there is still a massive Great Western heritage remaining for all to enjoy.

Left *A 1985 main line steam-hauled excursion, 'The Western Stalwart', heading south from Hereford to Cardiff with No. 4930,* Hagley Hall, *and No. 7029,* Clun Castle.

Below *No. 7819,* Hinton Manor, *departs from Swindon with a Gloucester-bound excursion during August 1985.*

Appendix

Letter of application from Daniel Gooch to I.K. Brunel for the post of manager at the proposed Great Western Locomotive Works.

Reproduced by courtesy of the Great Western Museum, Swindon.

Manchester & Leeds Railway Office,
Rochdale. July 18th. 1837.

I K Brunel Esq.

Dear Sir,

I have just been informed it is your intention to erect an engine manufactory at or near Bristol and that you wish to engage a person as Manager. I take the earliest opportunity of offering my services for the situation.

I have until the last two months been constantly engaged in engine building and have worked at each branch of the business, but principally at locomotive engine work. The first three years of my time I was with Mr Homphry at Tredegar Iron Works, Monmouthshire. I left him to go to Mr R Stephenson and was at the Vulcan Foundry 12 months when I obtained leave from Mr Stephenson to go down to Mr Stirling of the Dundee Foundry Co, Dundee, to get a knowledge of steam boat work. I remained with him 12 months and returned to Mr Stephenson's works at Newcastle where I remained until last October when I left having had an offer from a party in Newcastle to take the management of a locomotive manufactory which they intended erecting, but which owing to some unavoidable circumstances they have now given up the idea of proceeding with, and we have countermanded the order for machinery. This left me without a situation, and I am anxious to engage myself to some company where I will have the manag ement of the building of engines. At present I am with my brother on the Manchester & Leeds line, where I have employment until I meet with something more suitable.

I will be glad to refer you to any of the forementioned places for testimonials.

Should you approve of my application I shall be glad to hear from you stating the salary and any other information you may think necessary.

I am, Sir, Yours obly,
Danl Gooch.

Footnote References

Chapter 1.

1. I. Brunel, *The Life of Isambard Kingdom Brunel* (Longman, 1870), p.64.
2. R.B. Wilson, *Memoirs & Diary of Sir Daniel Gooch* (David & Charles, 1972), p.31.
3. Brunel Personal Letter Book, 5-6 March 1850 (Bristol Univ. Lib.).
4. Brunel, *The Life of I.K. Brunel*, p.70.
5. Brunel, *The Life of I.K. Brunel*, p.78.
6. Gauge Commissioners' Report, 1846.
7. L.T.C. Rolt, *Isambard Kingdom Brunel* (Longman, 1957), p.210.
8. *The Engineer*, 27 May 1892, p.448.
9. F.Wishaw, *Railways of Great Britain and Ireland* (Weale, 1842), p.152.
10. Simmons, *Birth of the Great Western Railway* (Adams & Dart, 1971), p.43.
11. Simmons, *Birth of the GWR*, p.61.
12. Simmons, *Birth of the GWR*, p.64.
13. Brunel Diary, 26 December 1835; quoted by Rolt on p.119.
14. E.T. MacDermot, *History of the Great Western Railway* vol. 1 (Ian Allan), p.103.
15. Brunel, *The Life of I.K. Brunel*, pp.137-142.
16. Quoted by Rolt on p.215.
17. Quoted by Rolt on p.219.
18. R.A. Forrester, *What was an Atmospheric Railway?* (Starcross Atmospheric Railway Museum).
19. Brunel, *The Life of I.K. Brunel*, p.159.
20. Brunel, *The Life of I.K. Brunel*, p.165.
21. *Great Western Railway Magazine*, 1910, vol. 22, p.82.
22. *GWR Magazine*, 1910, vol.22. p.82.
23. *GWR Magazine*, 1910, vol.22, p.83.
24. Simmons, *Birth of the GWR*, p.48.
25. MacDermot, *History of the GWR*, p.392.
26. MacDermot, *History of the GWR*, p.386.
27. Quoted by MacDermot on p.377.

Chapter 2.

1. R.B. Wilson, *Memoirs & Diary of Sir Daniel Gooch* (David & Charles, 1972), p.27.
2. *Great Western Railway Magazine*, 1890, vol.3, p.3.
3. Wilson, *Memoirs*, p.48.
4. Wilson, *Memoirs*, p.26.
5. Wilson, *Memoirs*, p.28.
6. Wilson, *Memoirs*, p.34.
7. Simmons, *Birth of the Great Western Railway* (Adams & Dart, 1971), p.63.
8. Wilson, *Memoirs*, p.35.
9. D.K. Clark, *Railway Machinery* (Blackie, 1851-5), p.291.
10. Wilson, *Memoirs*, p.41.
11. BRB document HRP1/6: now in PRO Rail Collection.
12. Wilson, *Memoirs*, p.53.
13. Wilson, *Memoirs*, pp.65-66.
14. Wilson, *Memoirs*, pp.75-76.
15. Wilson, *Memoirs*, p.92.
16. *Great Western Railway Magazine*, 1890, vol.3, p.5.
17. *North Wilts Herald*, 3 September 1864.
18. *Great Western Railway Magazine*, 1941, vol.53, p.180.
19. Wilson, *Memoirs*, p.66.
20. *Great Western Railway Magazine*, 1899, vol.2, p.4.
21. H.Holcroft, *The Armstrongs of the Great Western* (Railway World, 1953), pp.25-27.
22. *Great Western Railway Magazine*, 1891, vol.3, p.101.
23. *GWR Magazine*, 1891, vol.3, p.102.
24. *GWR Magazine*, 1891, vol.3, p.102. Holcroft, *The Armstrongs of the GW*, p.30.
25. *Great Western Railway Magazine*, 1891, vol.3, p.102.
26. *Swindon Works and its place in Great Western History* (GWR, 1935), p.55.
27. *North Wilts Herald*, 9 June 1877.
28. *Great Western Railway Magazine*, 1891, vol.3, p.102.
29. Holcroft, *The Armstrongs of the GW*, pp.73-74.
30. *Great Western Railway Magazine*, 1902, vol.14, p.105.
31. *Great Western Railway Magazine*, 1891, vol.3, p.102.
32. *North Wilts Herald*, 11 June 1877.
33. *Great Western Railway Magazine*, 1943, vol.55, p.125.
34. Holcroft, *The Armstrongs of the GW*, p.88.
35. Holcroft, *The Armstrongs of the GW*, p.88.
36. Holcroft, *The Armstrongs of the GW*, p.94.
37. *North Wilts Herald*, 6 January 1888.
38. Holcroft, *The Armstrongs of the GW*, p.83.
39. *The Engineer*, 29 September 1905, p.316.
40. *The Engineer*, 29 September 1905, p.316.
41. *Great Western Railway Magazine*, 1902, vol.14, p.17.
42. Private Correspondence, Research Office, National Army Museum, 10 September 1985.
43. *Great Western Railway Magazine*, 1902, vol.14. p.104.
44. *Great Western Railway Magazine*, 1913, vol.25, pp.169-171.
45. A.S. Peck, *The Great Western & Swindon Works* (OPC, 1983), pp.90, 97.

46. *Great Western Railway Magazine*, 1916, vol.28, p.163.
47. H. Holcroft, *An Outline of GWR Locomotive Practice 1837-1947* (Locomotive Publishing Co., 1957), p.54.
48. *The Locomotive*, January 1940.
49. *Great Western Railway Magazine*, 1902, vol.14, p.17.
50. *GWR Magazine*, 1902, vol.14, p.105.
51. Peck, *The GW & Swindon Works*, p.122.

Chapter 3.

1. *Cassiers Magazine*, December 1904, vol.27, p.168.
2. Sir W.A. Stanier, *G.J. Churchward, CME of the Great Western Railway* (Newcomen Society, 1960), vol.30, p.1.
3. Stanier, *G.J. Churchward*, p.2.
4. *Great Western Railway Magazine*, 1922, vol.34, p.22.
5. *Great Western Railway Magazine*, 1920, vol.32, p.229.
6. *GWR Magazine*, 1920, vol.32, p.229.
7. H. Holcroft, *An Outline of GWR Locomotive Practice 1837-1947* (Locomotive Publishing Co., 1957), p.97.
8. Felix Pole, *His Book* (Town & Country Press, 1968), p.41.
9. Pole, *His Book*, p.44.
10. H.A. Bulleid, *Master Builders of Steam* (Ian Allan, 1963), p.108.
11. K.J. Cook, *The late G.J. Churchward's Locomotive Development on the GWR* (Institute of Locomotive Engineers, 1950), paper 492, p.171.
12. A.S. Peck, *The Great Western & Swindon Works* (OPC, 1983), p.188.
13. Cook, *Loco. Development on the GWR*, p.172.
14. *Great Western Railway Magazine*, 1920, vol.32, p.229.
15. *Great Western Railway Magazine*, 1922, vol.34, p.245.
16. Stanier, *G.J. Churchward*, p.8.
17. Bulleid, *Master Builders of Steam*, p.126
18. Cook, *Loco. Development on the GWR*, p.173.
19. Cook, *Loco. Development on the GWR*, p.182.
20. Cook, *Loco. Development on the GWR*, p.200.
21. G.J. Churchward, *Large Locomotive Boilers* (Institute of Mechanical Engineers, February 1906), p.225.
22. Cook, *Loco. Development on the GWR*, p.178.
23. Rail Coll., PRO Kew, quoted in Rogers, *G.J. Churchward* (Allen & Unwin, 1975), p.115.
24. *North Wilts Herald*, 22 December 1933.
25. *North Wilts Herald*, 29 December 1933.
26. Private correspondence, Librarian, Merchant Taylors School, 30 November 1985.
27. *Great Western Railway Magazine*, 1941, vol.53, p.179.
28. *GWR Magazine*, 1941, vol.53, p.159.
29. *Who Was Who*, 1951-60, p.230.
30. K.J. Cook, *Swindon Steam 1921-51* (Ian Allan, 1974), p.46.
31. Cook, *Swindon Steam*, p.47.
32. *Who Was Who*, 1951-60, p.230.
33. *Great Western Railway Magazine*, 1927, vol.39, p.103.
34. *GWR Magazine*, 1927, vol.39, p.108.
35. Cook, *Swindon Steam*, pp.130-131.
36. Cook, *Swindon Steam*, pp.118-119.
37. Pole, *His Book*, pp.87-88.
38. O.S. Nock, *British Locomotives of the 20th Century* vol.2 (Patrick Stephens, 1984), p.93.
39. Nock, *British Locomotives* vol.2, p.91.
40. *GWR Magazine*, 1941, vol.53, p.179.
41. Pole, *His Book*, pp.75-76.
42. O.S. Nock, *Sir William Stanier* (Ian Allan, 1964), p.58.
43. Cook, *Swindon Steam*, p.107.
44. Nock, *British Locomotives* vol.2, p.90.
45. H.C.B. Rogers, *G.J. Churchward, A Locomotive Biography* (Allen & Unwin, 1975), pp.129-130.
46. O.S. Nock, *The GWR Stars, Castles & Kings* (David & Charles, 1980), p.90.
47. Cook, *Swindon Steam*, pp.149-150.
48. Cook, *Swindon Steam*, p.47.
49. *B.R. Western Region Magazine*, 1952, p.199.
50. *GWR Magazine*, 1941, vol.53, p.180.
51. O.S. Nock, *British Locomotives of the 20th Century* vol.1 (Patrick Stephens, 1983), p.163.
52. *GWR Magazine*, 1941, vol.53, p.180.
53. *Swindon Evening Advertiser*, 3 December 1960.
54. *Swindon Evening Advertiser*, 10 December 1949.
55. Nock, *British Locomotives* vol.1, p.234.
56. Nock, *British Locomotives* vol.2, p.103.
57. Nock, *British Locomotives* vol.2, p.96.
58. *Locomotives of the Great Western Railway*, part 9 (Railway Correspondence and Travel Society, 1962), p.J54.
59. O.S. Nock, *Tales of the GWR* (David & Charles, 1984), p.110.
60. *Great Western Railway Magazine*, 1907, vol.19, p.190.
61. O.S. Nock, *GWR Steam* (David & Charles, 1972), p.207.
62. *Railway Magazine*, August 1976, p.484.

Chapter 4.

1. R.B. Wilson, *Memoirs & Diary of Sir Daniel Gooch* (David & Charles, 1972), p.27.
2. Wilson, *Memoirs*, p.35.

3. A.S. Peck, *The Great Western at Swindon Works* (OPC, 1983), p.8.
4. Peck, *The Great Western*, p.7.
5. *Swindon Works and its Place in Great Western History* (GWR, 1935), p.7.
6. *Great Western Railway Magazine*, 1935, vol.67, pp.478-479.
7. *Swindon Works*, p.7.
8. Wilson, *Memoirs*, p.53.
9. *Locomotives of the GWR*, part 2 (RCTS, 1953), p.B21.
10. H. Holcroft, *The Armstrongs of the Great Western* (Railway World, 1953), p.42.
11. *Great Western Railway Magazine*, 1935, vol.67, p.93.
12. E.T. MacDermot, *History of the Great Western Railway*, vol.2 (Ian Allen), pp.16, 19.
13. Felix Pole, *His Book* (Town & Country Press, 1968), p.40.
14. MacDermot, *History of the GWR*, pp.276, 279.
15. Peck, *The Great Western*, p.111.
16. Peck, *The Great Western*, p.133.
17. K.J. Cook, *Swindon Steam 1921-1951* (Ian Allan, 1974), p.151.
18. Cook, *Swindon Steam*, p.85.
19. Peck, *The Great Western*, p.47.
20. Peck, *The Great Western*, pp.141-143.
21. Holcroft, *The Armstrongs of the GW*, pp.94-95.
22. Pole, *His Book*, p.46.
23. Peck, *The Great Western*, p.192.
24. Peck, *The Great Western*, p.197.
25. *The Engineer*, supplement, 16 December 1910, p.10.
26. A. Vaughan, *Grub, Water & Relief* (Murray, 1985) p.157.
27. Cook, *Swindon Steam*, p.47.

Chapter 5.

1. H. Holcroft, *An Outline of GWR Locomotive Practice 1837-1947* (Locomotive Publishing Co., 1957), p.66.
2. *Locos of the GWR*, part 2 (RCTS, 1953), p.B22.
3. I.K. Brunel, *Report to GWR Directors, 13 December 1838* (GWR, 1839), pp.23-25.
4. *The Engineer*, 16 December 1910, p.10.
5. R. Coffin, *Kings of the Great Western* (6000 Loco. Soc., 1977), p.141.
6. Felix Pole, *His Book* (Town & Country Press, 1968), p.75.
7. Holcroft, *An Outline of GWR Locomotive Practice*, p.46.
8. Holcroft, *An Outline of GWR Locomotive Practice*, p.47.
9. Holcroft, *An Outline of GWR Locomotive Practice*, p.75.

10. W.H. Pearce, *Favourable Points in 4 Cylinder Designed Locos* (Swindon Engineering Society, 1924). Reported in *GWR Mag.* 1924, vol.36, p.129.
11. Holcroft, *An Outline of GWR Locomotive Practice*, p.143.
12. G.J. Churchward, *Large Locomotive Boilers* (Proceedings Institute of Mechanical Engineers, February 1906), p.166.
13. S.O. Ell, *Developments in Locomotive Testing* (Proceedings Institute of Locomotive Engineers, 1953), paper 527, p.567.
14. Ell, *Developments*, p.572.
15. Holcroft, *An Outline of GWR Locomotive Practice*, p.40.
16. Holcroft, *An Outline of GWR Locomotive Practice*, p.23.
17. Holcroft, *An Outline of GWR Locomotive Practice*, p.64.
18. *Great Western Railway Magazine*, 1936, pp.125-127; D.K. Clark, *Railway Machinery* (Blackie, 1851), p.238; F. Wishaw, *Railways of Great Britain* (Weale, 1842), plate 9.
19. K.J. Cook, *The late G.J. Churchward's Locomotive Developments on the GWR* (Proceedings Institute Locomotive Engineers, 1950), paper 492, p.158.
20. Cook, *Churchward's Loco. Developments*, p.178.
21. Holcroft, *An Outline of GWR Locomotive Practice*, p.84.
22. Cook, *Churchward's Loco. Developments*, p.200.
23. *Great Western Railway Magazine*, 1916, vol.28, p.163.
24. Churchward, *Large Locomotive Boilers*, p.224.
25. Cook, *Churchward's Loco. Developments*, p.191.
26. *Great Western Railway Magazine*, 1913, vol.25, p.136.
27. K.J. Cook, *Swindon Steam 1921-1951* (Ian Allan, 1974), p.114.
28. Cook, *Swindon Steam*, p.64.
29. Cook, *Churchward's Loco. Developments*, p.163.
30. H. Fowler, *Superheating Steam in Locomotives* (Proc' Institute Civil Engineers, 1914), vol.196, paper 4082.
31. *The Engineer*, GWR Supplement, 16 December 1910, p.16.
32. Cook, *Churchward's Loco. Developments*, p.178.
33. Fowler, *Superheating Steam*, pp.128-131.
34. Cook, *Swindon Steam*, p.82.
35. Cook, *Swindon Steam*, p.94.
36. Cook, *Swindon Steam*, p.96.

Chapter 6.

Locomotive details have been taken from *Locomotives of the Great Western Railway*, parts 2,4,5,6 &

7, published by The Railway Correspondence and Travel Society between 1953 and 1959.

1. Brunel letter dated 12 November 1836, Box GWR at NRM, York.
2. Brunel letter dated 16 January 1840, Box GWR at NRM, York.
3. *The Engineer*, 27 May 1892, p.447.
4. Gauge Commissioners' Report, 1846, answer 107, p.7.
5. R.B. Wilson, *Memoirs & Diary of Sir Daniel Gooch* (David & Charles, 1972), p.55.
6. Gauge Commissioners' Report, 1846.
7. E.T. MacDermot, *History of the Great Western Railway* vol.1 (Ian Allan), p.400.
8. MacDermot, *History of the GWR*, p.401.
9. D.K. Clark, *Railway Machinery* (Blackie, 1851-5), p.311.
10. MacDermot, *History of the GWR*, p.404.
11. E.L. Ahrons, *British Steam Railway Locomotive 1825-1925* (Locomotive Publishing Co., 1927), p.63.
12. Wilson, *Memoirs*, p.54.
13. H. Holcroft, *An Outline of GWR Locomotive Practice 1837-1947* (Locomotive Publishing Co., 1957), p.5.
14. Official locomotive report from Gooch to GWR directors, dated 19 November 1849; mentioned in *Locos of GWR* part 2 (RCTS).
15. Ahrons, *British Steam Railway Loco.*, p.70.
16. Wilson, *Memoirs*, p.85.
17. Holcroft, *An Outline of GWR Locomotive Practice*, p.16.
18. H. Holcroft, *Armstrongs of the Great Western* (Railway World, 1953), p.45.
19. Holcroft, *An Outline of GWR Locomotive Practice*, p.26.
20. Ahrons, *British Steam Railway Loco.*, p.186.
21. Holcroft, *An Outline of GWR Locomotive Practice*, p.34.
22. Holcroft, *An Outline of GWR Locomotive Practice*, p.35.
23. Holcroft, *An Outline of GWR Locomotive Practice*, p.46.
24. Holcroft, *An Outline of GWR Locomotive Practice*, p.47.
25. *Railway Magazine*, November 1908, p.398.
26. *Railway Magazine*, January 1909, p.69.
27. Holcroft, *An Outline of GWR Locomotive Practice*, p.62.
28. Holcroft, *An Outline of GWR Locomotive Practice*, p.67.
29. *Railway Magazine, July 1897, pp.62-66*.
30. G.J. Churchward, *Large Locomotive Boilers* (Proceedings Institute of Mechanical Engineers, February 1906), p.167.

Chapter 7.

Details of actual and proposed locomotives have been taken from *Locomotives of the Great Western Railway*, parts 4,5,7,8,9 & 11, published by The Railway Correspondence and Travel Society between 1953 and 1962.

1. G.J. Churchward *Large Locomotive Boilers* (Proceedings Institute of Mechanical Engineers, February 1906), p.165.
2. K.J. Cook, *The late G.J. Churchward's Locomotive Developments on the GWR* (Proceedings Institute of Locomotive Engineers, 1950), paper 492, p.134.
3. Cook, *Churchward's Locomotive Developments*, p.171.
4. G.H. Burrows, *GWR Locomotives* (Swindon Junior Engineering Society, 1903-4), paper 52, pp.148-149.
5. Burrows, *GWR Locomotives*, p.167.
6. Churchward, *Large Locomotive Boilers*, p.225.
7. O.S. Nock, *The GWR Stars, Castles & Kings* (David & Charles, 1980), p.25.
8. Nock, *The GWR Stars, etc.*, pp.25-26.
9. O.S. Nock, *British Locomotives of the 20th Century*, vol.1 (Patrick Stephens, 1983), pp.163-165.
10. Goodman & Veal, *Heavy Freight* (Great Western Society, 1980), p.8.
11. Cook, *Churchward's Loco. Developments*, p.153.
12. K.J. Cook, *Swindon Steam 1921-1951* (Ian Allan, 1974), p.32.
13. Cook, *Swindon Steam*, p.117.
14. Cook, *Churchward's Loco. Developments*, p.181.
15. *The Engineer*, 16 October 1903, p.380.
16. H. Holcroft, *An Outline of GWR Locomotive Practice 1837-1947* (Locomotive Publishing Co., 1957), p.137.
17. C.B. Collett, *Testing of Locomotives on the Great Western Railway*, World Power Conference, London, 1924, pp.882-888.
18. Cook, *Swindon Steam*, p.116.
19. Felix Pole, *His Book* (Town & Country Press, 1968), p.88.
20. Cook, *Swindon Steam*, p.53.
21. Nock, *The GWR Stars, etc.*, pp.130-132.
22. O.S. Nock, *British Locomotives of the 20th Century*, vol. 2 (Patrick Stephens, 1984), p.76.
23. *GWR Magazine*, vol.47, 1935, pp.206-207.
24. Holcroft, *An Outline of GWR Locomotive Practice*, p.142.
25. Cook, *Swindon Steam*, p.60.

Chapter 8.

1. C. Babbage, *Passages in the Life of a Philosopher* (Longman, 1864), pp.320-321.
2. Babbage, *Passages*, p.330.
3. Babbage, *Passages*, p.334.

4. D.K. Clark, *Railway Machinery* (Blackie, 1851-5), p.292.
5. Clark, *Railway Machinery*, pp.63-65.
6. Clark, *Railway Machinery*, pp.292-293.
7. Clark, *Railway Machinery*, pp.292-298.
8. *The Engineer*, GWR supplement, 16 December 1910, p.11.
9. C.B. Collett, *Testing of Locomotives on the Great Western Railway*, World Power Conference, London, 1924, pp.884-887.
10. K.J. Cook, *Swindon Steam 1921-1951* (Ian Allan, 1974), p.37.
11. Letter from N. Gresley to G.J. Churchward, 7 April 1914. Box Test/Test 4, NRM, York.
12. *Great Western Railway Magazine*, 1924, vol.36, pp.168-171.
13. Collett, *Testing Locos*, p.893.
14. O.S. Nock, *The GWR Stars, Castles & Kings* (David & Charles, 1980), p.46.
15. Collett, *Testing Locos*, p.893.
16. G.J. Churchward, *The Testing Plant on the GWR at Swindon* (Institute Mechanical Engineers, June 1904); *The Engineer*, 22 December 1905, p.621.
17. Sir W.A. Stanier, *G.J. Churchward, CME of the Great Western Railway* (Newcomen Society, vol.30, 1960), p.10.
18. Churchward, *The Testing Plant*, p.939.
19. A.S. Peck, *The Great Western at Swindon Works* (OPC, 1983), p.147.
20. *The Engineer*, 22 December 1905, p.621.
21. O.S. Nock, *British Locomotives of the 20th Century*, vol.2 (Patrick Stephens, 1984), p.93.
22. *Great Western Railway Magazine*, 1934, vol.46, pp.500-503.
23. Cook, *Swindon Steam*, p.92.
24. *Railway Gazette*, 18 January 1946, pp64-69.
25. H. Holcroft, *The Armstrongs of the Great Western* (Railway World, 1953), pp.136-140.
26. *Great Western Railway Magazine*, 1922, vol.34, p.136.
27. G.A. Gammon, *Standardization & Design of B.R. Goods & Min. Wagons* (Institute Locomotive Engineers, 1950), paper 496, pp.444, 469.
28. K.J. Cook, *The late G.J. Churchward's Locomotive Development on the GWR* (Institute Locomotive Engineers, 1950), paper 492, p.164; also Stanier, *G.J. Churchward*, p.7.
29. Cook, *Churchward's Loco. Development*, p.164.
30. Stanier, *G.J. Churchward*, p.4.
31. Cook, *Churchward's Loco. Development*, p.166.
32. *The Engineer, 16 June 1914, p.80.*

Chapter 9.

1. E.T. MacDermot, *History of the Great Western Railway*, vol.1 (Ian Allan), p.431.
2. MacDermot, *History of the GWR*, vol.1, p.433.
3. *Great Western Railway Magazine*, 1935, vol.47, p.505.
4. L.T.C. Rolt, *Isambard Kingdom Brunel* (Pelican, 1957), p.157.
5. J.H. Russell, *Pictorial Record of GWR Coaches*, part 1 (OPC, 1972), p.6.
6. MacDermot, *History of the GWR*, p.444.
7. Russell, *Pictorial Record*, p.5.
8. MacDermot, *History of the GWR*, vol.1, p.444.
9. MacDermot, *History of the GWR*, vol.1, p.445.
10. Hamilton-Ellis, *Railway Carriages in the British Isles from 1830 to 1914* (George Allen & Unwin, 1965), p.67.
11. Hamilton-Ellis, *Railway Carriages*, p.86.
12. Hamilton-Ellis, *Railway Carriages*, pp.137-138.
13. *Railway Magazine*, July 1897, p.63.
14. MacDermot, *History of the GWR*, vol.1, p.302.
15. *The English Illustrated Magazine*, 1891-92, p.563.
16. *Railway Magazine*, July 1897, p.63.
17. G.J. Churchward, *Modern Railway Carriages* (Swindon Junior Engineering Society, Pamphlet No. 11, 9 September 1896).
18. Hamilton-Ellis, *Railway Carriages*, p.223.
19. *Great Western Railway Magazine*, 1934, vol.46, pp.557-558.
20. *Great Western Railway Magazine*, 1907, vol.19, pp.14-15.
21. M. Harris, *GWR Coaches 1890-1954* (David & Charles, 1966), p.22.
22. Hamilton-Ellis, *Railway Carriages*, p.558.
23. Determined using official weight and capacity data.
24. Harris, *GWR Coaches 1890-1954*, p.18.
25. *Great Western Railway Magazine*, 1935, vol.47, p.526.
26. Quoted in Harris, *GWR Coache;s 1890-1954*, p.20.
27. *Great Western Railway Magazine*, 1923, vol.35, pp.252-256.
28. H.C.B. Rogers, *G.J. Churchward, A Locomotive Biography* (Allen & Unwin, 1975), pp.64-65.

Chapter 10.

1. E.S. Cox, *British Railways Standard Steam Locomotives* (Ian Allan, 1966), pp.13-14.
2. L.T.C. Rolt, *Isambard Kingdom Brunel* (Pelican, 1970), pp.231-232.
3. R.B. Wilson, *Memoirs & Diary of Sir Daniel Gooch* (David & Charles, 1972), p.34.
4. Wilson, *Memoirs*, p.35.
5. *Great Western Railway Magazine*, 1936, vol.47, p.125.
6. H. Holcroft, *An Outline of GWR Locomotive Practice 1837-1947* (Locomotive Publishing Co., 1957), p.16.

7. H. Holcroft, *The Armstrongs of the Great Western* (Railway World, 1953), pp.66-68.
8. Holcroft, *The Armstrongs of the GW*, p.86.
9. Holcroft, *An Outline of GWR Locomotive Practice*, p.55.
10. *Great Western Railway Magazine*, 1913, vol.25, p.68: 'The Standardization of GW Locomotives by A.J.L. White'.
11. K.J. Cook, *The Late G.J. Churchward's Locomotive Development on the GWR* (Institute of Locomotive Engineers, 1950), paper 492, p.171.
12. Holcroft, *The Armstrongs of the GW*, p.69.
13. Cook, *Churchward's Loco. Development*, p.153.
14. G.J. Churchward, *Large Locomotive Boilers* (Proceedings Institute of Mechanical Engineers, February 1906), p.168.
15. *GWR Magazine*, 1913, vol.25, p.69.
16. Holcroft, *An Outline of GWR Locomotive Practice*, p.120.
17. Cox, *British Railways Standard Steam Locos*, p.15.
18. K.J. Cook, *Swindon Steam 1921-1951* (Ian Allan, 1974), p.60.

Chapter 11.

1. J.G.H. Warren, *A Century of Locomotive Building by Robert Stephenson & Co.* (David & Charles Reprints, 1970), p.386.
2. Warren, *A Century of Locomotive Building*, p.391.
3. J. Nasmyth, *James Nasmyth, Engineer. An Autobiography* (John Murray, 1889), p.229.
4. Nasmyth, *James Nasmyth, Engineer*, pp.230-231.
5. C. Hamilton-Ellis, *Twenty Locomotive Men* (Ian Allan, 1958), p.69.
6. F.A.S. Brown, *Great Northern Locomotive Engineers*, vol.1 (Allen & Unwin, 1966), pp.55-72.
7. Brown, *Great Engineers*, vol.1, pp.95-96.
8. Brown, *Great Engineers*, vol.1, p.99.
9. Brown, *Great Engineers*, vol.1, pp.49-51.

10. A.S. Peck, *The Great Western at Swindon Works* (OPC, 1983), pp.105-106.
11. Heap & Van Riemsdijk, *Pre-Grouping Railways*, part 2 (HMSO, 1980), p.23.
12. O.S. Nock, *British Locomotives of the 20th Century* vol.2 (Patrick Stephens, 1984), p.67.
13. O.S. Nock, *Sir William Stanier* (Ian Allan, 1964), p.58.
14. Nock, *Stanier*, p.62.
15. Bellwood & Jenkinson, *Gresley & Stanier* (HMSO, 1976), p.19.
16. Bellwood, *Gresley & Stanier*, pp.20-21.
17. G.J. Churchward, *Large Locomotive Boilers* (Proceedings Institute of Mechanical Engineers, February 1906), p.165.
18. Bellwood, *Gresley & Stanier*, p.65.
19. K.J. Cook, *The Late G.J. Churchward's Locomotive Developments on the GWR* (Proc' Institute Locomotive Engineers, 1950), paper 492, P.182.
20. H. Holcroft, *An Outline of GWR Locomotive Practice 1837-1947* (Locomotive Publishing Co., 1957), p.138.
21. O.S. Nock, *Gresley Pacifics* (David & Charles, 1982), pp.14-15.
22. Nock, *Gresley Pacifics*, pp.236-240.
23. Nock, *Gresley Pacifics*, pp.241-253.
24. O.S. Nock, *Stars, Castles & Kings* (David & Charles, 1980), pp.47-48.
25. Nock, *Stars, etc.*, pp.48-49.
26. Nock, *Stars, etc.*, p.100.
27. O.S. Nock, *British Locomotives of the 20th Century*, vol.1 (Patrick Stephens, 1983), pp.215-216.

Chapter 12.

Throughout this chapter reference is made to guides and stock books produced by the preservation societies of the railways concerned.

Index

GWR ENGINEERS

I. K. Brunel

appointment as engineer, 7
atmospheric railway, 11, 12, 14
baulk road design, 9, 63
choice of gauge 9
coach designs, 129
concern about broad gauge, 10
control of loco ordering, 50
death, 22
'Flying Hearse', 8
GWR loco specification, 14, 73
layout of line, 61
letter to Mather, Dixon & Co, 73
letter to T. E. Harrison, 16
list of projects, 11
royal carriage 1840, 130
selection of Gooch, 17
viaduct construction, 143
work with Gooch, 21

Daniel Gooch

accidents, 19
apointment to GWR, 20, 50
apprenticeship, 19
Atlantic cable, 23, 156
baronetcy, 23
birth, 19
black book, 60
chairman of GWR, 23, 54
children, 22
death, 23
death of Brunel, 22
design of 'Firefly' class, 21, 50, 173, 143
Dundee foundry appointment, 20
dynamometer car, 21, 115
engagement to Margaret Tanner, 20
experiments, 21, 51, 113
faith in Brunel, 10
father's death, 19
freemasonry, 23
ill-health, 20
indicator device, 113
letter of application, 175
locomotive stock report, 20, 50, 143
MP for Cricklade, 23
resignation from GWR, 22, 53
salary with GWR, 22
scolding from Brunel, 8

selection by Brunel, 17
standard locos, 144
views on patents, 21

Joseph Armstrong

appointment as GWR Loco Superintendent, 23, 24, 53
appointment to Hull & Selby Railway, 24
birth. 24
chairman of Swindon New Town Board, 25
civic responsibilities, 25
continuous brakes, 123
convertible coaches, 132
death, 27, 30
driver on L & M Railway, 24
gauge conversion, 26
Inst of Mech Eng, 26
land purchase, 56
lay preacher, 25
lifeboat *Joseph Armstrong*, 27
locomotive design, 26
move to Swindon, 24
Newburn House, 25
relationship with directors, 54
standard locomotives, 144

William Dean

apprenticeship, 29
Armstrong's chief assistant, 26, 30
compound locomotives, 32, 84, 90
death, 33
illness, 32
Inst of Mech Eng paper, 32
Inst of Mech Eng President, 30
laboratory, 32, 55
locomotive building, 31
locomotive No 9 (4-2-4), 89
manager of Stafford Road works, 28, 30
marriage, 30
retirement, 33
St John Ambulance Assoc, 30, 33
scholastic prizes, 30
standardization, 145
suspension bogie, 132
Swindon workforce, 31
volunteer army major, 30
water testing, 69

George Jackson Churchward

American and French

influence, 67, 118, 136
appointment as CME, 36
axle-box tests, 35, 140
brake patents, 126, 140
carriage works manager, 34
CBE award, 37
conflict with Inglis, 36
'County' class design, 37
de Glehn compounds, 37
Dean's assistant, 32
death, 39
destruction of broad gauge locos, 39, 163
disciplinary attitude, 60
dynamometer car, 115, 116
freedom of Swindon, 37
hobbies, 38
horizontal cylinders, 39, 69
Locomotive Superintendent, 35
locomotive testing, 116
move to Swindon, 34
pupil engineer, 34
retirement, 38
standard loco classes, 95, 146, 147, 151
stationary test plant, 39, 118
steam car, 34
Swindon's first mayor, 35
work with Joseph Armstrong, 29, 30, 34, 123

Charles Benjamin Collett

appointment as CME, 38, 41
apprenticeship, 40
bridge weight restrictions, 43
cancer cured, 42
'Castle' class design, 43
conference paper, 44
death, 45
'Dukedog' class, 43
dynamometer car, 117
early GWR appointments, 40
education, 40
Inst of Loco Eng, 45
locomotive designs, 44
locomotive tests, 117
marriage, 41
munitions work, 43
OBE award, 37
philosophical views, 42
rebuilding *The Great Bear*, 45, 100
relations with trades unions, 41
retirement, 45
standard locomotives, 151, 152

streamlining, 44, 107
whitewash coach, 45
wife's death, 42

Frederick William Hawksworth

apprenticeship, 45
compound 'Castle' design, 46
freedom of Swindon, 46
gas turbine loco, 48
Gooch prize, 45
hobbies, 46
interchange trials, 49
new design ideas, 47
oil firing, 47, 118
'Pacific' design, 47, 48, 56
retirement, 49
standard locomotives, 151, 152
teaching, 46

PERSONALITIES

Adams, W., 157
Armstrong, G., 26, 28, 29, 54, 56, 67, 87, 145
Armstrong, J. ('Young Joe'), 26, 29, 30, 34, 39, 54, 123, 132
Auld, J., 45, 46, 60
Babbage, C., 113
Bowen-Cooke, C. J., 160
Bulleid, O.V.S., 47, 48
Carlton, S., 35, 53
Clayton, T. G., 54
Cook, K. J., 42, 45, 69, 103, 159
Cox, E. S., 143
Crampton, T., 21, 50, 74, 156
Deeley, R. M., 99
Drummond, D., 104
Ell, S. O., 65
Fowler, H. (Sir), 161
Gibbs, G. H., 10, 20
Gibson, J., 24, 53, 131
Gooch, J., 77
Gooch, T., 19
Gooch, W., 22, 23, 52
Goss (Prof), 69, 118
Gray, G., 24, 66
Gresley, N. (Sir), 40, 116, 119, 120, 159, 162
Harrison, T. E., 14
Hawkshaw, J., 10
Holcroft, H., 25, 38, 39, 63, 69, 103, 105, 109, 159
Holden, J., 26, 34, 55, 90, 132, 133, 157
Hurst, J., 20, 22, 60

Inglis, J. (Sir), 36
Ivatt, H. A., 37
Johnson, S. W., 37, 99, 157
Joy, D., 89
Lardner, D., 11
Locke, J., 8, 19
Malan, A. H., 133
Marillier, F. W., 37
Maunsell, R. E. L., 40, 159,
    161, 162
Milne, J. (Sir), 48, 56, 164
Nasmyth, J., 155
Nock, O. S., 48, 100
Pearson, G. H., 159
Pearson, J., 54
Pole, F. (Sir), 36, 42, 43, 45,
    56, 62, 106, 161
Potter, R., 22
Raven, V. (Sir), 117
Rea, M., 52
Roch, N., 7
Riddles, R. A., 49
Sacre, C. R., 22
Say, J., 122
Stanier, W. A. (Sir), 32, 37,
    38, 40, 41, 42, 45, 119, 120,
    146, 157, 162
Stanier, W. H., 32, 54
Stephenson, G., 7, 8, 12, 19,
    20, 24, 154
Stephenson, R., 20, 13, 14, 20,
    24, 73
Stirling, J., 39
Stroudley, W., 90
Sturrock, A., 50, 51, 52, 155
Townsend, W. H., 7
Vignoles, C., 8
Walker, J., 10
Webb, F. W., 37, 146
Wilson, E., 24, 53
Woods, N., 10
Worsdell, W., 37, 157
Wright, J., 34, 54

LOCOMOTIVES
Ajax, 16, 73
Ariel, 73
Berkeley Castle, 39
Caerphilly Castle, 43, 105, 160,
    164
Caldicot Castle, 105, 117
City of Truro, 94, 160
Corsair, 61, 79, 80
Flying Scotsman, 43, 105, 160
Great Western, 21, 51, 77, 79,
    90, 155
Hurricane, 16, 73
King George V, 62, 105, 106
Knight of St Patrick, 117
Launceston Castle, 105, 161
Mars, 73
Mercury, 73
Morning Star, 73

No 9 (4-2-4), 83
Nos 14 & 16 (2-4-0), 83
North Star, 14, 20, 39, 73, 163
Pendennis Castle, 105, 160
Planet, 73
Premier, 16, 73
Snake, 14
The Great Bear, 45, 46, 48, 64,
    100, 101, 149
Thunderer,, 73
Viper, 14
Wigmore Castle, 90

LOCOMOTIVE CLASSES
'360' (0-6-0), 86
'388' (0-6-0), 26, 86
'517' (0-4-2), 88
'717' (2-4-0), 86
'927' (0-6-0), 86
'1500' (0-6-0T), 69. 72, 111
'2251' (0-6-0), 110
'2800' (2-8-0), 101, 122
'3031' (4-2-2), 90
'3100' (2-6-2T), 103
'4200' (2-8-0T), 103, 122
'4300' (2-6-0), 103, 107
'4500' (2-6-2T), 52, 103
'4700' (2-8-0), 101, 150
'5600' (0-6-2T), 109, 152
'5700' (0-6-0T), 56, 110
'9400' (0-6-0T), 56, 110
2-10-2T (proposed), 112
'Aberdare' (2-6-0), 93, 95,
    103, 148
'Atbara' (4-4-0), 93, 94, 103,
    148
'Badminton' (4-4-0), 92,
'Barnum' (2-4-0), 90,
'Buffalo' or '1076' (0-6-0T),
    86, 89, 145
'Bulldog' (4-4-0), 92, 95, 103,
    148
'Caesar' (0-6-0), 80
'Castle' (4-6-0), 43, 64, 105,
    122, 152, 160
'City' (4-4-0), 93, 94, 148
'convertibles' , 31, 63, 82, 145
'County', (4-4-0), 37, 101, 146
'County', (4-6-0), 47, 64, 72,
    98, 111
'County tank', (4-4-2T), 101
Dean compounds, 32, 84, 90
'Dean Goods', or '2301' (0-6-
    0) 90, 110, 146
de Glehn compounds, 37, 97
'Duke', (4-4-0), 61, 90, 92
'Earl' or 'Dukedog', (4-4-0),
    43, 92
'Firefly', (2-2-2), 21, 50, 74,
    80
'Grange', (4-6-0), 108, 153
'Hall', (4-6-0), 108, 123, 153
'Hall', Modified (4-6-0), 108,

    111, 152, 153
'Hercules', (0-6-0), 77, 80
'King', (4-6-0), 64, 105, 150,
    152
'Kruger', (4-6-0), 94
'Leo', (2-4-0), 75
'Manor', (4-6-0), 108, 153
Metropolitan tank, (2-4-0T),
    82
'Premier', (0-6-0), 52, 77
'Prince', (2-2-2), 52, 79
'Pyracmon', (0-6-0), 77, 80
'Queen', (2-2-2), 26, 86, 88
'Saint', (4-6-0), 37, 71, 98, 108
'Sir Daniel', (2-2-2), 86, 145
'Sir Watkin', (0-6-0T), 82
'Standard Goods', (0-6-0), 80,
    83, 145
'Star', (4-6-0), 64, 100, 104,
    117
'Sun', (2-2-2), 75
'Swindon', (0-6-0), 83
'Victoria', (2-4-0), 80, 83
'Waverley', (4-4-0), 80

COACHES
'Centenary Stock', 62, 139
convertible type, 132, 133,
    157
corridor, 133
'Dreadnought'. 62, 136
'Long Charlies', 131
'Ocean Liner Saloons', 62
papier mâché bodies, 131
'Royal Jubilee' train, 133
royal saloon 1840, 130
sleeping cars, 132
slip coaches, 135
Third class iron, 130
Third class parliamentary,
    130
'Toplight' coaches, 136

GENERAL
Association of Railway
    Locomotive Engineers, 109
atmospheric railway, 11, 12,
    13
automatic train control, 127,
    139
axle-boxes, 140
axle loading, 106

Baltimore & Ohio Railway,
    106
baulk road design, 9
Beyer, Peacock & Co, 52, 84
Birmingham Railway
    Museum, 164
blast pipe, jumper top, 126
bogie design, 136
boilers, standard range, 69,

    105, 147
Bristol & Exeter Railway, 11,
    12, 26, 52, 54, 104
Bristol & Gloucester Railway,
    7, 12
Broadbent, H. & Co, 122
broad gauge, 8, 61, 65
Brown Boveri Ltd, 48
buckeye couplers, 139
cabs, locomotive, 66
carriage works, Oxford, 53
carriage works, Swindon, 54
Churchill Machine Tools, 121
coach construction, 139
coach livery, 137
coke firing, 66
compounding, 32, 37, 67
condensing locomotives, 81,
    156
continuous brakes, 123
contract system, 52

Dart Valley Railway, 170
draughting arrangement, 65
drawing office staff, 50
driver offences, 60
Duke of Edinburgh Regiment,
    30
Dundee foundry, 290, 50, 155
dynamometer car, 21, 55, 113,
    115, 116, 117, 171

either-side brake, 140

Fenton, Murray & Jackson,
    74

gas works, 56
Gauge Commissioners, 77,
    84, 154
gauge war, 154
gearing, driving whels, 15
Great Britain, SS, 155
Great Eastern, SS, 22, 23
Great Eastern Railway, 157
Great Northern Railway, 116,
    156
Great Western Society, 164
grouping, 59, 109
GWR loco specification, 14
GWR Parliamentary Bill, 8
GWR Museum, 171

Haigh Foundry, 14, 14, 73
hammer blow, 64
Hawthorn, R. & W., 14, 24,
    73, 75
Hull & Selby Railway, 24, 66
hydrostatic lubrication, 71

indicator, 113
instanter coupling, 126
Institute of Experimental

Metaphysics, 42
Institution of Civil Engineers, 45
Institution of Locomotive Engineers, 26, 32, 69, 94
interchange trials, 160, 161

L & NWR, 146, 160
land purchases,
L & SWR, 77
lifeboat *Joseph Armstrong*, 26
Liverpool & Manchester Railway, 20, 24
LMS, 105, 158, 161
LNER, 105, 139, 160, 164
load gauges, broad and narrow gauge, 62
Locomotive Committee, 56
London & Birmingham Railway, 9
London & Brighton Railway, 24
London Metaphysical Group, 42

Manchester & Leeds

Railway, 19
Mather, Dixon & Co, 14, 16, 73, 74
Maudslay, Sons & Field, 40, 72
Mechanics' Institute, Swindon, 23, 25, 30, 42
Metropolitan Railway, 80, 156
Metropolitan Vickers, 49
mid-feather, 80
Midland Railway, 99

narrow gauge locos, first GWR, 52
Nasmyth, Gaskell & Co, 77, 155
North Eastern Railway, 14, 116
Northern Division, 52, 145

oil firing, 47, 65, 122
optical alignment (Zeiss), 72, 121, 160

piston valves, 67, 94, 126

plate wheels, 16

railcar, diesel, 104, 166
railcar, steam, 104
repair costs, locos, 44, 70
Rothwell & Co, 79

Sanders-Bolitho brake system, 123, 132
sandwich frames, 63
Severn Tunnel, 55, 65
Severn Valley Railway, 168
Sharp, Roberts & Co, 14, 73
Shrewsbury & Birmingham Railway, 23, 52
Shrewsbury & Chester Railway, 23, 24, 28, 52, 85
South Devon Railway, 11, 12, 26, 34, 54, 61
Stafford Road Works, 28, 30, 52, 54, 55, 84
standard loco classes, 95, 143
stationary test plant, 69, 118, 120
steam tender, 156
steeling, 21, 67, 74

streamlining, 44, 107
superheating, 70, 100
suspension bogie, 132, 136
Swindon works established, 51

Taff Vale Railway, 9
taper boiler, 67
Tayleur & Co, 14
testing locomotives, 55
Tredegar Iron Works, 19

valve gear, Gooch, 66, 77, 84
valve gear, scissors, 99
valve gear, Stephenson, 66, 83, 97, 109
valve gear, Walschaerts, 99, 112
Vulcan Foundry, 14, 19, 73.

wagon design, 140, 141, 142
water treatment, 69
Welsh coal, 65, 118
West Midland Railway, 24, 53
wheel construction, 67
whitewash coach, 45